Problem-Solving Cour[...] Justice, and the International Gold Standard

This book presents findings from a process evaluation carried out at a problem-solving court located in England: Manchester Review Court. Unlike the widely documented successes of similar international models, there is no detail of Manchester Review Court in the accessible literature, not in any policy document, nor is there a court handbook or website outlining objectives and expected practice. In adopting the seminal 'wine' and 'bottle' analytical framework propounded by therapeutic jurisprudence scholars, and by carrying out a detailed comparative analysis comparing the court to successful international problem-solving courts, the original empirical data brings clarity to an overlooked area. A fidelity analysis is also offered for the forerunning English and Welsh drug courts, which were established during the early 2000s, but then shortly fell by the wayside without satisfactory explanation for why. Findings from the book shed new light on the causes of the English and Welsh drug court downfalls pending recent calls to roll out a fresh suite of problem-solving courts. In light of the international evidence base and national struggles in the field, the book proposes a renewed, UK-specific, fidelity matrix to forge the impetus for new practice in this area, whilst accounting for past failures and acknowledging current issues. Therefore, this book not only breaks new ground by advancing knowledge of a significantly uncharted area but provides important inroads for helping policy-makers with their strategies in tackling recidivism, addiction, victimisation, and austerity, as widespread social and human issues currently facing both Manchester and the UK more broadly.

Presenting significant advancements in theory, policy, and practice at both national and international scale, the book will be a valuable resource for academics and practitioners working in the fields of Therapeutic Justice, Criminal Law, Criminology, Criminal Justice, and Socio-Legal Studies.

Dr. Anna Grace Kawałek is Lecturer in the Law School, Leeds Beckett University, UK.

Problem-Solving Courts, Criminal Justice, and the International Gold Standard

Reframing the English and Welsh Drug Courts

Anna Grace Kawałek

Routledge
Taylor & Francis Group

LONDON AND NEW YORK

First published 2021
by Routledge
2 Park Square, Milton Park, Abingdon, Oxon OX14 4RN

and by Routledge
52 Vanderbilt Avenue, New York, NY 10017

Routledge is an imprint of the Taylor & Francis Group, an informa
business

British Library Cataloguing-in-Publication Data
A catalogue record for this book is available from the British Library

Library of Congress Cataloging-in-Publication Data
Names: Kawałek, Anna Grace, author.
Title: Problem-solving courts, criminal justice, and the international
gold
standard: reframing the English and Welsh drug courts/Anna Grace
Kawałek.
Description: Milton Park, Abingdon, Oxon; New York, NY:
Routledge, 2021. | Includes bibliographical references and index.
Identifiers: LCCN 2020032310 (print) | LCCN 2020032311 (ebook) |
ISBN 9780367466107 (hardback) | ISBN 9781003029946 (ebook)
Subjects: LCSH: Drug courts–England. | Drug courts–Wales. |
Criminal justice, Administration of–England. | Criminal justice,
Administration of–Wales. | Gold Standard.
Classification: LCC KD3460 .K39 2021 (print) |
LCC KD3460 (ebook) | DDC 345.42/0277–dc23
LC record available at https://lccn.loc.gov/2020032310
LC ebook record available at https://lccn.loc.gov/2020032311

ISBN: 978-0-367-46610-7 (hbk)
ISBN: 978-1-003-02994-6 (ebk)

Typeset in Galliard
by Deanta Global Publishing Services, Chennai, India

I dedicate this book to my mum, who is my wisest friend, and to my dad, who is my biggest inspiration. It is your continuous love and support over the years that has enabled me to write this book to a standard that I am proud of – thank you.

Thank you also to David for the ongoing support and encouragement.

I am lucky to have such wonderful people in my life.

Contents

1 Introduction

1.1 Introduction

The purpose of this chapter is to assemble the aims, objectives, and presiding themes of this book. It will introduce the successes demonstrated by the international problem-solving court movement, before overviewing some of the difficulties that England and Wales have faced in the area. Like many similar rehabilitative initiatives in Britain, problem-solving courts appear to have been a non-prioritised, undervalued, and misunderstood area. Although in 2011 it was documented that six English and Welsh drug court pilots were in operation,[1] since then, a series of newspaper articles have informally declared their close-downs.[2] To date, we know little more than this and certainly there has been no formal explanation from the Ministry of Justice. As such, the chapter raises some preliminary questions around the chequered history of the national problem-solving courts compared to the international attempts at the same. It will also introduce the setting explored, where the empirical work for this study is based: Manchester Review Court.

1.2 Paradigm shifts

Psychology paradigms have historically been premised upon an illness ideology, whereby disease of the mind, biological defects, and human pathological traits were considered the causes of mental health problems.[3] Related psychological

---

1 Jane Kerr, Charlotte Tompkins, Wojtek Tomaszewski, Sarah Dickens, Roger Grimshaw, Nat Wright, & Matt Barnard 'The dedicated drug courts pilot evaluation process study' (2011) Ministry of Justice Research Series, 1. London: Ministry of Justice.
2 Jon Robins, 'Where next for community justice? Pioneering court closes' *The Justice Gap* (24 October 2013); Jon Robins, 'Whatever happened to community justice?' *The Justice Gap* (3 October 2012); Owen Bowcott, 'US-style problem solving courts plan losing momentum' (*The Guardian*, 12 October 2016) <https://tinyurl.com/y3e68qc4> Accessed 2 June 2019; Owen Bowcott, 'Why are special courts that can help drug users at risk of being scrapped?' (*The Guardian*, 10 June 2014) <https://tinyurl.com/y3n6o9bp> Accessed 3 September 2019.
3 Peter Kinderman, *A prescription for psychiatry: why we need a whole new approach to mental health and wellbeing* (London: Palgrave Macmillan, 2014). doi:10.1057/9781137408716;

treatment thus sought to reverse human deficits through psychotherapy correction models,[4] although this transformation was deemed difficult, if not an impossible one to make. In 1998, Seligman posited the positive psychology model, stressing that traditional psychology frameworks had overemphasised biologic human deficits.[5] Perspectives shifted from an illness ideology when Seligman concluded that mental health is a contextually shaped, social phenomenon, and it is thus changeable.[6] Psychotherapy practices that followed became increasingly strengths-based, seeking to identify, nurture, and cultivate positive aspects of human character by assuming that those with mental health problems are able to develop, change, and flourish when subject to positive social conditions.[7] Elsewhere and in a similar vein, addiction and desistence experts have put forward similar models.[8] Mirroring the positive psychology domain, these new paradigm assume that substance addiction and tendencies towards criminal behaviour are states rather than traits, and individuals can achieve cessation or desistance by relying upon positive characteristics, circumstances, social situations, and strengths-based treatment.[9]

Paradigm shifts in psychology, desistance and addiction recovery run parallel to, and indeed underpin, those from the criminal justice sphere. David Garland, arguably the world's current leading contemporary criminologist, differentiates two types of punishment: positive and negative.[10] Negative punishment is more punitive and embodies a traditional Durkheimian approach to crime and punishment, assuming that offenders are rational actors who make fully informed

---

Charles Rapp, *The strengths model: case management with people suffering from severe and persistent mental illness* (Oxford: Oxford University Press, 1997).

4 Ibid.

5 Martin Seligman, 'Building human strength: psychology's forgotten mission' (1998) APA Monitor, 29(1).

6 Ibid.

7 Christopher Peterson & Martin Seligman, *Character strengths and virtues: a handbook and classification.* (Worcester, MA: American Psychological Association; Oxford: Oxford University Press, 2004); Martin Seligman & Mihaly Csikszentmihalyi, 'Positive psychology: an introduction' (2000) American Psychologist, 55(1), 5–14. doi: 10.1037/0003-066X.55.1.5; Jeffery Froh, 'The history of positive psychology: truth be told' (2004) NYS Psychologist, 16(3), 18–20; Kennon Sheldon & Laura King, 'Why positive psychology is necessary' (2001) American Psychologist, 56(3), 216–217. doi: 10.1037/0003-066X.56.3.216.

8 William Cloud & Robert Granfield, 'Conceptualizing recovery capital: expansion of a theoretical construct' (2008) Substance Use and Misuse, 43(12–13), 1971–1986. doi: 10.1080/10826080802289762; William Cloud & Robert Granfield, 'Social context and "natural recovery": the role of social capital in the resolution of drug-associated problems' (2001). Substance Use and Misuse, 36(11), 1543–1570.

9 William White, 'Addiction recovery: its definition and conceptual boundaries' (2007) Journal of Substance Abuse Treatment, 33, 229–241; Shadd Maruna, *Making good: how ex-convicts reform and rebuild their lives.* (Washington, DC: American Psychological Association, 2011). doi: 10.1037/10430-000.

10 Fergus McNeill, 'Positive criminology, positive criminal justice?' in Natti Ronel & Dana Segev (eds.) *Positive criminology* (Routledge, 2015).

decisions towards the committal of crime; therefore, criminals are inherently wrongdoing people.[11] To that end, negative punishment is functional, punitive, harsh, and a deterrent, taking something away from offenders through imprisonment, social rejection, and a criminal record.[12] Comparatively, positive punishment takes a more holistic view of crime and punishment by embedding strengths-based efforts into crime and justice, assuming offenders have the potential to rehabilitate and desist when empowered and exposed to the right set of social circumstances.[13] By incorporating strengths-based agendas rooted in positive criminology, positive psychology, desistance and recovery capital models, the positive branch provides relief from Durkheimian sentiments.[14] As these paradigms have shifted, so has the tone, structure, and delivery of many punishment disposals.[15] Critics claim that many Western jurisdictions have now made a 'serious effort' to advance strengths-based approaches within justice measures,[16] which has led to the emergence of a multitude of new interventions, the centrepiece of which is, arguably, the problem-solving court model.

1.3 Rationale for the book: problem-solving courts: the UK and beyond

Problem-solving courts in various guises have had a long-standing history across jurisdictions worldwide and a traffic of literature details their successes.[17] Pioneering this movement is the drug court, established in Miami-Dade County,

11 Emile Durkheim, *The division of labor in society* (New York: Free Press of Glencoe Collier-Macmillan, 1964).
12 McNeill (n 10); Granfield & Cloud 2008 (n 8).
13 Natti Ronel & Ety Elisha, 'A different perspective: introducing positive criminology' (2011) *International Journal of Offender Therapy and Comparative Criminology*, 55(2), 305–325. doi: 10.1177/0306624X09357772; Natti Ronel, Noa Frid, & Uri Timor, 'The practice of positive criminology: a vipassana course in prison' (2013) International Journal of Offender Therapy and Comparative Criminology, 57(2), 133–153; Jane Donoghue, *Transforming criminal justice?: Problem-solving and court specialization* (Routledge, 2014), 16.
14 Shadd Maruna & Thomas Lebel, 'Strengths-based restorative approaches to reentry: the evolution of creative restitution, reintegration and destigmatization' in Natti Ronel & Dana Segev (eds.) *Positive criminology* (Routledge, 2015); Maruna (n 9)
15 Donoghue, (n 13); Ronel & Segev (n 10); Howard Zehr, *The little book of restorative justice* (Intercourse, PA: Good Books, 2002); Ronel & Elisha (n 13); Ronel, et al. (n 13).
16 David B. Wexler & Bruce J. Winick, *Judging in a therapeutic key: therapeutic jurisprudence and the courts* (Durham, NC: Carolina Academic Press, 2003) cited in Jane Donoghue (n 13).
17 Denise Gottfredson, Kearley Brooke, Stacey Najaka, & Carlos Rocha, 'How drug treatment courts work: an analysis of mediators' (2007) Journal of Research in Crime and Delinquency, 44(1), 3–3; Douglas Marlowe, 'Research update on adult drug courts' (2010) National Association of Drug Court Professionals; Eric Sevigy, Harold Pollack, & Peter Reuter, 'Can drug courts help to reduce prison and jail populations?' (2013) Sage Journals; KPMG Consulting, 'Evaluation of the drug court of Victoria. Government Advisory Services. Final Report' (2014) Magistrates' Court of Victoria, 18.

United States, in the late 1980s. At this time, the Reagan administration's 'War on Drugs' resulted in a crack cocaine epidemic overburdening the criminal justice system. The revolving-door phenomena, in which the justice system sees the same repeat offenders time after time, caused repercussions for Miami's prison and court docket overcrowding crisis, and oversaw drug arrests increase by 134% between 1980 and 1989.[18] As research began to evidence the close link between drug use and repeat offending, policymakers were galvanised to reconsider the existing repressive responses to drug-using offenders. Miami's drug court was established on experimental terms; through a trajectory combining treatment and criminal justice measures, the drug court would be a pathfinder to long-term change by tackling underlying addictive behaviours.[19]

The international drug courts success rates are strong. That there are now 3,142 drug courts in the United States alone speaks its own truth in terms of prosperity,[20] and they have shown particular success for reducing repeat offending and drug use.[21] Drug courts have also been piloted across jurisdictions worldwide, including: the UK, Belgium,[22] New Zealand, Canada,[23] and Australia[24] and the model now also exists as part of a wider problem-solving court family inclusive of: domestic violence, community, veteran, mental health, and girl courts.[25] Perhaps most significantly, these new courts represent a departure away from mainstream jurisprudence by recognising drug addiction as an addictive disorder and that traditional punishment measures have often failed to address the root cause of illicit behaviours, thus adopting Garland's conceptualisation of positive punishment within the above-mentioned paradigm shifts.

Whilst the problem-solving court movement evolved without any particular philosophical underpinning in mind, it soon required a theoretical framework to justify and support the fact that it radically departed away from the traditional court process, beginning to operate under the auspices of therapeutic jurisprudence. Established by mental health law professors, Wexler and Winick,

---

18 Phillip Bean, 'Drug courts USA' Drug Link, Institute for the Study of Drug Dependence (May/June 1995).
19 Wexler & Winick (n 16).
20 National Institute of Justice, 'Overview of drug courts' (NIJ 14 May 2012). <https://nij.ojp.gov/topics/articles/overview-drug-courts> Accessed 3 September 2019.
21 KPMG (n 17).
22 Kerr et al. (n 1); and Anne Dekkers, Jasmein Beerens, Ciska Wittouck, & Wouter Vanderplasschen, 'Recovery through the eyes of drug treatment court clients' (2016) Cahiers Politiestudies, (40), 191–210.
23 National Crime Prevention Centre, 'Drug Treatment Court of Vancouver' (Public Safety Canada, 31 January 2018) <https://www.publicsafety.gc.ca/cnt/rsrcs/pblctns/drgtrt mnt-vncvr/index-en.aspx> Accessed 2 September 2019.
24 KPMG (n 17).
25 Donoghue (n 13); Erin Collins, 'Status courts' (2017) Geo. Law Journal, 105, 1481–1528; Arie Freiberg, 'Problem-oriented courts: innovative solutions to intractable problems?' (2001) Journal of Judicial Administration, 11(8); Michael Perlin, '"The judge, he cast his robe aside": mental health courts, dignity and due process' (2013) Mental Health Law and Policy Journal, 3(1), 1–29.

independently, but around the same time as the first American drug court in the late 1980s,[26] therapeutic jurisprudence is an academic doctrine that rationalises that legal rules, procedures, roles, as well as the law itself have adverse therapeutic and anti-therapeutic effects on people, whether intentional or not, 'know it or not, like it or not'.[27] To this end, the growing body of therapeutic jurisprudence scholarship has examined how we can apply the law in a way that enhances emotional wellbeing and promotes rehabilitative, remedial, and restorative outcomes. As problem-solving courts have been increasingly understood as therapeutic vehicles, the shared vision has allowed therapeutic jurisprudence principles to enrich problem-solving court practice worldwide through an arsenal of -matured and well-researched principles.

Close at hand, analogous models, adopting key problem-solving styles and therapeutic jurisprudence principles, have begun proliferating globally, perhaps representing a modernised version of the drug court; examples are: Judicial Monitoring (Victoria, Australia),[28] Supervision, Monitoring, Accountability, Responsibility, and Treatment ('SMART') (Kentucky, United States),[29] Special Sanctions Court (Fort Bend County, United States),[30] Hawaii's Opportunity with Probation Enforcement ('HOPE')[31] (Hawaii, Pacific United States), and Probation Accountability with Certain Enforcement ('PACE') (Alaska, United States).[32] Arguably these splintering sister models are beginning to supplant drug courts, though are rooted in the same rationale and modelled on similar principles, ethos, and goals to the orthodox drug court. Whilst the original drug court model has expanded, matured, and refined over time, for any new or old version

26 David B. Wexler, 'Wine and bottles: a metaphor and a methodology for mainstreaming TJ' (2015) Arizona Legal Studies Discussion Paper No. 15 (05). https://ssrn.com/abstract=2553868; Peggy F. Hora, William G. Schma, & John T. Rosenthal, 'Therapeutic jurisprudence and the drug treatment court movement: revolutionizing the criminal justice system's response to drug abuse and crime in America' (1999) 74 Notre Dame Law Review, 439. Available at: http://scholarship.law.nd.edu/ndlr/vol74/iss2/4; Winick & Wexler (n 10).
27 David Wexler, 'Therapeutic jurisprudence: an overview' (2000) Thomas M. Cooley Law Review 17(3).
28 Judicial College, 'Judicial monitoring condition' (2015). Retrieved from: http://www.judicialcollege.vic.edu.au/eManuals/VSM/7157.htm
29 Lisa Shannon, Shelia Hulbig, Shira Birdswhistell, Jennifer Newell, & Connie Neal, 'Implementation of an enhanced probation program: evaluating process and preliminary outcomes' (2015) Evaluation and Programme Planning, 49, 50–62.
30 Clete Snell, 'Fort Bend county community supervision and corrections special sanctions court program evaluation report' (2007) University of Houston.
31 Lorana Bartels, 'Looking at Hawaii's opportunity with probation enforcement (HOPE) program through a therapeutic jurisprudence lens' (2016) QUT Law Review, 16, 30; Lorana Bartels, *Swift, certain and fair: does project HOPE provide a therapeutic paradigm for managing offenders?* (Springer, 2017); Lorana Bartels, 'HOPE-ful bottles: examining the potential for Hawaii's opportunity probation with enforcement (HOPE) to help mainstream therapeutic jurisprudence' International Journal of Law and Psychiatry, 63, 26–34.
32 Teresa Carns & Stephanie Martin, 'Probation accountability with certain enforcement: a preliminary evaluation of the Anchorage pilot PACE project' (2011) Alaska Judicial Council.

to be considered under the broader umbrella term 'problem-solving court' it must incorporate each of the following dimensions:

- Specialisation of the court model around a target group;
- Collaborative intervention and supervision;
- Accountability through judicial monitoring;
- A procedurally fair environment;
- A focus on outcomes.[33]

This book presents findings from a process evaluation carried out at a court in the jurisdiction of England and Wales: Manchester Review Court. The court operates each of the above indicators and can thus be considered a problem-solving court. By bringing offenders back for regular review of recovery progress and law compliance on the core drug rehabilitation requirement ('DRR') component under section 210 of the Criminal Justice Act 2003,[34] Manchester Review Court offers an innovative approach to English and Welsh criminal justice by mobilising key problem-solving principles. However, despite the court having been in operation since (we think) 2005, the UK literature has continuously failed to acknowledge its existence. Indeed, there is no track record of Manchester Review Court in the available literature repositories evidencing its existence, no empirical research, no mention in the media or any policy document, and nor is there a court handbook at the site outlining objectives and expected practice. The most helpful written material is enshrined in section 210 of the Criminal Justice Act 2003 where provisions refer only to DRR court reviews more broadly, and not Manchester Review Court specifically.[35] As such, Manchester Review Court is somewhat of an enigma; we are left unclear on its origins, purpose and expected practice, leaving a big literature gap to fill.

Hallmarked by a similar theme, the literature for all English and Welsh problem-solving courts, particularly drug courts, is patchy, vague, and inconsistent. Like many rehabilitative approaches to criminal justice in England and Wales, and unlike the international models, the English and Welsh drug courts are an under-researched, non-prioritised, and misunderstood area, where perhaps

---

33 Phil Bowen & Steve Whitehead, 'Problem-solving courts: an evidence review' (Centre for Justice Innovation, 2015).
34 Criminal Justice Act 2003, s210.
35 Ibid. 'Drug Rehabilitation Requirement: Provision for Review by Court:(1) A community order or suspended sentence order imposing a drug rehabilitation requirement may (and must if the treatment and testing period is more than 12 months) –(a) Provide for the requirement to be reviewed periodically at intervals of not less than one month;(b) Provide for each review of the requirement to be made, subject to section 211(6), at a hearing held for the purpose by the court responsible for the order (a "review hearing");(c) Require the offender to attend each review hearing;(d) Provide for the responsible officer to make to the court responsible for the order, before each review, a report in writing on the offender's progress under the requirement, and;(e) Provide for each such report to include the test results communicated to the responsible officer under section 209(6) or otherwise and the views of the treatment provider as to the treatment and testing of the offender.'

consequentially, perhaps causally, there has been little published literature. We do know that six pilot drug court sites were alive, and seemingly well, in 2011, delineated by an empirical evaluation by Kerr et al.[36] However, since publication of the Kerr, et al. paper, a series of newspaper articles have informally declared closedown of most (but not all) of the original English and Welsh drug courts, but without proper explanation of why.[37] We know little more than this and certainly there has been no formal explanation. The success of drug courts in jurisdictions worldwide makes this particularly suspicious and perplexing from an international perspective.

Since the Kerr, et al. publication there have also been significant changes to the British landscapes, including: five new justice secretaries under the current Conservative government alone, withdrawal from the European Union, and significant austerity measures, cutbacks, centralisation, and privatisation reforms to sectors that pillar problem-solving court sustainability. Alongside this, Britain has been unreceptive to a rehabilitation revolution, an effect symptomatic of deepseated penal populism causing drastic changes in political responses, appetites, and agendas in this area. Before publication of this book, Manchester Review Court was a mystery from an academic perspective, and despite my best efforts, it still remains unclear whether it is the ghost of the predecessor Salford drug court, or a different method of justice innovation. This question, stemming from the lack of UK literature in this area, is engaged and debated throughout this book through a drug court fidelity analysis for Manchester Review Court and the previous drug court models.

The dearth of UK literature, problems underscoring Manchester Review Court's definition, alongside the lack of formal explanation for the drug court closedowns highlights the need to advance knowledge in this field. By addressing these gaps, this book makes important inroads, providing insight into a significantly underexplored area of British scholarship, justice innovation, and criminal justice practice.

1.4 When is a drug court not a drug court?

The next chapter will posit that one of this book's objectives is to unravel the ontological definition of Manchester Review Court through a fidelity analysis. As such, at this early stage, it is worth spending some time discussing what it means to 'be' a 'drug court'. This of course is different to the more expansive term 'problem-solving court', which offers a broader purview of defining indicators.

As drug courts operate with best-practice principles in mind and have expanded in rapid and organic growth, models can differ in practical approach and emphasis. From a research perspective, this poses problems for external validity and replicability. However, perhaps more pressingly, it leaves unclear when a

36 Kerr et al. (n 1).
37 (n 2) – all.

'drug court' can appropriately be defined by that name.[38] A typical drug court is captured by the Ten Key Components, a matrix stipulated for both systematic measurement and impactful implementation worldwide.[39] Experts suggest that for any problem-solving court to be considered and defined as a 'drug court', it must possess each of the following facets:

1. Drug courts integrate alcohol and other drug treatment services with justice system case processing;
2. Using a non-adversarial approach, prosecution and defence counsel promote public safety whilst protecting participants' due process rights;
3. Eligible participants are identified early and promptly placed in the drug court program;
4. Drug courts provide access to a continuum of alcohol, drug, and other related treatment and rehabilitation services;
5. Abstinence is monitored by frequent alcohol and other drug testing;
6. A coordinated strategy governs drug court responses to participants' compliance;
7. Ongoing judicial interaction with each drug court participant is essential;
8. Monitoring and evaluation measure the achievement of program goals and gauge effectiveness;
9. Continuing interdisciplinary education promotes effective drug court planning, implementation, and operations;
10. Forging partnerships among drug courts, public agencies, and community-based organizations generates local support and enhances drug court program effectiveness.[40]

A widely agreed viewpoint is that all ten components are paramount for success in terms of recidivism and recovery outcomes and it has been stated that 'each of these hypothesised key components has been studied by researchers or evaluators to determine whether it is, in fact, necessary for effective results. Results have confirmed that

38 John Goldkamp, Michael White, & Jennifer Robinson, 'Do drug courts work? Getting inside the drug court black box' (2000) Journal of Drug Issues, 31(1), 27–72; John Goldkamp, 'Challenges for research and innovation: when is a drug court not a drug court?' in W. Clinton Terry (eds.) *The early drug courts: case studies in judicial innovation* (Sage, 1999); Shannon M. Carey, Michael W. Finigan, & Kimberly Pukstas, 'Exploring the key components of drug courts: a comparative study of 18 adult drug courts on practices, outcomes and costs' (2008) NPC Research; Peggy Hora, 'A dozen years of drug treatment courts: uncovering our theoretical foundation and the construction of a mainstream paradigm' (2002) Substance Use and Misuse, 37, 12 & 13; 1469–488; Matthew Hiller, Steven Belenko, Faye Taxman, Douglas Young, Matthew Perdoni, & Christine Saum, 'Measuring drug court structure and operations: key components and beyond' (2010) Criminal Justice and Behaviour; Freiberg (n 25); Susan Witkin & Scott Hays, 'Drug court through the eyes of participants' (2017) Criminal Justice Policy Review, 30(7), 971–989. doi: 10.1177/0887403417731802.
39 John Ashcroft, Deborah Daniels, & Domingo Herriaz, 'Defining drug courts: the key components. U.S. Department of Justice' (2004). Retrieved from: https://www.ncjrs.gov/pdf files1/bja/205621.pdf
40 Ibid.

fidelity to the full drug model is necessary for optimum outcomes'.[41] Therefore, emphatically, drug courts require ascription to all ten key components to allow successful operation. This crucial point will come into play later in this book. In a 2008 local UK report, McSweeney et al.[42] asserted that differences in drug court delivery impacts effectiveness; this indicates not only that drug court success is interlaced with fidelity to the matrix, but that this fact was known to some UK experts during the time that the British drug courts were incepted, again a crucial point.

However, the components are not without criticism. In particular, their prescriptiveness overlooks subtler details around intensity, vigour, and strength for elements such as 'ongoing judicial interaction' (under Component 7).[43] They also fail to account for the different milieus that models operate within. In response, experts have developed a new typology for determining 'when a drug court is not a drug court' and the structural ingredients that linchpin effectiveness.[44] Experts arguing for tighter explanations of drug court factors have rationalised that: 'without such a framework to isolate the critical instrumental elements of the approach, findings from scattered evaluations will accumulate like apples and oranges and other ingredients for a mixed fruit salad of research'.[45] However, whilst the lack of specification and reliability problems have been the strongest criticism of the component monograph, it is exactly these factors that have facilitated the agency of local and cultural knowledge, best practice, experimentation, and innovation to guide their practice. In other words, although the components are not airtight, they continue to uphold strong international credentials by offering just the right degree of specification. Particularly for new, up-and-coming, or poorly understood courts, they are a valuable mechanism for constructing and evaluating drug courts from the ground up by ensuring drug courts operate with best practice in mind. Furthermore, from an ontological perspective, they aid and enrich understanding of what it means to 'be' a 'drug court'.

1.5 Concluding remarks for Chapter 1

We can conclude this chapter by stating that paradigm shifts have reconceptualised the 'criminal man' into a restorable human being, causing movement within criminal justice towards innovative practical solutions. This has manifested itself most prominently in the international drug court example. However, there is a discrepancy between the burgeoning international, particularly American, problem-solving courts, which have expanded in rapid and organic growth, and the British examples, which have lagged far behind and have faced formidable challenges. There is little literature, and certainly nothing of an empirical nature, that explains or rationalises these jurisdictional differences. We can see from the

---

41 Marlowe (n 17) [3].
42 Tim McSweeney, Alex Stevens, Neil Hunt, & Paul Turnbell, 'Drug testing and court review hearings: uses and limitations' (2008) *Probation Journal*, 55(1), 39–53.
43 Ashcroft et al. (n 39).
44 Goldkamp 1999 (n 38).
45 Ibid [28].

evidence base those facets a drug court 'should' possess to match the international mould, as well as the theoretical underpinnings of the models. However, despite being able to understand the conceptual features of problem-solving courts from the literature more broadly, we are left with little understanding of the British problem-solving courts. We do know that drug courts were once in existence, but have now fallen by the wayside – why? Manchester Review Court is still alive, although it is uncertain if it is well. And what exactly is this court – is it linked to the predecessor drug courts or is it something different? What happened to the drug courts? This chapter has raised more questions than it has answered, but by showing that this is an area worthy of further scrutiny, these questions are the rationale for empirical study and the basis for the rest of the book.

Bibliography

Ashcroft J., Daniels D. and Herriaz D., 'Defining drug courts: the key components. U.S. department of justice' (2004). https://www.ncjrs.gov/pdffiles1/bja/2056 21.pdf.

Bartels L., 'HOPE-ful bottles: examining the potential for Hawaii's opportunity probation with enforcement (HOPE) to help mainstream therapeutic jurisprudence' (2019) 63 International Journal of Law and Psychiatry, 26–34.

Bartels L., 'Looking at Hawaii's opportunity with probation enforcement (HOPE) program through a therapeutic jurisprudence lens' (2016) 16 QUT Law Review, 30.

Bartels L., *Swift, certain and fair: does project HOPE provide a therapeutic paradigm for managing offenders?* (Springer, 2017).

Bean P., 'Drug courts USA' Drug Link, Institute for the Study of Drug Dependence (May/June 1995).

Bowcott O., 'US-style problem solving courts plan losing momentum' *Guardian* (12 October 2016). https://tinyurl.com/y3e68qc4, Accessed 2 June 2019.

Bowen P. and Whitehead S., *Problem-solving courts: an evidence review* (Centre for Justice Innovation, 2015).

Carey S.M., Finigan M.W. and Pukstas K., 'Exploring the key component s of drug courts: a comparative study of 18 adult drug courts on practices, outcomes and costs' (2008) NPC Research.

Carns T. and Martin S., 'Probation accountability with certain enforcement a preliminary evaluation of the anchorage pilot PACE project' (2011) Alaska Judicial Council.

Cloud W. and Granfield R., 'Social context and "natural recovery": the role of social capital in the resolution of drug-associated problems' (2001) 36(11) Substance Use and Misuse, 1543–1570.

Cloud W. and Granfield R., 'Conceptualizing recovery capital: expansion of a theoretical construct' (2008) 43(12–13) Substance Use and Misuse, 1971–1986. doi:10.1080/10826080802289762.

Collins E., 'Status courts' (2017) 105 Geo Law Journal, 1481–1528.

Dekkers A., Beerens B., Wittouck C. and Vanderplasschen W., 'Recovery through the eyes of drug treatment court clients' (2016) 40 Cahiers Politiestudies, 191–210.

Donoghue J., *Transforming criminal justice?: problem-solving and court specialization* (Routledge, 2014).

Durkheim E., *The division of labor in society* (New York: Free Press of Glencoe Collier-Macmillan, 1964).

Freiberg A., 'Problem-oriented courts: innovative solutions to intractable problems?' (2001) 11(8) Journal of Judicial Administration, 8–27.

Froh J., 'The history of positive psychology: truth be told' (2004) 16(3) NYS Psychologist, 18–20.

Goldkamp J., 'Challenges for research and innovation: when is a drug court not a drug court?' in W.C. Terry (ed.) *The early drug courts: case studies in judicial innovation* (Sage, 1999).

Goldkamp J., White M. and Robinson J., 'Do drug courts work? Getting inside the drug court black box' (2000) 31(1) Journal of Drug Issues, 27–72.

Gottfredson D., Brooke K., Najaka S. and Rocha C., 'How drug treatment courts work: an analysis of mediators' (2007) 44(1) Journal of Research in Crime and Delinquency, 3.

Hiller M., Belenko S., Taxman F., Young D., Perdoni M. and Saum C., 'Measuring drug court structure and operations: key components and beyond' (2010) Criminal Justice and Behavior.

Hora H., 'A dozen years of drug treatment courts: uncovering our theoretical foundation and the construction of a mainstream paradigm' (2002) 37 Substance Use and Misuse, 12 & 13, 1469–1488.

Hora P.F., Schma W.G. and Rosenthal J.T., 'Therapeutic jurisprudence and the drug treatment court movement: revolutionizing the criminal justice system's response to drug abuse and crime in America' (1999) 74 Notre Dame Law Review, 439. http://scholarship.law.nd.edu/ndlr/vol74/iss2/4.

Judicial College, 'Judicial monitoring condition' (2015). http://www.judicialcolleg e.vic.edu.au/eManuals/VSM/7157.htm.

Kerr J., Tompkins C., Tomaszewski W., Dickens S., Grimshaw, R. Wright N. and Barnard, M. 'The dedicated drug courts pilot evaluation process study' (2011) Ministry of Justice Research Series, 1. London: Ministry of Justice.

Kinderman P., *A prescription for psychiatry: why we need a whole new approach to mental health and wellbeing* (Palgrave Macmillan, 2014). doi:10.1057/9781137408716.

KPMG Consulting, 'Evaluation of the drug court of Victoria. Government advisory services. final report' (2014) Magistrates' Court of Victoria, 18.

Marlowe D., *Research update on adult drug courts* (National Association of Drug Court Professionals, 2010).

Maruna S., *Making good: how ex-convicts reform and rebuild their lives* (American Psychological Association, 2011). doi:10.1037/10430-000.

Maruna S. and Lebel T., 'Strengths-based restorative approaches to reentry: the evolution of creative restitution, reintegration and destigmatization' in N. Ronel and D. Segev (eds.) *Positive criminology* (Routledge, 2015).

McNeill F., 'Positive criminology, positive criminal justice?' in Natti Ronel and Dana Segev (eds.) *Positive criminology* (Routledge, 2015).

McSweeney T., Stevens A., Hunt N. and Turnbell P., 'Drug testing and court review hearings: uses and limitations' (2008) 55(1) Probation Journal, 39–53.

National Crime Prevention Centre, 'Drug treatment court of Vancouver' *Public Safety Canada* (31 January 2018). https://www.publicsafety.gc.ca/cnt/rsrcs/ pblctns/drgtrtmnt-vncvr/index-en.aspx, Accessed 2 September 2019.

National Institute of Justice, 'Overview of drug courts' *NIJ* (14 May 2012). https:// nij.ojp.gov/topics/articles/overview-drug-courts, Accessed 3 September 2019.

Owen B., 'Why are special courts that can help drug users at risk of being scrapped?' *Guardian* (10 June 2014). https://tinyurl.com/y3n6o9bp, Accessed 3 September 2019.

Perlin M., '"The judge, he cast his robe aside": mental health courts, dignity and due process' (2013) 3(1) Mental Health Law and Policy Journal, 1–29.

Peterson C. and Seligman M., *Character strengths and virtues: a handbook and classification* (American Psychological Association; Oxford University Press, 2004).

Rapp C., *The strengths model: case management with people suffering from severe and persistent mental illness* (Oxford: Oxford University Press, 1997).

Robins J., 'Where next for community justice? Pioneering court closes' *The Justice Gap* (24 October 2013).

Robins J., 'Whatever happened to community justice?' *The Justice Gap* (3 October 2012).

Ronel N. and Elisha E., 'A different perspective: introducing positive criminology' (2011) 55(2) International Journal of Offender Therapy and Comparative Criminology, 305–325. doi:10.1177/0306624X09357772.

Ronel N., Frid N. and Timor U., 'The practice of positive criminology: a vipassana course in prison' (2013) 57(2) International Journal of Offender Therapy and Comparative Criminology, 133–153.

Seligman M., 'Building human strength: psychology's forgotten mission' (1998) 29(1) APA Monitor, 2.

Seligman M. and Csikszentmihalyi M., 'Positive psychology: an introduction' (2000) 55(1) American Psychologist, 5–14. doi:10.1037/0003-066X.55.1.5.

Sevigy E., Pollack H. and Reuter P., 'Can drug courts help to reduce prison and jail populations?' (2013) Sage Journals.

Shannon L., Hulbig S., Birdswhistell S., Newell K. and Neal C., 'Implementation of an enhanced probation program: evaluating process and preliminary outcomes' (2015) 49 Evaluation and Programme Planning, 50–62.

Sheldon K. and King L., 'Why positive psychology is necessary' (2001) 56(3) American Psychologist, 216–217. doi:10.1037/0003-066X.56.3.216.

Snell C., *Fort bend county community supervision and corrections special sanctions court program evaluation report* (University of Houston, 2007).

Wexler D.B., 'Therapeutic jurisprudence: an overview' (2000) 17(3) Thomas M. Cooley Law Review, 125–134.

Wexler D.B., 'Wine and bottles: a metaphor and a methodology for mainstreaming TJ' (2015) Arizona Legal Studies Discussion Paper No. 15 (05). https://ssrn.com/abstract=2553868.

Wexler D.B. and Winick B.J., *Judging in a therapeutic key: therapeutic jurisprudence and the courts* (Carolina Academic Press, 2003).

White W., 'Addiction recovery: its definition and conceptual boundaries' (2007) 33 Journal of Substance Abuse Treatment, 229–241.

Witkin S. and Hays S., 'Drug court through the eyes of participants' (2017) 30(7) Criminal Justice Policy Review, 971–989. doi:10.1177/0887403417731802.

Zehr H., *The little book of restorative justice* (Intercourse, PA: Good Books, 2002).

2　The evidence so far
A critical review

2.1 Introduction

This chapter will build on the themes identified in the previous chapter by expressly acknowledging the prevailing literature gaps for problem-solving courts in England and Wales. It will begin by detailing some recent statistics released by the Ministry of Justice for UK drug-fuelled offending to justify that an intelligent justice revolution is required. This chapter will give a more detailed synopsis of national and worldwide problem-solving court history compared to the previous chapter, delineating some of the UK legislation and policy put forward by British justice ministers before and around the time that they formally opened the original six drug courts.

The chapter seeks to take the reader through the conflicting messages put forward by the Blair Labour government, the Coalition government, and the more recent Conservative governments, and will conclude that the British rehabilitation revolution, including problem-solving courts agendas, have been stop–start with efforts often abandoned before they have been given a chance to succeed. By dissecting the history in this field, the chapter will show that the jettisoned British drug court schemes were merely the tip of the iceberg amongst a much broader history of UK failures in this area. This in turn will raise questions as to what went wrong for the English and Welsh drug courts, whilst asking whether British cultural modalities and public conversations are overshadowed by punitive populism.

The chapter will ask whether problem-solving courts are now an obsolete phenomenon for England and Wales or if they are still relevant to research, policy, and practice. In scrutinising the literature repositories, it transpires that a very recent range of policy reports and initiatives are keen to reinstate UK problem-solving courts, and that this effort has not totally lost traction, despite the downfalls of the England and Wales drug courts. Very recent plans to progress these efforts, including the September 2020 White Paper, serve to highlight that problem-solving is an area that Britain has not yet abandoned but in fact feature in current policy. This, and the fact that the drug court efforts were unsuccessful, renders empirical research germane. To this effect, the chapter will set up key research questions to be explored, engaged with, and discussed throughout the book, and will introduce the methods, methodology, and evaluative framework used to collect the data for this book. It will discuss the three methodological phases leveraged during the empirical work and will acknowledge their limitations.

2.2 The backdrop: English and Welsh crime and drug statistics

During a criminal justice climate accentuated by austerity measures, England and Wales currently face high recidivism rates. In their latest report, the Ministry of Justice detailed that (adult and youth) offenders recidivate at a rate of 29.3%.[1] The Ministry of Justice have further reported that adults released from custodial sentences of less than 12 months reoffend at a rate of 62.2%.[2] Although recidivism rates remain high, fluctuating between 26% and 28% since 2003, there has been an overall decline in England and Wales' crime rates since 2007.[3] The fact that crime rates have fallen in the same timeframe that reoffending rates have climbed the statistical ladder makes recidivist criminals an interesting, albeit frustrating, cohort for policymakers, legislators, and government ministers, forcing them to ask: who are these individuals, what causes them to reoffend, and what can be done to stop them?

Although it is ubiquitous across current UK criminal justice policy,[4] the current lexicon for tackling recidivist individuals offers nothing particularly new. In fact, reducing offending amongst this cohort has foregrounded the agendas of the National Offender Management Service (now called Her Majesty's Prison and Probation Service) and Her Majesty's Court and Tribunal Service since they were founded in 2004 and 2011 respectively.[5] This means that despite the ostensible best efforts of the UK over nine years and more, reoffending rates remain consistently and unmanageably high. It is reported that this issue is lethargic, burdensome, and frustrating for legal practitioners, for those who fall victim to these crimes, and to wider communities that become increasingly unsafe environments.[6] But we must not forget that the system is also failing the offenders.

1 Ministry of Justice, 'Proven reoffending statistics quarterly bulletin, July 2017 to September 2017' (2019) National Statistics.
2 Ibid.
3 Ministry of Justice, 'Criminal justice statistics quarterly, England and Wales' (2017) National Statistics.
4 Ministry of Justice, 'Transforming rehabilitation: a strategy for reform' (2013). Retrieved from https://consult.justice.gov.uk/digital-communications/transforming-rehabilitation/results/transforming-rehabilitation-response.pdf; Ministry of Justice, 'Prison safety and reform' (2016); Offender Rehabilitation Act, 2014; Criminal Justice Act, 2003; Ministry of Justice, 'New partnership to boost offender rehabilitation' (2019). Retrieved from: https://www.gov.uk/government/news/new-partnership-to-boost-offender-rehabilitation; David Gauke, 'Smarter sentences, safer streets' Ministry of Justice (2019). Retrieved from https://www.gov.uk/government/speeches/smarter-sentences-safer-streets (Government Speech); Georgina Eaton & Aiden Mews, 'The impact of short custodial sentences, community orders and suspended sentence orders on reoffending' (2019) Ministry of Justice.
5 Patrick Carter, 'Managing offenders, reducing crime: a new approach' (2007) Strategy Unit; Ministry of Justice 'Her majesty's courts and tribunals service: about us' (2011) Gov.UK.
6 Ashley Cowburn, 'Prison population should be cut by half to "Margaret Thatcher levels", urge senior politicians (*The Independent*, 22 December 2016). https://www.independent.c

A plethora of research demonstrably links drug use to criminal activity.[7] The literature suggests that around three-quarters of all offenders have substance abuse problems[8] and approximately 60% of individuals arrested for most crimes test positive for illegal drugs under the Misuse of Drugs Act 1971 upon arrest.[9] The relationship between drug use and criminal behaviour is complex, manifesting itself as: drug sales, theft property crimes, prostitution, child abuse, violence, domestic violence, and drink driving.[10] More specifically, research shows that a large number of acquisitive crimes (such as: shoplifting, burglary, vehicle crime, and robbery) are related to feeding an addiction.[11] Evidence also suggests that 81% of arrestees using heroin and/or crack at least once a week reported committing an acquisitive offence within the previous 12 months (compared with 30% of other arrestees).[12] Whilst acquisitive crime is generally classified as low-level, resulting in shorter-term sentencing in view of its non-violent nature,[13] it

o.uk/news/uk/politics/prison-population-cut-40000-overcrowding-margaret-thatcher -levels-nick-clegg-ken-clarke-a7489636.html)> Accessed 4 September 2019.

7 National Council on Alcohol and Drug Dependence, 'Alcohol, drugs and crime' (National Council on Alcohol and Drug Dependence, 2015), <https://tinyurl.com/yy76h5ar> Accessed 6 June 2019; Phillip Bean, *Drugs and crime* (Routledge, 2014); National Institute on Drug Abuse, 'Criminal justice' (National Institute on Drug Abuse, 2014) <https:// tinyurl.com/y289r7jy> Accessed 12 June 2019; The Scottish Consortium on Crime and Criminal Justice, 'Making sense of drugs and crime: drugs, crime and penal policy' (2003) <https://tinyurl.com/y4xtwfur> Accessed 12 June 2019; Douglas Anglin & and Yih-Ing Hser, 'Criminal justice and the drug-abusing offender: policy issues of coerced treatment' (1991) Behavioural Sciences and the Law 9(3), 243–267; Tim McSweeney, Alex Stevens, Neil Hunt, & Paul Turnbull, 'Drug testing and court review hearings: uses and limitations' (2008) Probation Journal, 55(1), 39–53; Howard Parker & Perpetua Kirby, 'Methadone maintenance and crime reduction on Merseyside' (1996) Home Office, Police Research Group; Katy Holloway, Trevor Bennett, & Claire Lower, 'Trends in drug use and offending: the results of the NEW-ADAM programme, 1999–2002' (2004) Home Office; House of Commons, Health Committee, 'Public health: twelfth report of session 2010–2012' (2012. No. 1) London: House of Commons <https://tinyurl.com/y5hdh56a> Accessed 12 July 2019; Shadd Maruna, 'Making good: how ex-convicts reform and rebuild their lives' (Washington, DC: American Psychological Association, 2001). doi:10.1037/10430-000.

8 Susan Young, June Wells, & Gisli Hannes Gudjonnson, 'Predictors of offending among prisoners: the role of attention-deficit hyperactivity disorder and substance use' (2011) *Journal of Psychopharmacology*.

9 Trevor Bennet & Katy Holloway, 'Drug use and offending: summary results of the first two years of the NEW-ADAM programme' (2004) Home Office.

10 Mangai Natarajtan & Mike Hough, *Illegal drug markets: from research to prevention policy* (Monsey: NY: Criminal Justice Press/Willow Tree Press, 2000).

11 Michael Gossop, 'The National Treatment Outcomes Research Study (NTORS) and its influence on addiction treatment policy in the United Kingdom' (2015) National Addiction Centre, Institute of Psychiatry.

12 UK Drugs Policy Commission, 'Reducing drug use, reducing reoffending' (2008) UK Policy Commission <https://www.ukdpc.org.uk/wp-content/uploads/Policy%20report%20-%2 0Reducing%20drug%20use,%20reducing%20reoffending%20(summary).pdf> Accessed 4 September 2019.

13 Mark Bryan, Emilia Bono, & Stephen Pudney, 'Drug-related crime' (2013) No. 2013-08 Institute for Social and Economic Research.

is expensive – inflicting losses to the country of nearly 14 billion pounds a year through repeated muggings, robberies, and theft.[14]

These statistics spawn broader questions: could the criminal justice system be a window of opportunity to rehabilitate offenders; could the criminal justice system itself be a vehicle for recovery; and can we marry together therapy and justice? Ideas at the heart of these questions have been instilled most prominently within international practice, such as that of the American drug courts.

As the international drug court successes have been so widely documented, there is little point regurgitating old academic turf in this book; however, restating some of their most prominent impacts is important to the key themes. Responding to the notion that punitive measures alone do not appropriately tackle drug fuelled acquisitive crime, the evidence base for drug courts is strong, particularly across primary outcome delivery, namely: substance use and reoffending.[15] According to Marlowe's report,[16] over three-quarters of the American drug courts (78%) reduced criminal activity. The leading models have demonstrated reductions of between 35% and 40%.[17] Reductions in recidivism have been evidenced to last for three years post entry.[18] Elsewhere, studies also show that non-completers are more likely to recidivate than those who graduate[19] and researchers have identified low relapse rates amongst drug participants.[20] It has also been illustrated that drug courts are the most effective way of addressing the recidivism problem over any other criminal justice approach in isolation.[21] Research suggests that the US drug courts are six times more likely to keep offenders in treatment long enough for them to get better.[22] Drug courts are also proven vehicles in which offenders can reintegrate back into communities and make other positive

---

14 Owen Bowcott, 'Why are special courts that can help drug users at risk of being scrapped?' (*The Guardian*, 10 June 2014) <https://tinyurl.com/y3n6o9bp> Accessed 3 September 2019).

15 Steven Belenko, 'Research on drug courts: a critical review' (1998) National Drug Court Institute Review, 1(1), 1–42. Brown, 2010; David Wilson, Ojmarrh Mitchell, & Doris MacKenzie, 'A systematic review of drug court effects on recidivism' (2006) *Journal of Experimental Criminology*, 2(4), 459–487; Christopher Lowenkamp, Alexander Holsinger, & Edward Latessa, 'Are drug courts effective: a meta-analytic review' (2005) *Journal of Community Corrections*, 15(1), 5–11; Deborah Koetzle Shaffer, 'Reconsidering drug court effectiveness: a meta-analytic review' (2006) Doctoral thesis retrieved from https://etd.ohiolink.edu/

16 Douglas Marlowe, 'Research update on adult drug courts' (2010) National Association of Drug Court Professionals.

17 Lowenkamp et al. (n 15); Shaffer (n 15).

18 Marlowe (n 16).

19 Belenko (n 15).

20 Karen Freeman, 'Health and well-being outcomes for drug-dependent offenders on the NSW drug court programme' (2003) Drug and Alcohol Review, 22(4), 409–416; Belenko (n 15).

21 KPMG Consulting, 'Evaluation of the drug court of Victoria. Government Advisory Services. Final Report.' (2014) Magistrates' Court of Victoria, 18.

22 Marlowe (n 16).

life changes.[23] Whilst these successes are hard to argue with, the UK problems with drug-fuelled offending remained problematic despite the English and Welsh drug courts efforts in the early 2000s. However, the jurisdiction would seemingly benefit from a similar intervention given the track record of drug courts and the UK statistics. However, this simply opens up further questions: why have UK ministerial efforts been circumspect compared to those of international jurisdictions? Why did the English and Welsh models fall by the wayside?

2.3 The history of England and Wales' problem-solving courts: an overview

The literature for the English and Welsh problem-solving courts is scant, patchy, and inconsistent. This statement is particularly true for the six, now-closed, English and Welsh drug courts. As a neglected area of British scholarship, the reasons for their failures have been left unclear. We know that six pilot drug court sites were alive, and seemingly well, in 2011, delineated by an empirical evaluation by Kerr et al.[24] However, since publication of the Kerr et al. paper, a series of newspaper articles have informally declared closedown of each British drug court, but without proper explanation of why.[25] We know little more than this and, certainly, there has been no formal explanation from the Ministry of Justice. When reporting on the closure of the West London drug court, UK magistrate and scholar, Gibbs, stated: 'the closure signals, yet again, how difficult it is for innovation to flourish in our courts system, and how resistant some parts of the system are to the specialist court model'.[26] Whilst Gibbs' statement certainly holds true, there is little satisfactory explanation for why the burgeoning international models have left England and Wales lagging so far behind, and the cause of such difficulties.

Despite their chequered history, and perhaps surprisingly, problem-solving courts have featured in UK history for over 20 years. Donoghue's 2014 book provides a comprehensive overview of UK agendas in this field.[27] She and other

23 John Goldkamp, Michael White, & Jennifer Robinson, 'Do drug courts work? Getting inside the drug court black box' (2000) *Journal of Drug Issues*, 31(1), 27–72.
24 Jane Kerr, Charlotte Tompkins, Wojtek Tomaszewski, Sarah Dickens, Roger Grimshaw, Nat Wright, & Matt Barnard, 'The dedicated drug courts pilot evaluation process study' (2011) Ministry of Justice Research Series, 1. London: Ministry of Justice.
25 Jon Robins, 'Where next for community justice? Pioneering court closes' *The Justice Gap* (24 October 2013); Jon Robins, 'Whatever happened to community justice?' *The Justice Gap* (3 October 2012); Owen Bowcott, 'US-style problem solving courts plan losing momentum' (*The Guardian*, 12 October 2016) <https://tinyurl.com/y3e68qc4> Accessed 2 June 2019; Bowcott (n 14).
26 Penelope Gibbs, 'Has the West London drugs court closed and does it matter?' (Transforming Justice, 10 June 2014) <http://www.transformjustice.org.uk/has-the-west-london-drugs-court-closed-and-does-it-matter/>Accessed 4 September 2019.
27 Jane Donoghue, *Transforming criminal justice?: problem-solving and court specialization* (Routledge, 2014).

UK experts have argued that section 89 of Crime and Disorder Act (1998) (intro-
duced under the Labour Government) represented the first British attempt at
court specialism by introducing drug treatment and testing orders ('DTTOS').[28]
As a newly available sentence tackling addicted offenders in the community, the
DTTO took influence from the international drug courts by enabling drug testing to become a court requirement and emphasising proactive judicial leadership,
bringing offenders back to court for regular review to monitor progress.[29] Whilst
the DTTOs were criticised by UK experts for being 'very weak version(s)' of the
international drug courts',[30] they never pretended to be drug courts. Arguably,
they instead lay the foundations for UK 'drug courts' to soon follow. At this
point experts noted that: 'although problem-solving justice is a relatively new
phenomenon in England and Wales, it already shows signs of following a similar
arc to the U.S. Beginning with the passage of the 1998 Crime and Disorder
Act'.[31] As such, the British future thus looked promising due to legislation of
section 89 and implementation of the DTTO.

Some years later, in 2005, the Criminal Justice Act 2003[32] replaced DTTOs
with the now widely used drug rehabilitation requirement (DRR), which the
Ministry of Justice have asserted are: 'the primary means for sentenced offenders
to address identified drug misuse within community sentencing'.[33] Like its DTTO
predecessor, DRRs were designed to address drug dependency in the community
by forming part of a community order or suspended sentence, and were (are)
funded, overseen, and supervised by the probation services who mandate drug
testing, court reviews, and appointments.[34] However, the DRR has wider ambit;
whereas the DTTO only provided for Class A users, the DRR provides more
opportunities for rehabilitation by tackling low-level persistent offenders including the homeless, as well as more prolific offenders.[35] Since its legislation, under
section 210 of the Criminal Justice Act 2003,[36] courts can formally impose DRRs
on the basis that:

28 Crime and Disorder Act 1998, s89.
29 McSweeney et al. (n 7); Mike Hough, Anna Clancy, Tim McSweeney, & Paul Turnbull,
    'Impact of drug treatment and testing orders on offending: two-year reconviction results'
    (2003) National Criminal Justice Reference Service, Home Office Findings 184.
30 Philip Bean, 'Drug treatment courts, British style: the drug treatment court movement in
    Britain' (2002) *Substance Use & Misuse*, 37(12–13) [1592].
31 Greg Berman & Aubrey Fox, 'Lasting change or passing fad? Problem-solving justice in
    England and Wales' (2009) Policy Exchange, London [27].
32 Criminal Justice Act, 2003.
33 Ministry of Justice, 'National Offender Management Service annual report 2011/12: man-
    agement information addendum' (2012) Ministry of Justice Information Release [22].
34 McSweeney et al. (n 7).
35 Melanie Hollingworth, 'An examination of the potential impact of the drug rehabilitation
    requirement on homeless illicit drug-using offenders' (2008) *Probation Journal: The Journal
    of Community and Criminal Justice*.
36 (n 32) section 210.

1. There is certainty that the offender has a dependency on drugs/a tendency to misuse illicit substances;
2. The court believes that the offender would benefit from the DRR; and
3. The offender expresses willingness to comply with the DRR/has a desire to pursue recovery.[37]

Under the act,[38] a DRR is a sentence mandating structured treatment with a regular drug testing component. It can be added to one of two primary sentencing options: (i) community order, or (ii) suspended sentence order.[39] Failure to comply with the DRR requirement could mean that the original sentence is enforced.[40] DRR service-users are usually identified during conviction where the mainstream court is obliged to consider criminal background; if there is history of acquisitive crime to fund a drug habit, the individual might be assessed for DRR suitability.[41] The DRR must be agreed by all, including the service-user and the court, but the final decision is made by the probation services under section 209 of the Criminal Justice Act.[42] The DRR thus resembles a traditional drug model; both are diversion programmes that seek to rehabilitate offenders from drug use where sentences can be carried out in the community so long as participants comply with the requirements, but where failure to comply risks reinstatement of the original sentence or more onerous requirements.

What is important for this study, and the aspect that bears the most semblance to the international drug courts, is that the DRR has an optional requirement for regular court review under section 210 of the Criminal Justice Act.[43] It is worth being clear at this stage that the empirical work in this study is interested exclusively in the court review aspect of the DRR, not the DRR core component. Most significantly from a court innovation perspective, section 210 of the Criminal Justice Act 2003 provides that offenders with DRRs of over 12 months must legally attend intermittent court review sessions in which recovery progress and law-abiding behaviour on the DRR is monitored by magistrates.[44] Importantly, though, despite the 12-month threshold for compulsory review under section 210, courts can

---

37 National Offender Management Service, 'Supporting community order treatment requirements' (2014) Commissioning Group.
38 (n 32).
39 'The Community Order replaces all existing community sentences for adults. It consists of one or more of 12 possible requirements and may last for as short a time as 12 hours or for as long as three years' ... 'The Suspended Sentence Order (SSO) is a custodial sentence and should only be used where the court is minded to pass a custodial sentence of less than 12 months. However, it is made up of the same requirements as the Community Order, so in the absence of breach is served wholly in the community', George Mair & Helen Mills, 'The community order and the suspended sentence order three years on: the views and experiences of probation officers and offenders' (2008) Centre for Crime and Justice Studies.
40 (n 32).
41 Ibid.
42 Ibid, section 209.
43 Ibid, section 210.
44 Ibid.

also mandate regular court reviews for service-users carrying out a DRR of under 12 months at their discretion. The process of review thus resembles the international drug court because it brings addicted offenders back before the judicial body to try to inaugurate long-term personal and social change through judicial monitoring and motivation. Notably, further powers are given to magistrates to regularly review progress in court under the Criminal Justice Act 2003 subject to the same 12-month restrictions: section 178 gives power to review a community order and section 191 a suspended sentence order.

Despite the DTTOs and DRRs having been in the background for several years, the 2002 White Paper: Justice for All,[45] was the first official endorsement for drug courts in England and Wales. Donoghue has stated that the drug courts were incepted based on similar rationales to the international attempts by seeking to respond to: public and professional dissatisfaction with legal processes and reoffending rates; inability to sufficiently deal with causations of crime; and law compliance issues.[46] Following publication of the 2002 White Paper, drug courts began formally proliferating in the UK, ostensibly with strong influence from the United States.[47] In 2005, under the Blair administration, the first two official drug courts were launched within West London and Leeds magistrates' courthouses.[48] They were purposefully housed within the mainstream court buildings and courtrooms themselves to preserve costs and overheads.[49] The drug courts, housed within the mainstream courts, would host the DRR review requirement under section 210 of the Criminal Justice Act 2003.[50] Thus, the courts fostered a specialist approach by singlehandedly catering for drug-using offenders sentenced to a DRR. However, the courts would expand from the DRR itself by operating further drug court components. It was reported that the drug court pilots progressed organically from existing responses to drug-using offenders,[51] presumably by building upon the existing DRR option to avoid enactment of new legislation or creating new sentences. As an aside, one could speculate that the optional DRR review requirement has become less popular with the drug court closedowns as there are fewer specialist courthouses to host it.

Within the same breath, government established the North Liverpool Community Justice Centre, which was modelled upon New York's Red Hook Community Center in Brooklyn, also launched in 2005. Like the New York version, the Liverpool counterpart aimed to tackle entrenched criminogenic needs by collaborating inter-agency working between the youth, the Crown Court,

---

45 Great Britain Home Office, 'Justice for all: a white paper on the criminal justice system' (2002) The Stationary Office.
46 Donoghue (n 27).
47 Ibid.
48 Plotnikoff J. & Woolfson R., *Review of the effectiveness of specialist courts in other jurisdictions* (London: Department of Constitutional Affairs, 2005).
49 Kerr et al. (n 24).
50 (n 32), section 210.
51 Kerr et al. (n 24).

criminal justice agencies, and a range of social services.[52] Two Scottish drug court pilots were also established in Glasgow in 2001 and Fife in 2002.[53] Then, in circa 2012, the UK Centre of Justice Innovation was launched, taking direct influence from the Red Hook Community Justice Center sister model (in Brooklyn, of the United States), which became responsible for developing British problem-solving approaches, carrying out legal consultancy, promoting relevant research, and implementing, evaluating, and disseminating new smart justice ideas and practices in the UK.[54] At this point, it looked as if British justice had turned a corner, by supporting an assortment of problem-solving measures to address long-term problems ingrained within the tapestry of the justice system.

In 2008, after the West London and Leeds drug courts had been running for three years, Matrix Group, commissioned by the UK Ministry of Justice, published a process evaluation, which sought to examine their functionality, impact, and value for money alongside any operational issues before, and with the idea of, wider implementation across the county to move drug courts from the margins to the mainstream.[55] The researchers applied a complete range of qualitative and qualitative methods, including: offender and stakeholder interviews, observations, stakeholder workshops, focus groups, as well as analysis of case files and court records. An area of interest for the researchers, and important to research question 1 ('wine') of this book (see section 2.6 Methods and research questions: this chapter), was the impact of a consistent judiciary (Drug Court Component 7)[56] on offender DRR outcomes, offender motivation, and compliance.[57] Qualitative evidence suggested that Component 7 was achieved at both drug courts even if only partially (the same magistrate sitting for two consecutive hearings). Although the researchers expressed concern that consistency was sometimes difficult to achieve procedurally, and it was often at the most 'crucial junctures' when it was lacking,[58] judicial continuity was a 'strong planned feature' of the courts going forward due to its high impact.[59] Overall, the results from the report were positive; although throughput was lower than expected, the courts had no major fault lines and were reportedly 'in line with international understandings'.[60] These positive outcomes led the Secretary of State for Justice to announce the roll-out of four more drug courts in the magistrates' courts of Barnsley, Salford, Cardiff, and Bristol in 2009, using the same model as the

52 Lucy Booth, Adam Altoft, Rachel Dubourg, Miguel Gonçalves, & Catriona Mirrlees-Black, 'North Liverpool Community Justice Centre: analysis of re-offending rates and efficiency of court processes' (2012) Ministry of Justice Research Series, 10/12.

53 Gill McIvor, 'Therapeutic jurisprudence and procedural justice in Scottish drug courts' (2009) Criminology and Criminal Justice, 9(1), 29–49.

54 Donoghue (n 27).

55 Matrix Knowledge Group, 'Dedicated drug court pilots a process report' (2008) Ministry of Justice Research Series 7/08. London: Ministry of Justice.

56 Ibid.

57 Ibid.

58 Ibid [2].

59 Ibid [1].

60 Ibid.

original pilots.[61] There was no doubt at this point that British problem-solving courts appeared to hold a strong trajectory. To that effect, subsequent years oversaw an expansion of the UK model embryonically into mental health courts, anti-social behaviour courts, domestic violence courts, family drug and alcohol courts, with various degrees of effect.[62]

The latest (and last) empirical research for the England and Wales drug courts was carried out in 2011 and comprised of a process evaluation.[63] The report investigated all six drug courts simultaneously using a case study design. By applying a combination of qualitative and quantitative methods, researchers mapped implementation, operation, and core elements of the models. The qualitative component explored perceptions of frontline practitioners and offenders, through in-depth interviews as well as observations and focus groups. Quantitative findings were derived through analysis of pre-existing datasets, allowing researchers to generate descriptive statistics around judicial continuity and breaches. Interestingly, the key (quantitative and qualitative) findings cemented the previous report by suggesting that judicial continuity under Component 7 remained crucial for successful operation and increased the positive offender experiences. Researchers reiterated that continuity would be logistically difficult to achieve long term but advised that this was easier to implement when a single district judge presided rather than a panel of magistrates. Across five of the six sites, partial continuity was achieved for 90% of cases,[64] a finding replicating international research emphasising the importance of a consistent judicial bench under Drug Court Component 7.[65]

UK data also mirrored international research by demonstrating that the judiciary–offender relationship was key for reducing drug use and reoffending. In line with scholarly work for therapeutic jurisprudence 'wine',[66] Kerr et al. reported that strong interpersonal and interactional styles of judicial officers carried much gravity and were fundamental for influencing offenders' structure and goal setting, self-esteem and confidence, accountability, engagement, increasing judicial knowledge of specific cases as well as the working of partnerships. Specifically, five judicial styles of engagement were elicited by magistrates across the drug courts: motivational, personalised, interactive, authoritarian, and challenging, and key attributes of this interaction were reported as: an interested approach, listening to

61 Her Majesty's Courts Service, 'Her majesty's courts service business plan 2009–10' (2009) HMCS.
62 Donoghue (n 27).
63 Kerr, et al. (n 24).
64 Ibid.
65 Ibid. David B. Wexler & Bruce J., *Winick law in a therapeutic key: developments in therapeutic jurisprudence* (Durham, NC: Carolina Academic Press, 1999) <http://www.austlii.edu.au/au/journals/CICrimJust/1997/9.pdf>; John Ashcroft, Deborah Daniels, & Domingo Herriaz, 'Defining drug courts: the key components. U.S. Department of Justice' (2004). Retrieved from: https://www.ncjrs.gov/pdffiles1/bja/205621.pdf.
66 David B. Wexler, 'Wine and bottles: A metaphor and a methodology for mainstreaming TJ' (2015) Arizona Legal Studies Discussion Paper No. 15 (05) <https://ssrn.com/abstract=2553868>.

offenders, engaging with them genuinely and non-judgementally, and encouraging them to want to do well,[67] and service-users were refreshed by these court-room interactions.[68] In terms of costs, some initial funding had been given to the sites for start-up; however, funds were not deemed to be an ongoing requirement; the existing magistrates' courts would simply need to ensure enough space and scheduled time to house the drug court sessions, as well ensuring there were enough resources in place to ensure judicial continuity.[69]

Whilst these findings are all positive, casting a critical eye over the report from a fidelity perspective raises alarm bells. During their project, researchers evaluated (at most) four of the ten key drug court components (outlined in full in the previous chapter):

1. Continuity of the judiciary (i.e., Component 7);
2. Staff training (including the judiciary) (i.e., Component 9);
3. Partnership working (i.e., Component 10); and
4. Exclusivity of the model in handling drug cases (i.e., Component 1).

The reason for reporting exclusively on these components appears to be because they were the onset targets of Her Majesty's Court Service when implementing the drug courts in the first instance. In other words, justice ministers designed the English and Welsh drug courts with only five of the ten components in mind. This is open to critique: why did Her Majesty's Court Service itself, and latterly commissioned researchers, only implement and examine five drug court components when the international literature strongly evidences that all ten optimise success rates? This, and the fact that the report failed to mention therapeutic jurisprudence as the underpinning philosophy, could indicate poor understanding of the drug court model at the grassroots level by UK public bodies and researchers thereafter.

By hinting that the drug courts could lack fidelity to the international benchmark, the report raises suspicions about the authenticity of the drug court models: were the English and Welsh schemes really 'drug courts'; should they really be classed in this way; were their titles misleading? The answers to these questions could already begin to explain their failures. This is all the published data currently available in the public domain, but if we fast forward to 2020, each of the original drug court pilots has closed; all that remains is Manchester Review Court, which could be the ghost of Salford drug court. However, plans are currently in motion to implement a fresh suite of UK problem-solving courts. With this in mind, it is worth paying attention to what went wrong, and why, for the original schemes, with all that appears to be left of these models: Manchester Review Court.

---

67 Kerr et al. (n 24)
68 Ibid.
69 Ibid.

2.4 The UK: a rehabilitation revolution or punitive populism?

Having noted that Britain currently faces, and has for many years faced, high reoffending rates but that its drug courts have had a chequered history, it is worth considering whether Britain underwent the rehabilitation revolution promised with many of its earlier policies. If a rehabilitation revolution has taken place, why did it not reduce reoffending? If it has not, why not, given the international successes? Success of any therapeutic intervention relies upon wider systematic support and a political climate conducive to its operation; as such, considering whether a British rehabilitation revolution has occurred relates to sustainability of the problem-solving court 'bottle'.

The literature reports inconsistently on the existence, growth, and impact of England and Wales' rehabilitative drives, leaving the impression that the attempts have been stop–start. Bowen and Donohue have offered a particularly sceptical view of past governments, rationalising that a successful intelligent justice revolution would rely on devolved power structures that leave room for practitioners to centrepiece local and community justice in their work.[70] Positing that 'local and community justice can enable an innovative and responsive framework, provided that they reside within a broad and stable set of national legal and policy frameworks',[71] they conclude these initiatives have often stood in opposition to other competing political targets prioritising managerialism and marketisation; these themes will be picked up in subsequent chapters.

Bowen and Donoghue describe the rhetoric of the Labour government (1997 to 2010) as 'a set of mixed messages'[72] with some commitment towards integrating local justice (e.g. the Crime and Disorder Act, 1998) and community justice (e.g. neighbourhood policing, referral orders for young people) in law and policy. This energy was reflected by policy experts who suggested that problem-solving justice was slowly becoming part of the DNA of the British criminal justice system.[73] However, somewhat counter-intuitively, Labour also put forward reforms replacing localism with a coherent set of national standards for quality assurance.[74] The 2001 Review of the Criminal Courts of England and Wales (The Auld Report) proposed radical reform to the criminal courts in keeping with smart justice, but most of these were not accepted by parliament, which brings into question how serious Labour's alleged efforts to develop a rehabilitation revolution were.

Moving forward chronologically, Bowen and Donohue argue that the Coalition government (2010–2016) attempted to undo the marketisation and

---

70 Phil Bowen & Jane Donoghue, 'Digging up the grassroots? The impact of marketisation and managerialism on local justice, 1997 to 2013' (2013) *British Journal of Community Justice*, 9–21.

71 Ibid [10].

72 Ibid [13].

73 Berman & Fox (n 31).

74 Bowen & Donoghue (n 70).

ring-fencing strategies that had characterised previous Labour governments by devolving powers to local bodies.[75] Donoghue[76] has also argued that the Coalition came into power during a critical economic crisis whilst facing the expense of a financially unsustainable and congested criminal justice system, leaving them with no choice but to reframe ambitions towards creative justice measures. Thus, for some, election of the Coalition government in 2010 marked the beginning of the UK rehabilitation revolution. Indeed, the Green Paper from 2011 set out what appeared to be a highly rehabilitation-focused agenda that promised to break drug-related crime cycles. In 2012, the then Lord Chancellor Chris Grayling officially announced the beginning of the rehabilitation revolution, a year later releasing the now highly debated and widely criticised policy Transforming Rehabilitation 2013, promising to address reoffending rates through rehabilitative strategy.[77] Part of Transforming Rehabilitation's qualitative goals involved restructuring and splitting the probation trusts into two new categorisations through privatisation. Findings presented in later chapters of this book document some of the impacts that this controversial policy has had on UK problem-solving courts. Despite these pledges, and like the predecessor government, the Coalition government were conflicting in their messages, with critics suggesting that the ideas put forward were merely linguistic fiction aimed to appease justice experts and silence any insurgents.[78]

During the Conservative government (2015–2016) Prime Minister David Cameron again held out promise of justice revolution when he boldly stated that, under his government, the UK was undergoing the biggest transformation of normative criminal justice practice since Victorian times. Cameron argued that: 'we must offer chances for change, that for those trying hard to turn themselves around, we should offer hope (and) … help those who've made mistakes to find their way back onto the right path'.[79] However, these sentiments starkly contrast with those from a statement he had made only a few years earlier, which was dominated by punitive ideology and mentality, when he said: 'committing a crime is always a choice. That's why the primary, proper response to crime is not explanations or excuses, it is punishment – proportionate, meaningful punishment'.[80] Paradoxes within political rhetoric not only muddy the water

---

75 Ibid.

76 Donoghue (n 27).

77 Ministry of Justice 2013 (n 4).

78 Nicola Padfield, 'Wither the rehabilitation revolution?' (2011) Criminal Justice Matters, Issue 1; Penelope Gibbs, 'Return magistrates' courts to local control' *Law Gazette* (3 June 2013) <https://www.lawgazette.co.uk/analysis/return-magistrates-courts-to-local-control/71223.article> Accessed 4 September 2019.

79 David Cameron, 'Prison reform: Prime Minister's speech' (8 February 2016) <https://www.law.ox.ac.uk/sites/files/oxlaw/oscola_4th_edn_hart_2012quickreferenceguide.pdf> Accessed: 4 September 2019.

80 David Cameron, '2012 speech on crime and justice' (20 November 2015) <http://www.ukpol.co.uk/david-cameron-2012-speech-on-crime-and-justice/> Accessed: 4 September 2019.

when attempting to establish the true intentions of governments, but also exemplify that British political sentiment has so often been marked by drastic U-turns and contradictions. However, current statutory law and policy is scattered with punishment reform strategy,[81] including very recent plans to reinstate and roll out British problem-solving courts (detailed under the next subheading of this book). The Centre for Justice Innovation is also still going strong, and they have continued to support and disseminate relevant research from this domain, and have been the key driver for keeping the flame alive for problem-solving and related practice in the UK over recent years. Some believe that the rehabilitation revolution has begun, only it has been a slow-burner that is yet to make a difference[82] with ongoing turbulences in the wider landscapes, and governmental priorities for larger-scale projects such as Brexit, have aggravated any political inertia.

O'Neil et al.[83] empirically tested the hypothesis that there are discrepancies across UK expert opinion and public conversation when it comes to justice innovation. Despite most UK expert evidence evidencing that innovative penology offers the most sensible and plausible solution, they showed that political and public ideology still exhibit harsh sentiments. Indeed, it was noted by UK experts in 2010 that: 'the media and political environment is so overheated that criminal justice officials are rarely given the time and space to engage in a rigorous process of trial and error'.[84] Researchers reported that this creates a vicious cycle in which political rhetoric contours public opinion into punitive tick-boxes, which then spurs politicians either keen to get elected or who fear demotion, to react with projection plans, conversations, and communications marked by punitive zeal. By asking the important question: 'how can criminal justice reformers effectively argue for different solutions to reducing crime when they are up against widely shared views about the efficacy of harsh punishment?', researchers demonstrate that although negative cycles are difficult to break, they can be interrupted and dislodged by more productive ways of thinking.[85] As such, O'Neil et al.[86] respond with empirically tested communication tools for politicians to create space for public conversations that support constructive reform measures. Whilst implementing them will allegedly take 'time and

81 (n 4) – all.
82 The Centre for Social Justice, 'What happened to the rehabilitation revolution' (CSJ, September 2016) <https://www.centreforsocialjustice.org.uk/core/wp-content/uploads /2017/09/CSJJ5667-Rehab-Revolution-WEB.pdf> Accessed 4 September 2019.
83 Moira O'Neil, Nathaniel Kendall-Taylor, & Andrew Volmert, 'New narratives: changing the frame on crime and justice' (FrameWorksInstitute.org, 9 July 2018) <http://framewor ksinstitute.org/assets/files/PDF/UKCJ_MM_July_2016_Final.pdf > Accessed 4 September 2019.
84 Greg Berman & Aubrey Fox, 'The future of problem-solving justice: an international perspective' (2010) 10 University of Maryland Law Journal of Race Religion, Gender & Class 1.
85 O'Neil et al. (n 83) [4].
86 Ibid.

practice', the devised tools hold promise for a robust, coherent, and memorable series of communications supportive of rehabilitative agendas.[87] However, although this is positive, it serves to highlight that England and Wales' public opinion is currently overshadowed by punitive populism, putting up significant barriers for revolutionising justice in the UK, which relies on a political climate supportive of therapeutic jurisprudence.

Why does it matter if Britain has undergone or is undergoing a rehabilitation revolution? This question is important because it relates to the sustainability of the wider landscapes in which a therapeutic practice is situated.[88] If mainstream culture and projection plans stand contrary to the ethos underscoring a therapeutic model, then there is little motivation or patience to keep it alive. If legislators, lobbyists, and policymakers are unsure of and lack confidence in their own agendas and philosophies, a therapeutic solution stands little hope of longevity and becomes merely a fad that experts soon turn their back on.

If nothing else, the British rehabilitation revolution efforts, including the drug courts, have often been abandoned before they have been given a chance to succeed; the UK rehabilitation revolution has wrestled for space in a justice system that upholds many competing aims and objectives. This in turn has contributed to stop–start political agendas, mixed messages, and smart justice often failing to embed itself into the fabric of the British criminal justice system. As the UK faces (and has faced) a time of political uncertainty, upheaval, and black holes, past and present governments have put forward an unreliable set of mixed messages and it remains to be seen how any new strategies, documented in the next section, will unfold. The evolving question is whether English and Welsh problem-solving courts have now become obsolete phenomenon or are still of relevance to British research, policy, and practice. Are they thus worthy of further research and scrutiny, or is it time to move on?

2.5 Problem-solving courts in England and Wales: an obsolete phenomenon?

Despite the drug courts possessing a keen trajectory in the early 2000s, they soon began to peter out after the publication of the 2011 report, despite it showing good early results, but this was given little explanation. Yet the jettisoned British drug court schemes are merely the tip of the iceberg amongst a broader history of UK failures in the same area. The previously mentioned Liverpool and Salford community justice courts closed at a similar time to the drug courts and in a similar vein; they were quietly removed from public conversations and their closures lacked a formal, satisfactory, or well-reasoned justification.[89] Elsewhere, the two British mental health courts also fell by the wayside after their pilot period expired

87 Ibid [26].
88 Wexler (n 66).
89 Robins 2013 (n 25).

in 2013.[90] To date, the question of 'why' the national efforts have been unsuccessful remains largely outstanding for each of these schemes, but it has been raised by national and international policymakers alike, and is made pertinent by the desire to retest the schemes and is perplexing given the successes offered by the international models.

From a research perspective, arguably, these failures could render any new British work in the field obsolete and futile. However, I will show in this section, that despite these downfalls, problem-solving court practice has not completely evaporated from the British systems. Within independent, but neighbouring jurisdictions, Glasgow and Dublin drug courts are still running, and the former has been heralded for its far-reaching impact.[91] The literature also demonstrates success of the 15 English Family Drug and Alcohol Courts (FDAC), which have benefitted from high-quality research, a recent 15 million private reinvestment scheme to maintain operation after they threatened to close down,[92] and ongoing support for the Centre for Justice Innovation. In 2015, the Centre for Justice Innovation undertook a financial analysis of the London FDAC showing that the model saved money; for each £1 spent, £2.30 is saved.[93] In the south of England, Bedfordshire and Herefordshire have been running two problem-solving courts since 2007 and 2011 respectively as part of their community-led offender management schemes for prolific burglars: Choices and Consequences ('C2') and Prolific Intensive Scheme ('PI'). Incepted as a piecemeal response by Judge Baker and his frustration with a McDonaldized justice system,[94] C2 was assembled using a similar rationale to the original American drug courts. However, interestingly and somewhat tellingly of UK models more generally, this was without Judge Baker's knowledge of the international context.[95] Moreover, perhaps surprisingly given the turbulences, the Centre for Justice Innovation, has survived and is still alive and well, and they continue to effectively produce and disseminate relevant research and ideas and identify and support key practice within the area. Manchester Magistrates' Court also runs a women's problem-solving court,

90 Karen Snedker, 'Why the UK needs a separate justice system for people with mental illness' *The Conversation* (5 July 2018).

91 Susan Eley, Margaret Malloch, Gill McIvor, Rowdy Yates, & Alison Brown, 'The Glasgow drug court in action: the first six months' (2003) Crime and Criminal Justice Research Programme Research Findings No.70/2003.

92 Department for Education & Nadhim Zahawi, '£15 million investment to help keep families safely together' (GOV.UK, 2019).

93 Stephen Whitehead & Neil Reeder, 'Better courts: the financial impact of the London Family Drug and Alcohol Court' Centre for Justice Innovation. Retrieved from: https://justice innovation.org/sites/default/files/media/documents/2019-03/better-courts-the-financial-impact-of-the-london-fdac.pdf

94 Simon Conlan, 'The McDonaldization of criminal justice' (2019). Understanding Contemporary Societies.

95 Michael Baker, 'Choices and consequences – an account of an experimental sentences programme' (2014) Criminal Law Review Issue 1. Thomson Reuters (Professionals) UK Limited.

specialising in female offender, and this has been praised by the 2020 White Paper for its innovation and for ensuing good outcome responses, where the Ministry of Justice claimed that it possesses 'lower annual average reoffending rate for female offenders compared to similar urban areas, and England and Wales overall (15% compared to 23% for the April 2017 to March 2018 cohort)'.[96]

In 2015, following the drug court closures, the UK's Centre for Justice Innovation published a new delivery plan for problem-solving courts in the UK,[97] an agenda seemingly halted by cabinet shuffles and the reassignment of five new justice secretaries since its publication. A year later, in 2016, a proposal for UK Youth Referral Orders had problem-solving courts at its heart and recommended ongoing judicial supervision of offenders to help 'motivate the child to engage'.[98] The same report pushed for the roll-out of a revolutionised UK justice system more generally. In the youth justice sphere, the Centre for Justice Innovation continue their mission to drive forward problem-solving in the Youth Courts of England and Wales, which has been met with particular success in Northamptonshire.[99] In 2017, the UK's Centre for Social Justice released a paper positing ten new criteria to resuscitate the rehabilitation revolution; of these, most relevant to problem-solving courts was the fourth action point: 'reintroduction of problem-solving courts inclusive of four new pilots in the Crown Courts'.[100] Elsewhere, a Parliamentary report published in June 2019 proposed mainstreaming problem-solving into the courts, where it was concluded that 'we welcome the Government's willingness to explore whether elements of a problem-solving approach, including court progress reviews'.[101] In June 2019, it was announced that Falmouth was instating a new drug court, although this never appears to have been followed up.[102] The biggest breakthrough then occurred in September 2020, when the government published a White Paper, which pledged to establish five new problem-solving courts, alluding to a speciality in drug related offending, by taking influence from the international examples. It stated that: 'we now intend to pilot enhanced problem-solving based on these recommendations in up to five courts. Substance misuse has been the traditional focus of problem-solving courts and is the area providing most of the international evidence base'.[103] What the discussion in this section shows is that problem-solving is still on the UK agenda, and remains an area that Britain has not yet been completely abandoned.

96 Ministry of Justice, 'A smarter approach to sentencing' (2020) White Paper, 55.
97 Phil Bowen & Stephen Whitehead, 'Problem-solving courts: a delivery plan' (2016) Justice Innovation Charity.
98 Quentin Goodman, 'Proposed model for the national implementation of court reviews of Youth Rehabilitation Orders' (2016) Northamptonshire Youth Offending Service [9].
99 Ibid.
100 The Centre for Social Justice (n 82).
101 House of Commons Justice Committee, 'The role of the magistracy: follow-up session 2017–19' (London, 12 June 2019) Justice Committee.
102 Alex Newman, 'Falmouth is getting a drug court' (Patch, 30 April 2019) <https://patch.com/massachusetts/falmouth/falmouth-getting-drug-court> Accessed 5 September 2019.
103 Ministry of Justice (n 96).

Greater Manchester has long been recognised for spearheading the problem-solving court movement in England in which the now-closed Salford Community Court reportedly left a legacy of keen interest amongst practitioners.[104] Today, as already detailed, in addition to Manchester Review Court, Manchester has a problem-solving court specialising in female issues, and additionally, Stockport has a problem-solving court that supports persistent offenders with complex needs.[105] A Memorandum of Understanding between the Ministry of Justice and Greater Manchester Council was signed in 2016, which aimed to integrate treatment into Manchester's justice provisions. In 2019, Manchester's Deputy Mayor, Baroness Hughes, spoke about driving this agenda forward in a powerful statement:

> The commitments within this Memorandum of Understanding are central to our mission of unifying public services for the benefit of the people of Greater Manchester. It is a testament to the partnership that has been forged with the Ministry of Justice that there is a joint ambition to improve outcomes and experiences across all aspects of our justice system.[106]

Sanguine for British problem-solving, this statement epitomises how the UK is making headway, even if only in small pockets of the justice system. However, it is interesting that despite acknowledgement of Manchester's attempts at problem-solving including the female problem-solving court, which is housed in the same magistrates court as Manchester Review Court, every one of these references fails to mention Manchester Review Court. It appears to have slipped through the cracks and under the radar of the officials. It thus appears to have slipped through the cracks, operating off the radar of the officials, in a void. This – the fact that problem-solving is still extant in Britain – presents an area worthy of further scrutiny and renders topical any new research in the field.

Coming back to UK recidivism statistics posited in earlier sections of this chapter, the Centre for Social Justice have quite aptly reported that 'the need for a rehabilitation revolution is as pressing today as it ever has been' but that 'the revolution is at risk of stalling before it has really begun – and the government must do more than recommit to the consensus that exists and think boldly on making rehabilitation a reality'.[107] As the UK has faced times of political uncertainty, governments have continually changed their minds; what remains is a sense that England and Wales' rehabilitative drive, and the specialist courts that centrepiece that effort, is a misunderstood area. It remains to be seen how recent

---

104 Centre for Justice Innovation, 'Problem solving courts in Manchester' (London, 27 April 2018) <https://justiceinnovation.org/articles/problem-solving-courts-manchester> Accessed 5 September 2019.

105 Ibid.

106 Rochdale Online, 'New justice partnership for Greater Manchester' (Manchester, 4 June 2019) <https://www.rochdaleonline.co.uk/news-features/2/news-headlines/128218/new-justice-partnership-for-greater-manchester> Accessed 5 June 2019.

107 The Centre for Social Justice (n 82).

plans to institute a fresh suite of problem-solving courts will unfold. However, before Britain can move forward productively with this ambition, and to prevent a second iteration of failures, a full evaluation of what went wrong for the drug courts is required. This forms the rationale for this book; it will use Manchester Review Court as a case study to hypothesis on the drug court failures. However, it will go further by developing a renewed UK-specific problem-solving court fidelity matrix that accounts for the existing and historical problems in this field and current issues to forge the impetus for successful policy and practice in the future.

2.6 Methods and research questions

To achieve these goals, three phases of empirical methods were leveraged to collect the data for this book: court observations, surveys, and interviews, throughout which sampling was achieved opportunistically. Mixed methods within a case study design gave depth to an area where there is currently no published literature whilst cultivating a complete range of research questions for a topic where many questions remained unanswered.

The lenses and insights brokered by therapeutic jurisprudence underpin this book's methodological framework. Wexler has put forward a seminal metaphor comprising 'wine' and 'bottles', which provides a tool for examining the therapeutic proficiency of legal settings.[108] 'Wine' refers to the quality of practitioners' discretionary techniques, skills, or approaches, where insights are garnered by the cognitive behavioural sciences, including: the psychology of procedural justice, positive criminology, motivational interviewing, social work, and restorative justice.[109] 'Bottles' refers to wider structural factors that cannot easily be changed, developed, or manipulated, such as: laws themselves, provisions, rules, rule of law, and procedural norms and values. As such, whilst wine refers to the therapeutic application of the law, bottles refers to the therapeutic design of the law.[110]

Cooper[111] has acknowledged the analogy within the methodology of therapeutic jurisprudence field by exploring how bottle- and wine-level considerations can be translated into research questions, evaluation, and findings. Whereas the former refers to analysis of macro-level structures, including policy, organisational strategy, and legalisation, the latter refers to application of therapeutic jurisprudence principles in practice, including judicial skillsets and methods of engagement. Both levels contain therapeutic and anti-therapeutic value, but only through their strong combination can healing outcomes become mobilised.[112] By transposing this metaphor into an evaluative framework for the current project,

---

108 Wexler (n 66).
109 Ibid.
110 Ibid.
111 Caroline Cooper, 'Evaluating the application of TJ principles: lessons from the drug court experience' in Nigel Stobbs, Lorana Bartels & Michel Vols (eds.) *The methodology and practice of therapeutic jurisprudence* (pp. 287–204) (Durham, NC: Carolina Academic Press).
112 Wexler (n 66).

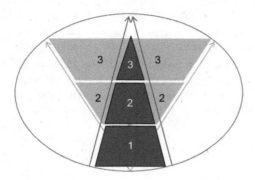

Diagram A: Visual representation of the methods.

the research questions for this book are structured around the two layers of therapeutic jurisprudence.

2.6.1 *Wine*

1. What impact does an inconsistent bench have on the therapeutic application of magistrates' interpersonal skills and behavioural styles?
    a. Does proficiency at these approaches change according to magistrates' gender?
2. What is the therapeutic quality of the wine?

2.6.2 *Bottle*

1. Does the court adhere to the international drug court gold standard?[113]
2. Is the review court the remains of the original drug courts?
3. What is the therapeutic quality of the bottle?

The Phase 1, 2, and 3 methods are represented visually in Diagram A, and are separated into two branches: 'wine' (the darker shaded areas) and 'bottle' (the lighter shaded areas), to reflect the dual focus of this study. The three main methodological phases are displayed by each block, 1, 2 and 3, to show that they were not independent but rather built upon one another. The 'wine' aspect was quantitative and examined the therapeutic quality of magistrates' interpersonal skills at Manchester Review Court and was considered throughout all data collection phases as a core thread to the study. The focus on the wine narrowed as the study progressed and began to ask broader qualitative questions about the quality of the 'bottle'. Unlike the darker 'wine' arrows that narrow, the lighter 'bottle' arrows broaden, to reflect the emphasis of each data collection phase. Throughout the

113 Ashcroft et al. (n 65).

Table 2.1 Wine Measurement Tool

Harnessing therapeutic support	Engaging therapeutic dialogue	Inspiring therapeutic change
Magistrates are interested in and compassionate towards my life circumstances	Magistrates give me a voice	I can ask questions when I need to
Magistrates understand what it's like to have drug and/or alcohol problems	Magistrates speak to me slowly, clearly, and loudly	Magistrates are realistic when we set my goals for next review
Magistrates have hope and faith that I will make progress	Magistrates do not rush or interrupt me when I am speaking	Magistrates help me build upon my strengths
Magistrates listen to my point of view	Magistrates are sincere and honest when they speak to me	Magistrates make me feel positive about my future
Magistrates praise me when I am doing well	Magistrates speak to me without pity or disdain	
Magistrates are personable	Magistrates are attentive when I am speaking	
Magistrates reiterate my goals so that they are clear		
Magistrates motivate me		

whole project, unstructured observations were being carried out, represented by the encompassing outer circle, which can be considered 'ethnography' although I am reluctant to call this 'a phase' due to its constancy.

2.7 Wine measurements

In my work elsewhere, I used two statistical techniques from the social sciences (principal component analysis and Cronbach's alpha) to validate a tool for measuring the therapeutic value of the wine in problem-solving court jurisdictions.[114] Through these statistical techniques, 18 variables, arranged on three respective scales, had high interrelated correlations, and were shown to be valid and reliable.[115] These three scales were used to measure the wine data for this book and the variables are presented in Table 2.1. Comparably, the bottle data was collected using a more fluid set of indicators and the data derived was more qualitative in nature. As such, as the discussion moves from wine to bottle, the substantiating data shifts from broadly quantitative to broadly qualitative.

114 Anna Kawalek, 'A tool for measuring therapeutic jurisprudence values during empirical research' (2020) International Journal of Law and Psychiatry, 71C, 101581.
115 One variable was removed for this study due to irrelevance.

2.8 Phase 1: observations

Without making any contact (verbal or nonverbal) with service-users or key personnel, the visual observations were carried out overtly by sitting in the courtroom public gallery, watching what happened as the interactions unfolded in their real-life capacity with the intention of being as much of a fly on the wall as possible. Observations could directly measure the court and allow real-life behaviour to be recorded, which was of special interest given the paucity of published literature in the area. During this stage, measurements were taken for wine only (see Table 2.1) and only the interactions between service-user and magistrates were recorded.

2.9 Phase 2: surveys

In Phase 2, data was collected using the survey method and measurements were taken using a standardised questionnaire. This phase above any other was interested in general structures of opinion and was disseminated to service-users only. The dearth of UK literature lent itself to this method, which could enable information to be gathered quickly and efficiently, from as many possible service-user respondents. The survey questions rolled out the 18 variables from the wine tool to measure this aspect as well as 12 questions for bottle measurements (hence a broadened focus on Diagram A).

2.10 Phase 3: interviews

In Phase 3, semi-structured interviews were carried out with a range of stakeholders. Interview schedules were largely consistent across participants, although they were tweaked according to their role at the court; whereas staff members were asked more focused questions about court or DRR practice respectively, service-users were asked questions about their court experiences. In all instances, there were some questions around the therapeutic quality of magistrates' interpersonal skills to maintain a core thread (wine), but, as the broadest phase, it was more concerned with court impact, operation, practice, and procedure (bottle).

2.11 Ethnography

During this aspect of data collection, I overtly collected qualitative notes documenting my experiences at court as I observed its operation in a real-life capacity without actively participating. This included not only observations at the site, but also conversations with key personnel worthy of note from both in person and email and telephone exchanges. This was not a phase of data collection, rather a state of continuous exploration, necessary to build a baseline of knowledge in a field where there is currently no literature. As such, methods and methodology became somewhat subordinate to my experience of the practical application of the setting.[116] The special form of data collection was complementary to, and necessarily richer, than the other stages.

2.12 Selection of location: Manchester Review Court

Given that Manchester Review Court is an enigma, it is worth addressing how it was selected as a location to base the empirical work. The first problem-solving court that I visited was 'Leeds drug court', which I knew existed from the 2011 report. In late 2015, I went to conduct informal court observations. Whilst struck by how few of the gold-standard drug court components were in operation considering it operated under the 'drug court' name, a distinguished feature was magistrates' interactional styles, which appeared to be operating therapeutic jurisprudence 'wine'. Despite its visible shortcomings, practitioners confirmed the court's international origins and considered it to 'be' a 'drug court'. Shortly after fieldwork at Leeds had commenced, the court was closed due to 'sustainability issues';[117] little more explanation was given, epitomising many of the problems characterising the UK in this field more generally. The seed that had already been planted in my mind based on the literature, pertaining to the struggles in the area, grew significantly at this point, and I started to ask big questions about why the English and Welsh drug courts had faced so many problems.

Following the closure of Leeds, I visited Salford Magistrates' Court, which had been (temporarily) renamed 'Salford and Manchester Magistrates' Court'; under UK court centralisation reforms[118] Salford Magistrates' had been merged into Manchester's Central Magistrates' Court, including (arguably) the drug court, and I knew there was a Salford drug court from the 2011 report.[119] At the court, Manchester Review Court operated. It presented itself very similarly to 'Leeds drug court': devoid of many of the key components, but with a renewed therapeutic orientation. It was unclear from informal observations and conversations with court staff whether Manchester Review Court was a recentralised version of Salford drug court. As the study progressed and the absence of many key components became increasingly transparent, my confidence in its definition as a 'drug court' began to deteriorate. The ambiguity later led to a drug court fidelity analysis to be carried out, findings from which are presented in Chapter 4. The following points summarise the rationale for the selected location:

- There was no literature explicitly addressing and acknowledging Manchester Review Court. The closest was outdated research for the drug courts, including Salford drug court.[120] Updating the literature through an original empirical-led study was thus necessary.

---

116 Uwe Flick, *Introducing research methodology: a beginner's guide to doing a research project* (London: Sage, 2011).
117 Ethnographic data collected by Anna Kawałek (file held with author).
118 Courts Act 2003.
119 During the course of this study, it then changed to 'Central Manchester Magistrates' Court'.
120 Kerr et al. (n 24).

- Manchester Review Court lacked many key drug court components but appeared to adopt a therapeutic jurisprudence orientation. As such, a fidelity analysis could shed light on the court's definition.
- There had been no proper explanation for the drug court failures; using Manchester Review Court as a case study could help aid and enrich understanding of this area.
- The city of Manchester had (and has) significant problems with drug use, particularly synthetic cannabis,[121] and according to Manchester City Council, approximately 42% of detected acquisitive crimes occurring in Manchester are linked to addiction.[122] Moreover, Manchester has a bold problem-solving court agenda which champions justice innovation technique in England. These factors make the city relevant to the court's effectiveness.

2.13 Triangulation

During analysis, the findings from each empirical vantage point were combined through data triangulation.[123] Findings from the phases either: agreed (converged), focused on different aspects of an issue (complemented) or contradicted one another (diverged).[124] Chapters 3 and 4 offer complex analyses where all data points are brought together to respectively analyse the 'wine' and 'bottle' data. Triangulation was also a discursive validity check to audit the full dataset to bring weight to all of the findings across the phases.

2.14 Limitations of methodology

Manchester Review Court was at times a frustrating site to work with empirically. It was (and still is) unclear whether it represents the remains of the English and Welsh drug courts (specifically Salford drug court centralised into Manchester Magistrates' Court) or a different of problem-solving method. Confusions were augmented by practitioners at the site, some of whom believed Manchester Review Court was the old Salford drug court and thus a 'drug court', whilst others believed that it was an independent practice. One notable interaction was with an erstwhile Salford drug court legal advisor, who was moved to Manchester

---

121 Frances Perraudin, '"It's worse than heroin": how spice is ravaging homeless communities' (*The Guardian*, April 15 2017) <https://www.theguardian.com/society/2017/apr/15/its-worse-than-heroin-how-spice-is-ravaging-homeless-communities> Accessed 4 September 2019.

122 Manchester City Council Heath Scrutiny Committee, 'Report on alcohol and drug services in Manchester' (2016) <https://secure.manchester.gov.uk/download/meetings/id/20099/6_alcohol_and_drug_related_crime > Accessed 1 June 2018.

123 Flick (n 116).

124 Udo Kelle & Christian Erzberger, 'Making inferences in mixed methods: the rules of integration' in Abbas Tashakkori & Charles Teddlie (eds.) *Handbook of mixed methods in social & behavioural research* (Thousand Oaks, CA: Sage, 2003).

Review Court under the court centralised initiatives; whilst setting up for the main sessions, this individual asked *me* if *I* was the drugs worker whilst I was data collecting. Drug workers did not feature at Manchester Review Court, only in the old drug courts; this therefore suggests that this participant believed Manchester Review Court was the predecessor Salford drug court centralised into the main Manchester court. However, it also felt fraudulent to conceptualise Manchester Review Court as a 'drug court' because it neglected too many key components, as will be demonstrated in later chapters.

The overall lack of UK guidance, of empirical or non-empirical nature, and its inconsistent definition, made measurement difficult and could obfuscate the issues at hand. However, defining Manchester Review Court was important from an empirical perspective because it helped clarify the appropriate framework and research to apply during analysis, and authenticates any suggestions for successful and sustainable delivery. Establishing clarity in this area often felt like an ongoing struggle and data collection a Kafkaesque experience. Manchester Review Court presented many empirical caveats; in addition to its unclear definition, there were significant attendance issues undermining data quantities, information storage problems, and both staff and service-users could often be confused as to its purpose. However, in turn, I realised that each of these frustrations became telling of the chequered history that had punctuated the narrative for the English and Welsh drug courts historically: they have often been misunderstood, confused, and indiscernible. As such, these obstacles became important qualitative findings, interwoven into this book's discussion, enabling me to speculate on past drug court failures.

2.15 Concluding remarks for Chapter 2

England and Wales currently face problems with drug-fuelled recidivism. There is a plethora of research, both national and international, pointing to the demonstrable link between drug addiction and recidivist crimes.[125] UK justice ministers seem acutely and keenly aware of this, reflected in policy documentation both past and present pregnant with example of plans to tackle reoffending at its root through rehabilitation.[126] However, where England and Wales have not always been successful is the marrying of justice and therapy, especially compared to its jurisdictional brother, America, which has been a trailblazer for delivering drug courts successfully.

---

125 National Council on Alcohol and Drug Dependence (n 7).

126 Ministry of Justice, 'Ministry of justice single departmental plan' (2018). Retrieved from: https://www.gov.uk/government/publications/ministry-of-justice-single-depar tmental-plan/ministry-of-justice-single-departmental-plan--2; McGuire J., 'What works in reducing reoffending in young adults? A rapid evidence assessment' (2015) National Offender Management Service: Analytical summary. Retrieved from: https://assets.publi shing.service.gov.uk/government/uploads/system/uploads/attachment_data/file/4493 47/reducing-reoffending-in-adults.pdf; Ministry of Justice, 2013 (n 4).

Like many similar justice interventions in England and Wales, Manchester Review Court is a misunderstood area, where perhaps consequentially, perhaps causally, there has been no published empirical literature. Although the UK drug courts were incepted in 2005, seemingly with good intentions, the UK landscapes have since been marked by sudden political U-turns, mixed messages, and unsatisfactory evidence bases to help support practice. This chapter has brought to hand these issues whilst showing that England and Wales have been unreceptive to a rehabilitation revolution, which could be due to deep-seated punitive attitudes, although some new agendas continue to push for rehabilitation, at least in theory. Despite the turbulences in the broader landscapes, there are glimmers of hope in some pockets of the UK justice system: some problem-solving courts remain running and a new iteration could be on the horizon, the UK Centre for Justice Innovation is still in operation, and the city of Manchester has been a long-standing advocate of problem-solving as the local mayor keenly attempts to push this initiative forward.

Original granular data has been gathered and will be presented in this book to address the existing gaps with the aim to drive forward policy, legislation, and practice in the field. Using Manchester Review Court as a case study, it will answer two tiers of research questions, the first relating to therapeutic wine at the micro level, and the other relating to the wider bottle at the structural level. To this effect, the next chapter (Chapter 3) will present the wine data. Thereafter, Chapter 4 will broaden its focus towards and evaluation of the bottle. Current issues with drug-fuelled recidivism must be faced and the international evidence base strongly suggests that this can be achieved when using justice methods that dovetail with rehabilitation. However, when shaping future strategy, UK policymakers cannot ignore the demise of the original England and Wales drug courts. No empirical evidence currently explains their downfalls. It is now time to take the bull by the horns; based on empirical data, this book will propose a UK-specific fidelity matrix accounting for past failures, acknowledging current issues, to enable a sustainable future for the delivery of the new suite of problem-solving courts pledged by the 2020 White Paper.

Bibliography

Anglin D. and Hser Y.I., 'Criminal justice and the drug-abusing offender: policy issues of coerced treatment' (1991) 9(3) Behavioral Sciences and the Law, 243–267.

Ashcroft J., Daniels D. and Herriaz D., 'Defining drug courts: the key components. U.S. department of justice' (2004). https://www.ncjrs.gov/pdffiles1/bja/2056 21.pdf.

Baker M., 'Choices and consequences – an account of an experimental sentences programme' (2014) (1) Criminal Law Review. Thomson Reuters (Professionals) UK Limited.

Bean P., 'Drug treatment courts, British style: the drug treatment court movement in BRITAIN' (2002) 37(12–13) Substance Use & Misuse, 1592.

Bean P., *Drugs and crime* (Routledge, 2014). National Institute on Drug Abuse, 'Criminal Justice' (National Institute on Drug Abuse, 2014). https://tinyurl. com/y289r7jy, Accessed 12 June 2019.

Belenko S., 'Research on drug courts: a critical review' (1998) 1(1) National Drug Court Institute Review, 1–42. Brown, 2010.

Bennet T. and Holloway K., 'Drug use and offending: summary results of the first two years of the NEW-ADAM programme' (2004) Home Office.

Berman G. and Fox A., *Lasting change or passing fad? Problem-solving justice in England and Wales* (London: Policy Exchange, 2009).

Berman G. and Fox A., 'The future of problem-solving justice: an international perspective' (2010) 10 University of Maryland Law Journal of Race Religion, Gender & Class, 1.

Booth L., Altoft A., Dubourg R., Gonçalves M. and Mirrlees-Black C., 'North Liverpool Community Justice Centre: analysis of re-offending rates and efficiency of court processes' (2012) Ministry of Justice Research Series 10/12.

Bowcott O., 'Why are special courts that can help drug users at risk of being scrapped?' *Guardian* (10 June 2014). https://tinyurl.com/y3n6o9bp, Accessed 3 September 2019.

Bowcott O., 'US-style problem solving courts plan losing momentum' *Guardian* (12 October 2016). https://tinyurl.com/y3e68qc4, Accessed 2 June 2019.

Bowen P. and Whitehead S., 'Problem-solving courts: a delivery plan' (2016) Justice Innovation Charity.

Bryan M., Bono E. and Pudney S., 'Drug-related crime' (2013) No. 2013-08, Institute for Social and Economic Research.

Cameron C., '2012 speech on crime and justice' (20 November 2015). http://www.ukpol.co.uk/david-cameron-2012-speech-on-crime-and-justice/, Accessed 4 September 2019.

Cameron D., 'Prison reform: Prime Minister's speech' (8 February 2016). https://www.law.ox.ac.uk/sites/files/oxlaw/oscola_4th_edn_hart_2012quickreferenc eguide.pdf, Accessed 4 September 2019.

Carter P., 'Managing offenders, reducing crime: a new approach' (2007) Strategy Unit; Ministry of Justice, 'Her majesty's courts and tribunals service: about us' (2011) Gov.UK.

Centre for Justice Innovation, 'Problem solving courts in Manchester' *London* (27 April 2018). https://justiceinnovation.org/articles/problem-solving-courts-man chester, Accessed 5 September 2019.

The Centre for Social Justice, 'What happened to the rehabilitation revolution' *CSJ* (September 2016). https://www.centreforsocialjustice.org.uk/core/wp-content/uploads/2017/09/CSJJ5667-Rehab-Revolution-WEB.pdf, Accessed 4 September 2019.

Conlan S., 'The McDonaldization of criminal justice' (2019) Understanding Contemporary Societies.

Cooper C., 'Evaluating the application of TJ principles: lessons from the drug court experience' in N. Stobbs, L. Bartels and M. Vols (eds.) (2019) *The methodology and practice of therapeutic jurisprudence* (Durham, NC: Carolina Academic Press), 287–204.

Cowburn A., 'Prison population should be cut by half to "Margaret Thatcher levels", urge senior politicians' *The Independent* (22 December 2016). https://www.ind ependent.co.uk/news/uk/politics/prison-population-cut-40000-overcrowdi ng-margaret-thatcher-levels-nick-clegg-ken-clarke-a7489636.html, Accessed 4 September 2019.

Department for Education and Zahawi N, *£15 million investment to help keep families safely together* (GOV.UK, 2019).

Donoghue J., *Transforming criminal justice?: problem-solving and court specialization* (London: Routledge, 2014).

Eley S., Malloch M., McIvor G., Yates R. and Brown A., 'The Glasgow drug court in action: the first six months' (2003) Crime and Criminal Justice Research Programme Research Findings No.70/2003.

Flick U., *Introducing research methodology: a beginner's guide to doing a research project* (London: SAGE, 2011).

Freeman K., 'Health and well-being outcomes for drug-dependent offenders on the NSW drug court programme' (2003) 22(4) Drug and Alcohol Review, 409–416.

Gibbs P., 'Managing magistrates' courts – has central control reduced local accountability?' (2013) Transform Justice.

Gibbs P., 'Return magistrates' courts to local control' *Law Gazette* (3 June 2013). https://www.lawgazette.co.uk/analysis/return-magistrates-courts-to-local-co ntrol/71223.article, Accessed 4 September 2019.

Gibbs P., 'Has the West London drugs court closed and does it matter?' *Transforming Justice* (10 June 2014). http://www.transformjustice.org.uk/has-the-west-lo ndon-drugs-court-closed-and-does-it-matter/, Accessed 4 September 2019.

Goldkamp J., White M. and Robinson J., 'Do drug courts work? Getting inside the drug court black box' (2000) 31(1) Journal of Drug Issues, 27–72.

Goodman Q., 'Proposed model for the national implementation of court reviews of youth rehabilitation orders' (2016) Northamptonshire Youth Offending Service.

Gossop M., 'The national treatment outcomes research study (NTORS) and its influence on addiction treatment policy in the United Kingdom' (2015) National Addiction Centre, Institute of Psychiatry.

Great Britain Home Office, 'Justice for all – a white paper on the criminal justice system' (2002) Stationary Office.

Guake D., 'Smarter sentences, safer streets' Ministry of Justice; Georgina Eaton & Aiden Mews, 'The impact of short custodial sentences, community orders and suspended sentence orders on reoffending' (2019) Ministry of Justice.

Her Majesty's Courts Service, 'Her Majesty's Courts Service business plan 2009–10' (2009) HMCS.

Hollingworth M., 'An examination of the potential impact of the drug rehabilitation requirement on homeless illicit drug-using offenders' (2008) Probation Journal: The Journal of Community and Criminal Justice.

Holloway K., Bennett T. and Lower C., 'Trends in drug use and offending: the results of the NEW-ADAM programme, 1999–2002' (2004) Home Office.

Hough M., Clancy A., McSweeney T. and Turnbell P., 'Impact of drug treatment and testing orders on offending: two-year reconviction results' (2003) National Criminal Justice Reference Service, Home Office Findings 184.

House of Commons, 'Department for Constitutional Affairs: key policies and priorities' (2005) DRUG COURTA Research Series 3/05, Department for Constitutional Affairs, London.

House of Commons; Health Committee, *Public health: twelfth report of session 2010–2012* (London: House of Commons, 2012. No. 1). https://tinyurl.com/ y5hdh56a, Accessed 12 July 2019.

House of Commons Justice Committee, *The role of the magistracy: follow-up session 2017–19* (London: Justice Committee, 12 June 2019).

Kawalek A., 'A tool for measuring therapeutic jurisprudence values during empirical research' (2020) 71C International Journal of Law and Psychiatry, 101581.

Kelle U. and Erzberger C., 'Making inferences in mixed methods: the rules of integration' in A. Tashakkori and C. Teddlie (eds.) *Handbook of mixed methods in social & behavioural research* (Thousand Oaks, CA: Sage, 2003).

Kerr J., Tompkins C., Tomaszewski W., Dickens S., Grimshaw R., Nat W. and Matt B. 'The dedicated drug courts pilot evaluation process study' (2011) Ministry of Justice Research Series, 1, Ministry of Justice, London.

KPMG Consulting, 'Evaluation of the drug court of Victoria: government advisory services. Final report.' (2014) Magistrates' Court of Victoria, 18.

Lowenkamp C., Holsinger A. and Latessa E., 'Are drug courts effective: a meta-analytic review' (2005) 15(1) Journal of Community Corrections, 5–11.

Mair G. and Mills H., 'The community order and the suspended sentence order three years on: the views and experiences of probation officers and offenders' (2008) Centre for Crime and Justice Studies.

Manchester City Council Heath Scrutiny Committee, 'Report on alcohol and drug services in Manchester' (2016). https://secure.manchester.gov.uk/download/meetings/id/20099/6_alcohol_and_drug_related_crime, Accessed 01 June 2018.

Marlowe D., 'Research update on adult drug courts' (2010) National Association of Drug Court Professionals.

Maruna S., *Making good: how ex-convicts reform and rebuild their lives* (Washington, DC: American Psychological Association, 2001). doi:10.1037/10430-000.

Matrix Knowledge Group, 'Dedicated drug court pilots a process report' (2008) Ministry of Justice Research Series 7/08. Ministry of Justice, London.

McGuire J., 'What works in reducing reoffending in young adults? A rapid evidence assessment' (2015) National Offender Management Service, Analytical Summary. https://assets.publishing.service.gov.uk/government/uploads/system/uploads/attachment_data/file/449347/reducing-reoffending-in-adults.pdf.

McIvor G., Barnsdale L., Eley S., Malloch M., Yates R. and Brown A., 'An evaluation of the glasgow and fife drug courts and their aim to reduce drug use and drug related reoffending' (2006) 9 Criminology and Criminal Justice, 29.

McSweeney T., Stevens A., Hunt N. and Turnbell P., 'Drug testing and court review hearings: uses and limitations' (2008) 55(1) Probation Journal, 39–53.

Ministry of Justice, 'National offender management service annual report 2011/12: management information addendum' (2012) Ministry of Justice Information Release.

Ministry of Justice, 'Transforming rehabilitation a strategy for reform' (2013) Ministry of Justice. https://consult.justice.gov.uk/digital-communications/transforming-rehabilitation/results/transforming-rehabilitation-response.pdf.

Ministry of Justice, (2015). https://assets.publishing.service.gov.uk/government/uploads/system/uploads/attachment_data/file/449347/reducing-reoffending-in-adults.pdf.

Ministry of Justice, 'Prison safety and reform' (2016). Offender Rehabilitation Act, 2014.

Ministry of Justice, 'Criminal justice statistics quarterly, England and Wales' (2017) National Statistics.

Ministry of Justice, 'Ministry of justice single departmental plan' (2018). https://www.gov&uk/government/publications/ministry-of-justice-single-departmental-plan/ministry-of-justice-single-departmental-plan--2.

Ministry of Justice, 'New partnership to boost offender rehabilitation' (2019) Ministry of Justice. https://www.gov.uk/government/news/new-partnership-to-boost-offender-rehabilitation.

Ministry of Justice, 'Proven reoffending statistics quarterly bulletin, July 2017 to September 2017' (2019) National Statistics.

Ministry of Justice, 'A smarter approach to sentencing' (2020) White Paper, 55.

Natarajtan M. and Hough M., *Illegal drug markets: from research to prevention policy* (Monsey, NY: Criminal Justice Press/Willow Tree Press, 2000).

National Council on Alcohol and Drug Dependence, *Alcohol drugs and crime* (National Council on Alcohol and Drug Dependence, 2015). https://tinyurl. com/yy76h5ar, Accessed 6 June 2019.

National Offender Management Service, 'Supporting community order treatment requirements' (2014) Commissioning Group.

Newman A., 'Falmouth is getting a drug court' *Patch* (30 April 2019). Offender Rehabilitation Act, 2014. https://patch.com/massachusetts/falmouth/falmouth-getting-drug-court, Accessed 5 September 2019.

O'Neil M., Kendall-Taylor N. and Volmert A., 'New narratives: changing the frame on crime and justice' *FrameWorksInstitute.org* (9 July 2018). http://framewor ksinstitute.org/assets/files/PDF/UKCJ_MM_July_2016_Final.pdf,   Accessed 4 September 2019.

Padfield N., 'Wither the rehabilitation revolution?' (2011) (1) Criminal Justice Matters.

Parker H. and Kirby P., 'Methadone maintenance and crime reduction on Merseyside' (1996) Home Office, Police Research Group.

Perraudin F., 'It's worse than heroin': how spice is ravaging homeless communities' *The Guardian* (April 15 2017). https://www.theguardian.com/society/2017 /apr/15/its-worse-than-heroin-how-spice-is-ravaging-homeless-communities, Accessed 4 September 2019.

Robins J., 'Whatever happened to community justice?' *The Justice Gap* (3 October 2012).

Robins J., 'Where next for community justice? Pioneering court closes' *The Justice Gap* (24 October 2013).

Rochdale Online, 'New justice partnership for greater Manchester' *Manchester* (4 June 2019). https://www.rochdaleonline.co.uk/news-features/2/news-headli nes/128218/new-justice-partnership-for-greater-manchester, Accessed 5 June 2019.

The Scottish Consortium on Crime and Criminal Justice, 'Making sense of drugs and crime: drugs, crime and penal policy' (2003). https://tinyurl.com/y4xtwfur, Accessed 12 June 2019.

Shaffer D.K., 'Reconsidering drug court effectiveness: a meta-analytic review' (2006) (Electronic Thesis or Dissertation). https://etd.ohiolink.edu/.

Snedker K., 'Why the UK needs a separate justice system for people with mental illness' *The Conversation* (5 July 2018).

UK Drugs Policy Commission, 'Reducing drug use, reducing reoffending' (2008) UK policy Commission. https://www.ukdpc.org.uk/wp-content/uploads/ Policy%20report%20-%20Reducing%20drug%20use,%20reducing%20reoffend ing%20(summary).pdf, Accessed 4 September 2019.

Wexler D.B., 'Wine and bottles: a metaphor and a methodology for mainstreaming TJ' (2015) Arizona Legal Studies Discussion Paper No. 15 (05). https://ssrn. com/abstract=2553868.

Wexler D.B. and Winick B., *Law in a therapeutic key: developments in therapeutic jurisprudence* (Durham, NC: Carolina Academic Press, 1999). http://www.austlii.edu.au/au/journals/CICrimJust/1997/9.pdf.

Wilson D., Mitchell O. and MacKenzie D., 'A systematic review of drug court effects on recidivism' (2006) 2(4) Journal of Experimental Criminology, 459–487.

Young S., Wells J. and Gudjonnson G.H., 'Predictors of offending among prisoners: the role of attention-deficit hyperactivity disorder and substance use' (2011) Journal of Psychopharmacology.

3 Analysis and discussion of the 'wine'

3.1 Introduction

In my work elsewhere, I developed a statistically validated tool to empirically measure the behavioural and interactional styles of judiciaries presiding in problem-solving court jurisdictions. Principal component analysis and Cronbach's alpha showed that the three measurement scales, entitled harnessing therapeutic support, engaging therapeutic dialogue, and inspiring therapeutic change, were valid and reliable. Using these measurement scales,[1] this chapter analyses, summarises, and discusses the findings for the wine data by knitting together data from three vantage points (Phases 1, 2, and 3) through a triangulation analysis. This will answer Research Questions 1, 1a, and 2 ('wine') posited originally in Chapter 2, but reiterated again:

1. What impact does an inconsistent bench have on the therapeutic application of magistrates' interpersonal skills and behavioural styles?
   a. Does proficiency at these approaches change according to magistrates' gender?
2. What is the broad therapeutic quality of these styles?

This chapter will first carry out a panel analysis to explore changes in approaches to therapeutic jurisprudence according to the magistrates sitting on the bench to answer Research Question 1 ('wine'). In doing so, a panel gender discrepancy will emerge, and Research Question 1a will clarify impact of gender through a confirmatory analysis. The chapter will then continue to examine proficiency of the measured skills: support, dialogue, and change, and their compounding variables to answer Research Question 2 ('wine'). Thereafter, Chapter 4 will then use the bottle data to ignite a wider discussion about the therapeutic jurisprudence/friendliness of the surrounding England and Wales landscapes. However, as the forthcoming discussions will show, wine and bottle counterparts are difficult to

---

1 Anna Kawałek, 'A tool for measuring therapeutic jurisprudence values during empirical research' (2020) International Journal of Law and Psychiatry, 71C, 101581.

unpick, and to maximise outputs their therapeutic application should be operated synchronously.

3.2 Research Question 1 ('wine')

3.2.1 Component 7

The National Association of Drug Court Professionals under Drug Court Component 7 stipulate that 'ongoing judicial interaction with each drug court participant is essential'.[2] In other words, one single judge should preside over all drug court proceedings. The international literature is fraught with evidence for how this component has enhanced drug court outcomes, arguably making it the most critical of the ten drug court components, where research suggests that higher levels of service-user contact with the same judge supports court outputs and lowers chances of recidivism.[3] The continuity element under Drug Court Component 7 has been shown to help build therapeutic relationships,[4] thus increasing offender accountability, coherency in goals, and raising of self-esteem.[5] The therapeutic jurisprudence literature augments that implementing the same judge to oversee all hearings engenders a therapist relationship style with service-users by allowing the judiciary to create bespoke court sessions by drawing upon their knowledge of the service-user from previous sessions.[6] In the rare local research that is available,

---

2 John Ashcroft, Deborah Daniels, & Domingo Herriaz, 'Defining drug courts: the key components. U.S. Department of Justice' (2004). Retrieved from: https://www.ncjrs.gov/pdf files1/bja/205621.pdf [15].

3 Gill McIvor, 'Therapeutic jurisprudence and procedural justice in Scottish drug courts' (2009) Criminology and Criminal Justice, 9(1), 5–25.

4 Jane Kerr, Charlotte Tompkins, Wojtek Tomaszewski, Sarah Dickens, Roger Grimshaw, Nat Wright, & Matt Barnard 'The dedicated drug courts pilot evaluation process study' (2011) Ministry of Justice Research Series, 1. London: Ministry of Justice; Matrix Knowledge Group, 'Dedicated drug court pilots: a process report' (2008) Ministry of Justice Research Series 7/08. London: Ministry of Justice; Bruce J. Winick & David B. Wexler 'Judging in a therapeutic key: Therapeutic jurisprudence and the Courts' (Durham, NC: Carolina Academic Press 2003) and Ibid.

5 Karen Stimler, 'Best practices for drug court: how drug court judges influence positive outcomes' (2013) (Master's thesis, Minnesota State University-Mankato Mankato, Minnesota; Peggy Hora, 'Courting new solutions using problem-solving justice: key components, guiding principles, strategies, responses, models, approaches, blueprints and tool kits' (2011) Chapman Journal of Criminal Justice, 2(1), 7–52; KPMG Consulting, 'Evaluation of the drug court of Victoria. Government Advisory Services. Final report' (2014) Magistrates' Court of Victoria, 18; Peggy Hora, William Schma, & John Rosenthal, 'Therapeutic jurisprudence and the drug treatment court movement: revolutionizing the criminal justice system's response to drug abuse and crime in America' (2011) Notre Dame Law Review, 74(2). Retrieved from: https://scholarship.law.nd.edu/cgi/viewcontent.cgi?article=1629&context=ndlr.

6 David B. Wexler & J. Bruce, *Winick Law in a therapeutic key: developments in therapeutic jurisprudence* (Durham, NC: Carolina Academic Press, 1999) <http://www.austlii.edu.au /au/journals/CICrimJust/1997/9.pdf>; Carrie Petrucci, 'Respect as a component in the judge-defendant interaction in a specialized domestic violence court that utilizes therapeutic jurisprudence' (2002) Criminal Law Bulletin, 38; Wexler and Winick (n 4).

the importance of a consistent bench in the UK has reverberated throughout the available empirical work. In a local Scottish context, research highlighted that the judicial interactional style and quality boasts compliance and motivation outputs amongst drug court participants.[7] This finding was reflected by English and Welsh research, which illustrated that offenders believed that this dialogue carried much gravity in the original drug courts.[8] For the English and Northern Irish Family Drug and Alcohol Courts (FDAC), researchers quoted that:

> the court reviews are the problem-solving, therapeutic aspect of the court process ... they also provide an opportunity for the judge to engage and moti-vate parents, for direct discussion between the judge and the parents, and for the identification of ways of resolving any problems that may have arisen'.[9]

In the 2008 English and Welsh report, Matrix Group[10] conducted a quantita-tive analysis measuring the impact of judicial continuity at the former Leeds drug court. The report demonstrated that a 10% increase in judiciary continuity resulted in: decreased chances of missing the next review (by 8–23%), lowered chance of failed heroin tests, increased likelihood of completing the sentence (by 11–29%), and less likelihood of being reconvicted (by 5–26%).

The therapeutic value of a consistent bench is not unique to drugs courts, and has also been emphasised within alternative methods of problem-solving practice internationally, such as Judicial Monitoring (Victoria, Australia),[11] Supervision, Monitoring, Accountability, Responsibility, and Treatment ('SMART') (Kentucky, United States),[12] Special Sanctions Court (Fort Bend County, United States),[13] Hawaii's Opportunity with Probation Enforcement ('HOPE')[14] (Hawaii, Pacific United States), and Probation Accountability with Certain Enforcement) ('PACE')

---

7 Gill McIvor, Lee Barnsdale, Susan Eley, Margaret Malloch, Rowdy Yates, & Alison Brown, 'An evaluation of the Glasgow and Fife drug courts and their aim to reduce drug use and drug related reoffending' (2006) Criminology and Criminal Justice, 2009(9), 29.
8 Kerr et al., Matrix Group (n 4).
9 Judith Harwin, Mary Ryan, Jo Tunnard, Subhash Pokhrel, Bachar Alrouh, Carla Matias, & Momenian-Schneider, 'The Family Drug & Alcohol Court (FDAC), evaluation project final report' (2011) Nuffield Foundation, Brunel University.
10 Matrix Knowledge Group (n 4).
11 Judicial College, 'Judicial monitoring condition' (2015) Retrieved from: http://www.judi cialcollege.vic.edu.au/eManuals/VSM/7157.htm
12 Lisa Shannon, Shelia Hulbig, Shira Birdswhistell, Jennifer Newell, & Connie Neal, 'Imple-mentation of an enhanced probation program: evaluating process and preliminary outcomes' (2015) Evaluation and Programme Planning, 49, 50–62.
13 Clete Snell, 'Fort Bend county community supervision and corrections special sanctions court program evaluation report' (2007) University of Houston.
14 Lorana Bartels, 'Looking at Hawaii's opportunity with probation enforcement (HOPE) pro-gram through a therapeutic jurisprudence lens' (2016) QUT Law Review, 16, 30; Lorana Bartels, *Swift, certain and fair: does project HOPE provide a therapeutic paradigm for manag-ing offenders?* (Springer, 2017); Lorana Bartels, 'HOPE-ful bottles: examining the potential for Hawaii's opportunity probation with enforcement (HOPE) to help mainstream thera-peutic jurisprudence' (2019) International Journal of Law and Psychiatry, 63, 26–34.

Table 3.1 Information Contextualising the Panels of Magistrates

Column 1	Column 2	Column 3
Panel number	Number of magistrates	Magistrates' gender
1	2	Female
2	3	Mixed
3	2	Male
4	2	Mixed
5	2	Female
6	2	Female
7	1	Male
8	3	Mixed
9	2	Female
10	3	Mixed

(Alaska, United States).[15] As such, both international and national research, along-side different versions of problem-solving courts, all emphasise the significance of the consistency of judicial benches Component 7, and its proper implementation has incurred good outcomes both internationally and specifically in the UK context.

In light of this evidence, Manchester Review Court was of concern because it was non-compliant to Component 7;[16] a bench of two to three lay magis-trates rotated fortnightly each time that the court sessions ran.[17] Service-users would therefore encounter different magistrates, not necessarily aware of their circumstances, context, and situation, each time they had contact with the court. Research question 1 was put in place to explore its impact on court operation: did the consistency of benches cause inconsistent application of therapeutic juris-prudence approaches?

To carry out the analyses, groups of cases were recoded into 'date group' and given a number (Column 1 of Table 3.1) because many cases (between three and seven individuals) could be seen by the same panel of magistrates on the same date. Therefore, each date group (or number) represented a different panel or composition of magistrates. Table 3.1 characterises the ten panels based on any additional information gathered during data collection (number of magistrates sitting, magistrates' gender) to contextualise the findings. Unfortunately, due to access restrictions, no further demographics of magistrates could be collected. However, since the purpose of this question was to explore broader impact of the breach of Component 7 on consistency of approaches rather than blaming certain judicial demographics for causing less therapeutic application, this was

---

15 Teresa Carns & Stephanie Martin, 'Probation accountability with certain enforcement a preliminary evaluation of the anchorage pilot PACE project' (2011) Alaska Judicial Council.
16 Ashcroft et al. (n 2).
17 The court ran fortnightly on a Wednesday afternoon.

Table 3.2 Means (M) of Therapeutic Scores when Controlling for Date Group (Panel)

Panel	Column 2 Phase 1 Mean	Column 3 Phase 2 Mean	Column 4 Difference Mean	Column 5 Final score Mean
1	3.2 (T)	no survey	NA	3.2(T)–0.4 = 2.8 (NT)
2	3.5 (T)	3.1 (T)	0.4 -	3.3 (T)
3	3.7 (T)	3.3(T)	0.4 -	3.5 (T)
4	3.4 (T)	2.9 (NT)	0.5 -	3.2 (T)
5	3.5 (T)	3.1 (T)	0.4 -	3.3 (T)
6	3 (least)	2.6 (NT) (least)	0.4 -	2.8 (least) (NT)
7	3.8 (T)	3.1 (T)	0.7 -	3.5 (T)
8	3.6 (T)	3.3 (T)	0.3 -	3.5 (T)
9	3 (least)	no survey	NA	3 (T)–0.4 = 2.6 (NT)
10	*4.2 (most)*	*3.4 (most)*	0.7 -	*3.8 (most)*
Total	3.5	3.1	0.4 -	3.31

not a substantial limitation, and the collected data was to sufficient to support the analysis for this research question.

Table 3.2 was generated to compare the overall mean of each of interpersonal and behavioural style measured using the three scales from my instrument.[18] It used the groupings from Table 3.1 to explore consistency of styles. Table 3.2 provides the mean difference between the Phase 1 and 2 scores (Column 4), and an average of the same two scores, which is taken as the 'final score' for that date (Column 5). The final score allowed the two scores together to give a collective average score per date (or panel) through data triangulation. Numerical scores were evaluated qualitatively by importing the qualitative diction from the Likert scale ('poor', 'fair', 'good', 'very good', and 'excellent')[19] to explore and animate the data, whilst giving authenticity to participant voices by retaining the original wording that they had used to answer the survey questions. A further code was also added; 3 or above represented a 'therapeutic' score and below 3 was 'non-therapeutic' based on the Likert scale wording.[20] For ease of readability, non-therapeutic scores are presented in bold and therapeutic scores in italic.

Table 3.2 shows that scores tended to concentrate in the good category (3). No scores fell into either of the extremities: poor (1) or excellent (5) and the lowest

18 Kawałek (n 1).
19 Wade Vagias, 'Likert-type scale response anchors. Clemson international institute for tourism and Research Development' (2006), Department of Parks, Recreation and Tourism Management, Clemson University.
20 Ibid.

scores were fair (2) and highest were very good (4).[21] The final score for each panel shows variation; scores range from 3 (good, therapeutic) and 2 (fair, non-therapeutic). The difference in Column 4 displays similarity of the scores for the same panel from the different methods of data collection. This shows that scores given during Phase 1 observations were consistently higher than for the Phase 2 surveys, but only by a small margin. The average difference between the Phase 1 and 2 scores was only 0.4 on the five-way Likert scale, and the biggest discrepancy was less than one point (0.7). The implication here is that the measurements that I took during the observations were slightly more generous than for those given by the service-users on the same variables. However, this difference was by less than a point at the most. Given that these scores were taken using two very separate methods, and two different observers, it shows a strong similarity across Phase 1 and 2 scores, suggesting convergent results in a triangulation analysis. What is particularly interesting is that both Phases 1 and 2 show, independently, that Panel 10 was the strongest panel and Panel 6 was the weakest, validating the results.

Contextualising these findings into panel type (Table 3.1) suggests that a mixed panel of three magistrates is the strongest composition (Panel 10) whereas an all-female panel of two (Panel 6) is the weakest. Where no data is available for Phase 2 (on Dates 1 and 9), we can hypothesise a score by subtracting the average difference (−0.4) from the Phase 1 score (Column 5). The scores in Column 5 show that Panels 1 (hypothesised), 6, and 9 were all non-therapeutic. The common characteristic between the non-therapeutic panels is that every panel is all-female. On the other hand, Panels 2, 3, 5, 7, and 10 were all therapeutic panels of mixed or male genders. The other characteristic gleaned is the number of magistrates sitting on the panel; however, this shows no pattern. Therefore, the data shows that most panels are therapeutic, although there is inconsistency in quality due to breach of Component 7,[22] the source of which could be gender.

So far, the Phase 1 and 2 quantitative datasets have both demonstrated differences in the therapeutic quality of interpersonal skills according to the bench sitting, where Panel 6 was the least therapeutic (non-therapeutic) and Panel 10 was the most therapeutic (therapeutic). These findings will now be embellished with qualitative data gathered for the wine.

During interviews, one participant suggested that 'without a shadow'[23] there were differences in approaches across benches. Other participants made similar suggestions:

> It [therapeutic quality] depends which magistrate you've got on the bench, it really does. Some are better than others, and others are worse than you'd expect.[24]

---

21 Ibid.
22 Ashcroft et al. (n 2).
23 Participant VI, interview data, collected by Anna Kawałek (file held with author).
24 Participant I, interview data, collected by Anna Kawałek (file held with author).

I think the vast majority of them are very good; however, there are one or two exceptions.[25]

Participants elaborated that a consistent bench would be beneficial as it would create more personalised reviews:

It allows magistrates to say: 'you look really well. When I first saw you months ago, there wasn't anything to you, but now look, you've got a glow in your cheek'.[26]
It's so they know your previous history.[27]

Other perceived benefits of a consistent bench were accountability and relationship building,[28] a fairer approach to individuals,[29] and a consistent review quality.[30] However, whilst all participants reported inconsistency in styles and approaches, this was capricious. Service-user 3 stated that 'they're all safe' (English slang for good), whereas Participants I and II indicated significant diversity across benches. One participant suggested that a consistent bench would only be advantageous if it was a therapeutic panel, otherwise: 'it would be the luck of the draw'.[31] Importantly, participants also reported that it would help them with recovery progress and reduce offending behaviour. Nonetheless, despite this, all participants from Phase 3 made clear that most panels were therapeutic, calibrating the Phase 1 and 2 findings. This suggests that breach of Component 7[32] results in inconsistent application of therapeutic jurisprudence wine at Manchester Review Court.

This finding builds upon the predecessor England and Wales drug court research by Kerr, et al.[33] Researchers examined only four (of the ten possible) key drug court components, one of which was Component 7. Although this alludes to broader fidelity problems, its incorporation alone underscores its importance to the UK drug courts. Researchers further marked the 'judiciary–offender relationship' as fundamental in a diagram mapping key drug court process elements on key outcome delivery, including reduced drug use and offending.[34] The research further stated that this dimension was key for providing offender structure and goal setting, self-esteem and confidence, accountability, engagement, increased judicial knowledge of specific cases as well as partnership working,[35] which are similar findings to those from this study.

25 Participant II, interview data, collected by Anna Kawałek (file held with author).
26 Participant II, interview data, collected by Anna Kawałek (file held with author).
27 Participant VI, interview data, collected by Anna Kawałek (file held with author).
28 Participant I, interview data, collected by Anna Kawałek (file held with author); Participant II, interview data, collected by Anna Kawałek (file held with author).
29 Participant I, interview data, collected by Anna Kawałek (file held with author).
30 Participant IV, interview data, collected by Anna Kawałek (file held with author).
31 Participant IV, interview data, collected by Anna Kawałek (file held with author).
32 Ashcroft et al. (n 2).
33 Kerr et al. (n 4).
34 Ibid. Figure 4.1 [24].
35 Kerr et al. (n 4).

Although the previous researchers highlighted the importance of Component 7, the findings were made in 2011 after only six years of operation for the original London and Leeds drug courts, and after only two years for the later iterations in Barnsley, Bristol, Cardiff, and Salford. Yet researchers had already also began to identify nascent issues that would thwart both current and longer-term operationalisation of Component 7. They detailed that its implementation would undermine, and was irreconcilable with, other court priorities, such as efficiency of administering breaches or logistical issues pertaining to 'magistrates' availability, conflicting priorities of other courts, bank holidays, the chaotic nature of offender lives, or an offender being in custody for another offence at the time of their review'.[36] Despite this, the quantitative analyses disclosed that partial continuity (where one member sits on the bench for two consecutive hearings) was achieved 90% of the time across the six models.[37] Although this is positive and surpasses the current model at Manchester, it still falls short of the ideal presented by the international blueprint, where a single charismatic judge oversees all hearings. Notably, neither model has ever tried using a single individual to oversee the DRR reviews but has always relied upon a bench of lay magistrates.

Interestingly, Salford drug court,[38] arguably the ancestor of Manchester Review Court (cf. Chapter 4), achieved the most continuity across the six pilot sites, where full bench continuity was achieved 29% of the time (dropping to 0% at Leeds drug court, who scored the lowest). This means there has been a significant decline in delivery of Component 7 within the region of Greater Manchester over the last eight years if Salford drug court and Manchester Review Court are considered separate models. Alternatively, it could indicate more specific declination within a single model if Manchester Review Court is Salford drug court's exact successor. This shows that the 2011 researchers correctly predicted difficulties mobilising Component 7 in the long term.

This is problematic; considering that the success of the international models is widely attributable to Component 7 as a key international component, and the UK knew this during onset implementation, why then has the UK continually failed to authentically deliver its problem-solving courts? A 2014 report for the (now-closed) West London drug court was scathing on this point; the author stated that the UK DRR reviews had 'almost perversely'[39] failed to respond to the strong international evidence base indicating the importance of a single presiding judge. Although England and Wales had faced great difficulties implementing a system whereby offenders are coherently reviewed under Component 7, it has counter-intuitively also acknowledged the profound impact of this breach. This not only raises fidelity questions but could also challenge the true

36 Ibid [15].
37 Ibid.
38 Also located in Greater Manchester.
39 Ben Estep, 'Better courts case-study: West London drug court' (2014). Centre for Justice Innovation. Retrieved from: https://b.3cdn.net/nefoundation/c5d489a84bc7c9aa59_cym6idhsz.pdf [2].

priorities of onset implementers, ostensibly unable or unwilling to push for successful delivery of a centrepiece drug court component when setting up the original drug courts.

Although existing research identified budding problems in the area, it was too soon to adequately address at full scale why its operationalisation was problematic for England and Wales. The data for this book can update this area; what emerged from the qualitative data is that such difficulties, both past and present, may be underpinned by fundamental problems at bottle level, namely, reforms under the Courts Act 2003, where a centralised rather than local court model has been emphasised. When I was data collecting, Salford (in 2012) and Bury (in 2017) Magistrates' Courts were already being integrated into the Central Manchester Magistrates' Court, and they were preparing for the imminent transfer of Bolton Magistrates' Court.[40] At this time, there were around 25 magistrates in the pool who would carry out the court reviews, from which 2 to 3 would be selected to form a bench.[41] However, the pool of 25 had broadened over time since the 2003 legislation had been enacted due to courts being combined. One of the most profound effects on Component 7 is that it makes it harder to achieve consistency as the pool of magistrates expands. In the words of my participant, the centralisation reforms have:

'Created a larger wheel to turn, to spin on'.[42]

Breach of Component 7 is likely to worsen in the long term as centralisation initiatives continue to be expedited across the nation, which is ultimately a bottle-level quandary. However, plans to reform this area were in the pipeline for some time before deployment of the original drug courts.[43] As my research confirms that issues implementing Component 7 have been exacerbated since Kerr, et al.,[44] this could suggest that the original drug courts were underpinned by a poorly thought-out conceptual model that failed to account for legislation that would frustrate fidelity to crucial areas. More broadly, ongoing infidelity to Component 7 could raise questions about the authenticity of the historical UK drug courts.[45]

The purpose of this analysis was to investigate whether non-adherence to Component 7 at Manchester Review Court impacted the consistency of therapeutic quality of benches; and, if there were differences, to contextualise why. In returning to the main research question, did inconsistency in benches cause inconsistency of therapeutic jurisprudence approaches? Yes, it did. Component 7 is designed to allow relationships to build between judicial officers and service-users

40 Ethnographic data collected by Anna Kawałek (file held with author).
41 Ethnographic data collected by Anna Kawałek (file held with author); Participant I, interview data, collected by Anna Kawałek (file held with author).
42 Participant I, interview data, collected by Anna Kawałek (file held with author).
43 Courts Act, 2003.
44 Kerr et al. (n 4).
45 Ashcroft et al. (n 2).

by offering continuity. Problem-solving court judges are expected to recast their role from neutral arbitrators of the law to that more similar to a therapist or social worker. But how can they foreseeably do this when the chances of seeing the same offender for the following review are miniscule? Results converged to suggest that inconsistency led to differences in the therapeutic quality of the styles and behaviours of Manchester Review Court magistrates. Participants felt that creating consistency under Component 7 would enhance the court as it would create more personalised reviews, accountability, and relationship building, a fairer approach, and more consistent review quality, which in turn would facilitate recovery and recidivism outcomes. Whilst the purpose of this question was to investigate the impact of an inconsistent bench, a potential panel gender discrepancy emerged, where all-females appeared to be the least therapeutic panel-type. This will be investigated through an explicit confirmatory analysis in the next section.

3.3 Research Question 1a ('wine')

Within the previous analysis, magistrates' gender emerged as a possible impactor on the therapeutic quality of judicial interpersonal and behavioural styles at Manchester Review Court. This section seeks to clarify these differences through a confirmatory analysis. The descriptive statistics (means) in Table 3.3 compare the scores from the Phase 1 (P1) and Phase 2 (P2) samples for gender. It splits the collective data from each phase into each of the three skills measured during data collection using my instrument.[46] The same indicators from the previous analysis (3 or above as 'therapeutic' and below 3 as 'non-therapeutic') were used as a mechanism to explore the numerical scores.

The results in Table 3.3 are interesting because both data sources show that an all-female panel is consistently weakest across Phases 1 and 2 for every skill It is also interesting to note that the only non-therapeutic (below 3) panels are

Table 3.3 Magistrates' Gender Means Scores for Therapeutic Support (TS), Therapeutic Dialogue (TD), and Therapeutic Change (TC)

	TS		TD		TC	
Data source	p1	p2	p1	p2	p1	p2
All male	3.22	3.8	3.95	3.3	3.31	3.3
All female	3.03	3	3.55	3.1	2.99 (NT)	2.8 (NT)
Mixed	3.63	3	3.87	3.4	3.6	3.1
Total	3.3	3.3	3.8	3.3	3.2	3.1

46 Abbreviations: harnessing therapeutic support (TS), engaging therapeutic dialogue (TD), and inspiring therapeutic change (TC).

all-female for the inspiring therapeutic change skill according to both the Phases 1 and 2 data (in bold). The results therefore converge to suggest that an all-female panel operating the therapeutic change skill is the weakest panel type. There is less pattern within the all-male and mixed groups, which changed from first to second place according to data source and skill. Interestingly, the average therapeutic support score for both Phase 1 and Phase 2 was exactly 3.3, indicating a perfect correlation. This not only demonstrates convergency within this item but increases confidence in the validity of the datasets more broadly. As both datasets on average gave a therapeutic (good) score to every skill and gender-type other than a non-therapeutic (fair) score for all-females within therapeutic change, they triangulate, and it can be concluded that female panels were the least proficient at 'inspiring therapeutic change' according to the descriptive statistics.

3.3.1 Tests of statistical significance: one-way ANOVA

Tests of statistical significance will be carried out to broaden the impact of these findings. The p value ($p=<0.05$) will demonstrate whether a finding within a dataset occurred by chance. If it did not occur by chance, we can assume that the same finding would occur within a broader parent population or a similar population measured at another time.[47] A parametric test (one-way ANOVA) will confirm whether there was statistical significance beyond the measured sample of magistrates.

- **Null hypothesis:** there is no statistically significant difference between magistrates' gender and application of the therapeutic support, dialogue, and change skills.
- **Alternative hypothesis:** there is a statistically significant difference between magistrates' gender and application of the therapeutic support, dialogue, and change skills.

According to Gravetter and Wallnau,[48] to carry out a parametric test, the data must satisfy the following criteria:

- Homoscedasticity (homogeneity of variances) within the independent variables;
- The dependent variable(s) must follow a normal distribution;
- The observations within each sample must be independent.

47 Sean Demack, 'Tests of statistical significance – their (ab)use in the social sciences – a comment' (2007) Retrieved from: https://www.jiscmail.ac.uk/cgi-bin/webadmin?A3=ind 0809&L=RADSTATS&E=base64&P=103048&B=------_%3D_NextPart_001_01C9 14DB.62AED010&T=application%2Fpdf;%20name=%22(ab)use%20of%20Significance%2 0Testing.pdf%22&N=(ab)use%20of%20Significance%20Testing.pdf&attachment=q.
48 Frederick J. Gravetter & Larry B. Wallnau, *Essentials of statistics for the behavioral sciences* (Boston, MA: Wadsworth, Cengage Learning, 2014).

Table 3.4 Tests of Normality Within the Distribution of the Independent Variables

Skill means	Skewness	Kurtosis
Support	–.236	–.512
Dialogue	–.354	–.153
Change	.178	–1.187

The first assumption was met by examining Levene's statistic[49] in which homoscedasticity (Appendix 1) showed equal variances across genders: $f(2, 48) = .263$, $p = .140$. For the second assumption, normality of the dependent variable can be checked in Table 3.4.

According to George and Mallery,[50] if skewness and kurtosis values are between –2 and +2, there is a normal univariate distribution. Table 3.4 shows that the dependent variables in this study met the second assumption and were appropriate for this analysis.[51]

However, for the third criterion, the data breached the independence of observations assumption because individual magistrates could appear in both all-gender and mixed panels, which could result in a Type 1 or Type 2 error.[52] Therefore, although the forthcoming results confirm differences in skills across panel genders, they must be treated tentatively due to breach of independence within Criterion 3.[53] This is not a major limitation because the descriptive statistics have already demonstrated that an all-female panel was the least therapeutic for the given sample with certainty, and findings will be imbricated with qualitative data to verify the results later.

The one-way ANOVA (Appendix 2) demonstrated a statistically significant difference between magistrates' gender for harnessing therapeutic support only: $p(2, 48) = 4.673$, $p = 0.14$. Levene's statistic had already confirmed homoscedasticity, which endorses the appropriateness of Tukey corrections for a post hoc test.[54] The Tukey corrections showed a statistically significant difference ($p = 0.12$) between all-female and mixed panels where the latter panel type is $m = 0.33$ more therapeutic (Appendix 3). Thus, the p value confirms that for harnessing therapeutic support, the relationship between a mixed and all-female panel did not occur by chance and it would therefore be likely to present itself within a broader parent population[55] or within another sample taken during a different timeframe.

49 Andy Field, *Discovering statistics using IBM SPSS statistics* (Sage, 2013).
50 Darren George & Paul Mallery, *IBM SPSS statistics 23 step by step: a simple guide and reference* (Routledge, 2016) doi:10.4324/9781315545899.
51 Gravetter & Wallnau (n 48).
52 Roderick McDonald, *Factor analysis and related methods* (New York: Psychology Press, 2014) (n 49).
53 Field (n 49); Gravetter & Wallnau (n 48).
54 Field (n 49).
55 Demack (47).

As such, the alternative hypothesis was accepted for harnessing therapeutic support skill and the null hypothesis was accepted for engaging therapeutic dialogue and inspiring therapeutic change skills. This means that there was strong reason to believe that for therapeutic support, female magistrates were less therapeutic that a mixed panel.

To summarise this section so far, the descriptive statistics demonstrated that gender impacted therapeutic quality of the wine at Manchester Review Court by indicating that all-female panels were less therapeutic than mixed and all-male panels when administering therapeutic support, dialogue, and change. For harnessing therapeutic support, all-female panels were shown to be less therapeutic than mixed panels, and this result was statistically significant. Although results from Phases 1 and 2 on these points triangulate, this will be now be aggregated by the Phase 3 data to check for validity. It is especially important to verify this finding with a third data source because the data breached the independence assumption for the third criterion required for parametric analysis.[56] Notably, although I did not ask participants if magistrates' gender impacted therapeutic skillsets during interviews because this finding surfaced later within the analytical phases, interestingly, it emerged nevertheless. Both Service-user 1 and Service-user 3 referenced male magistrates as particularly therapeutic.

> The main man today ... I just found him very likeable, which is a strange thing – and another difference between those [magistrates] in the normal courts.[57]
>
> He, you know that magistrate today, well instead of trying to put you down all the time, at least he'll listen.[58]
>
> I think he's positive about me.[59]

It is useful to contextualise these findings into further information obtained for panels. Service-user 3 made these comments on Date 3, where an all-male therapeutic panel comprising two magistrates presided, indicating strong influence of the main male magistrate on that day. Participant III made these remarks after he was seen by Panel 7, a single male presiding magistrate with a therapeutic score. This panel also gained the highest score (excellent) for motivation to triangulate with the above-mentioned quotation exhibiting motivational sentiments – 'he's positive about me'. However, importantly, the qualitative data did not indicate that female magistrates were non-therapeutic, but rather the participants derived a positive impression from certain male magistrate. As such, data sources (Phases 1, 2, and 3) verify one another to show that male magistrates effects quality of the wine at Manchester Review Court by increasing the therapeutic quality. Tentativeness

---

56 Gravetter & Wallnau (n 48).
57 Participant IV, interview data, collected by Anna Kawałek (file held with author).
58 Participant III, interview data, collected by Anna Kawałek (file held with author).
59 Participant III, interview data, collected by Anna Kawałek (file held with author).

left by the breach of independence assumption from the parametric test has thus been overcome through triangulation of this finding with other data sources.

However, this finding does not answer the question: why were male magistrates were more therapeutic? We can hypothesise based on the literature. Cultural stereotype dictates that women are more empathetic, compassionate, kind, and caring, compared to their male counterparts.[60] The same stereotype also governs that men are hardwired into traits associated with logic, rationality, practicality, and analytics.[61] Researchers have empirically tested this notion, and those seeking to provide causal explanation have tended to focus on the nature–nurture debate, although results in the field remain conflicting and inconclusive. A study comprising more than 680,000 people found that on average women have a greater ability to recognise what another person is thinking intuitively and to respond appropriately.[62] The study confirmed that 'typical females on average are more empathic, typical males on average are more systems-oriented' and 'we know from related studies that individual differences in empathy and systemizing are partly genetic, partly influenced by our prenatal hormonal exposure, and partly due to environmental experience'.[63] As such, any differences could arise from a variety of causes.

Elsewhere, researchers studying adolescents confirmed greater empathic responses in females compared to males of the same age, and these differences polarised with maturity.[64] Scientists in another study mapped the differences in the brain's structural connectivity and pathways by comparing male and female brains using MRI diffusion imaging, concluding that the right (creativity) and left (logic) hemispheres of women's brains are more interconnected than men, whose brain hemispheres are more independent to one another and inner connected.[65] The impact on human personality is allegedly that women can combine logical responses with emotional intuition, and are better at overlaying emotive responses during problem-solving, whereas men's over engagement of one side of the brain leads to quicker and more skilful solutions.[66] This could explain why females are believed to possess more emotional intelligence. Although these

60 Emma Seppälä, 'Are women really more compassionate?' (*Psychology Today*, 20 June 2013) <https://www.psychologytoday.com/gb/blog/feeling-it/201306/are-women-really-more-compassionate> Accessed 1 July 2020.
61 Madhura Ingalhalikar, Alex Smith, Drew Parker, Theodore D. Satterthwaite, Mark A. Elliott, Kosha Ruparel, Hakon Hakonarson, Raquel E. Gur, Ruben C. Gur, & Ragini Verma, 'Sex differences in the structural connectome of the human brain' (2014) Proceedings of the National Academy of Sciences, 111(2), 823–828. doi: 10.1073/pnas.1316909110
62 David M. Greenberga, Varun Warriera, Carrie Allisona, & Simon Baron-Cohen, 'Testing the empathizing–systemizing theory of sex differences and the extreme male brain theory of autism in half a million people' (2018) PNAS, 115(48), 12152–12157.
63 Ibid.
64 Maria Mestre, Paula Samper, Maria Frias, & Anna Tur, 'Are women more empathetic than men? A longitudinal study in adolescence' (2009) The Spanish Journal of Psychology, 12(1), 76–83. doi:10.1017/S1138741600001499
65 Ingalhalikar et al. [68] (n 61); Ragini Verma, 'Sex differences in the structural connectome of the human brain' (2014) PNAS, 111(2), 823–828. doi:10.1073/pnas.1316909110.
66 Ibid.

results are fairly compelling, and researchers used a large and representative sample to gather their data, it does not tell a comprehensive story.

A dissenting study also focused on neurological factors during an examination of compassion. Scientists compared brain structures of males and females using an fMRI scanner, whilst showing participants images connoting sadness. This study suggested that it is not true that one gender experiences compassion more than the other, despite neurological differences between the brains; however, genders may differ in how compassion is experienced, interpreted, and expressed,[67] suggesting that traits of empathy have a behavioural root. Another study suggested that females possess more pronounced facial electromyographic reactions compared to men. During interactions, this is reported to help women to convey empathy by mirroring expressions of their conversation recipient.[68] Another similar study found that differences in empathy levels and gender was not attributable to genetics or physiological factors; although women scored, on average, ten points higher than men in an emotional quotient test, there does not appear to be a genetic basis for those differences.[69] These studies could suggest that empathy is an environmentally learned characteristic and has a behavioural root; as such, although the scientific evidence suggests that there are gender differences across the lived experiences of empathy, with females tending to be more empathetic, there is no compelling or consistent explanation for what causes these differences.

We can infer from this that within therapeutic courts, and in the context of judge-craft, female leaders might be more emotive problem-solvers, and better able to overlay empathetic, caring, and compassionate sentiments during key court interactions, although we cannot conclude the root cause of this. Empirical proof of this hypothesis within the court context specifically is fairly scant, although there is some evidence of a gendered approach to morality. A leading scholar in this area is Carol Gilligan, who has argued that women and men approach moral problems differently; whereas women tend to define themselves through their connections with others and perceive morality through these interconnections, men tend to define themselves in terms of individual achievement and autonomy.[70] Owing to the discrepancies in neuropathways already identified by Ingalhalikar, et al. 2014., this theory seems plausible.

Researchers have also shown that the likelihood of a judge deciding in favour of a party alleging discrimination increases by about ten percentile points in female

67 Seppälä (n 60).
68 Lars-Olov Lundqvist, 'Facial EMG reactions to facial expressions: a case of facial emotional contagion?' (1996) Scandinavian Journal of Psychology, 36(2), 130–141. doi:10.1111/j.1467-9450.1995.tb00974.x.
69 Reuven Bar-On, Daniel Tranel, Natalie L. Denburg, & Antoine Bechara, 'Exploring the neurological substrate of emotional and social intelligence' (2003) Brain, 126(8), 1790–1800. doi:10.1093/brain/awg177
70 Carol Gilligan, *In a different voice: psychological theory and women's development* (Cambridge, MA: Harvard University Press, 1982).

judges compared to male judges,[71] which implies that male judges could be less emotive decision makers. Columbian judge, Vanessa Ruiz, recently shared her views on women's contributions to the judiciary with the United Nations Office on Drugs and Crime, stating that 'women judges bring those lived experiences to their judicial actions, experiences that tend toward a more comprehensive and empathetic perspective – one that encompasses not only the legal basis for judicial action, but also awareness of consequences on the people affected'.[72] Although this statement does not possess an empirical basis, it does serve to uphold the stereotype that women are more empathetic than men, which could then imply that women are more capable drug court judges.

However, each of these theories and inferences fall out of kilter with the findings from this book, which show the strengths of male magistrates at Manchester Review Court. Moreover, key judicial champions of therapeutic jurisprudence tend to be both male and female.[73] This finding for Manchester Review Court magistrates could be linked to the clientele of the court, which were exclusively male. Collins writes about girl courts in Oahu and Alameda,[74] which operate similar solution-focused principles to Manchester Review Court. Girl courts are staffed predominantly by women including female judges, 'who are expected to act as role models for the girls'.[75] In addition, female judges are rationalised as better able to deal with female participants, not only because they are more in tune with female issues but also because they are accustomed to female ways of speaking and behavioural styles, and can more easily strike up accountable, understanding, and empathetic relationships will fellow women.

If we take this finding and apply it here, perhaps male magistrates at Manchester Review Court were better equipped to deal with male offenders and more able to converse in relatable styles with this demographic. This hypothesis tallies with the Ingalhalikar, et al. gender study comparing hemispheres of male and female brains.[76] If, as found by the researchers, men rely more exclusively on one side of the brain when dealing with problems in front of them, and this leads to quicker and more skilful solutions, this could mean that males are more adept, proactive, and efficient problem-solvers.[77] This might bode particularly well when interacting with fellow male service-users, who mobilise the same parts of the brain to

---

71 Christina L. Boyd, Lee Epstein, & Andrew D. Martin, 'Untangling the causal effects of sex on judging' (2010) *American Journal of Political Science*, 54(2), 389–411.
72 Vanessa Ruiz, 'The role of women judges and a gender perspective in ensuring judicial independence and integrity' (UNODC) <https://www.unodc.org/dohadeclaration/en/news /2019/01/the-role-of-women-judges-and-a-gender-perspective-in-ensuring-judicial-indep endence-and-integrity.html> Accessed 1 July 2020.
73 See Pauline Spencer, Ginger Wren, Gregory Connellan, and in the more local context: David Fletcher, Michael Baker, and Philip Grey.
74 Erin Collins, 'Status courts' (2017) Geo. Law Journal, 105, 1481–1528; Arie Freiberg, 'Problem-oriented courts: innovative solutions to intractable problems?' (2001) *Journal of Judicial Administration*, 11(8).
75 Ibid [1498].
76 Ingalhalikar et al. [65].
77 Ibid.

find solutions, which is its own unique form of empathy. If this is true, it would be interesting to compare results for this book with a similar study investigating the women-only problem-solving court at Manchester Magistrates' Court; by drawing upon the same pool of magistrates for women offenders, could it be that the female magistrates are more therapeutic than males when dealing only with female clientele?

Despite the plausibility of this hypothesis, it is important to point out that the purpose of this analysis was not to accuse female (or any) magistrates of being unskilled or practising poorly. Rather the research question sought to comment on the impact of an inconsistent bench on the coherency across application of therapeutic jurisprudence in light of the court's breach of Component 7,[78] and to explore possible causes. Although it is interesting that a gender difference emerged, inconsistency of approaches may have been linked to other factors. The qualitative data tells a richer story where age, life experience, and attitudes to addiction each emerged as potential causes.

> They [magistrates] use their own experiences, they tend to be older.[79]
> Whether they see it as a medical issue rather than criminal.[80]
> Personality.[81]
> Insufficient training.[82]

These data samples suggest that differences across benches are deeper seated than gender. The last quotation suggests that judicial training could be a factor influencing panel inconsistencies. This is worth picking up because training was either very limited or non-existent at Manchester Review Court. This is despite the court representing a significant departure away from traditional justice methods, which would surely rely on enhanced knowledge bases. This leads onto a discussion of Component 9.

3.3.2 Component 9

Under Component 9, the international body states that for effective drug court practice, 'continuing interdisciplinary education promotes effective drug court planning, implementation, and operations'[83]. Elsewhere, Perlin reiterates the importance of training for therapeutic jurisprudence judges, insisting that 'judicial training is [made] compulsory'.[84] It is also widely documented by the

---

78 Ashcroft et al. (n 2).
79 Participant II, interview data, collected by Anna Kawałek (file held with author).
80 Participant IV, interview data, collected by Anna Kawałek (file held with author).
81 Participant I, interview data, collected by Anna Kawałek (file held with author).
82 Ethnographic data collected by Anna Kawałek (file held with author).
83 Ashcroft et al. (n 2) [21].
84 Michael Perlin, 'Mental health courts, dignity, and human rights' on page 193 in Bernadette McSherry & Ian Freckelton (eds.) *Coercive care: law and policy.* (Abingdon, Oxon: Routledge, 2013) [212].

international evidence base that: 'to serve effectively in this sort of court setting, the judge needs to develop enhanced interpersonal skills'.[85] As such, good quality training is of the essence.

Participants reported that the last training session for Manchester Review Court magistrates was in 2010, and no refresher had been provided.[86] Further, this training session would preclude some magistrates currently in the pool, which had naturally changed and broadened since 2010, catalysed by the England and Wales court centralisation reforms under the Courts Act.[87] This means that many of the magistrates on the bench had never received specialised training and were operating the problem-solving court based entirely on intuition.

It was further reported by Participant I that no specialised training for other court staff members (legal advisors or ushers) had ever been received. The same participant also told me that magistrates' specialist knowledge was instilled wholesale by reading leaflets for Manchester's rehabilitation centres left on tables in the staff room, as well as quarterly panel update meetings to ostensibly bolster judicial knowledge bases.

The lacuna of training opportunities undoubtedly fall significantly short of the ideal presented under Drug Court Component 9. It also corresponds to existing England and Wales literature where Kerr et al.[88] reported that there was limited evidence of formalised education for drug court judiciaries in the original models. This led researchers to recommend that national training provisions should be implemented to improve this area prior to roll-out. When talking to magistrates, I found that recipients of training tended to refer to outdated Salford drug court training; this is open to critique since Manchester Review Court is arguably a unique setting, with different team members, guiding principles, expectations and requirements. This is also telling of conflated understanding of definitions, and that magistrates believed that this court was a centralised version of the old Salford drug court, a point that will be addressed in the next chapter. However, this also suggests more opportunities were available prior to the centralisation. Combining this with the findings from this book highlights long-standing juris-dictional problems with judicial training. That training was so scarce both in the original and newer models raises alarm bells. How can we expect specialised courts to be operated effectively without education configuring the complexities of illicit substance recovery, methods of problem-solving interaction and behav-iours, strategies to mobilise outputs, and without drawing upon matured insights established by international best practice? – Is this somewhat telling of the down-falls of the original drug court efforts? In coming back to the central discussion point under Research Question 1, if certain panels have weaker styles and there are inconsistencies across benches, how can we blame them when they have been

---

85 Ibid. [206].
86 Ethnographic data collected by Anna Kawałek (file held with author).
87 (n 43), section 6.
88 Kerr et al. (n 4).

offered little training? And if there are inconsistencies across benches, do techniques vary according to the amount of rudimentary training received by magistrates? Moreover, does this finding say something broader about the perfunctory efforts of implementers during onset delivery of the problem-solving courts in their neglect of another key component? If it is telling of the failures in this area, this is not about the bandwidth of ground-level practitioners but to do with the lack of institutional support governing the area.

Although I will soon arrive at the conclusion that a single magistrate (or district judge) should preside over all hearings to circumvent consistency problems, a countermeasure under the current structure could be a rigorous national training programme to standardise approaches. Whilst this ultimately looks at improving the wine, it would require intervention at bottle level from the UK Judicial College. Under the Constitutional Reform Act 2005,[89] the Lord Chief Justice leading the Judicial College is responsible for providing training to UK judiciaries. They work closely with the Magistrates Association in developing relevant courses for magistrates. However, judicial training opportunities in recent years have been circumspect for the lay magistracy more generally, let alone in the field of problem-solving.

Figures indicate that UK training budgets have been subject to significant cuts.[90] The House of Commons' Justice Committee[91] reported that expenditure on magistrates' training has been reduced from £72 per sitting magistrate, per year, in 2009/10 to £30 per year in 2013/14. Although no official statistic has since been released, a newer figure of £26 per head, per year was suggested by the Justice Committee in 2019.[92] Although this statistic was critiqued for inaccuracy since training has now been moved in-house thereby reducing overheads, the shift to internal training alone is telling of the current economic environment. The raw figures suggest that spending in this area has depreciated by a third; this is sadly symptomatic of a criminal justice climate punctuated by austerity measures and cutbacks. Under the same agendas, it also goes hand in hand with the ongoing initiatives that are reducing the overall court staffing in this area, including judges and magistrates in line with the court centralisation reforms.[93]

In June 2019 the Justice Select Committee suggested that the source of the training issue is lack of governmental funding from the top, commenting that

89 Constitutional Reform Act, 2005.
90 House of Commons Justice Committee, 'The role of the magistracy Sixth Report of Session 2016–17' (2016) House of Commons. Retrieved from: https://publications.parliament.uk/pa/cm201617/cmselect/cmjust/165/165.pdf.
91 Ibid.
92 House of Commons Justice Committee, 'The role of the magistracy: follow-up eighteenth report of session 2017–19 (2019) House of Commons. Retrieved from: https://publications.parliament.uk/pa/cm201719/cmselect/cmjust/1654/1654.pdf.
93 Ibid.

'funding for magistrates' training was less than adequate'.[94] They went on to state that 'We recommend that the Ministry of Justice increase its funding to HMCTS and the Judicial Office to allow additional investment in magistrates' training'.[95] The follow-up response did not shoulder any responsibility, beginning with: 'magistrate training is a matter for the judiciary'.[96] However, the government also stated that more funding would be available if requested by the college, and the Judicial Colleges' strategy for 2018–2020, stated that 'the Faculty will develop pervasive elements of judgecraft training for use in induction and continuation seminars'[97]. If these statements are both true, then it is difficult to understand why magistrate training has been overlooked, other than simply a shortage of funds.

The diminishing opportunities for training magistrates mean that, whatever the root cause, the Constitutional Reform Act 2005 offers an unfriendly bottle for sustaining therapeutic jurisprudence wine. The cause seems to be austerity measures dominating the area, which, ushered in by the Coalition government, have caused resources to dwindle over time. Although the government have pledged more money to support training, and it is at the heart of the college's strategy, the impact on the lay magistracy both within and outside of problem-solving court domain remains to be seen. Given these problems, the findings in this book showing that the approach of magistrates was in alignment with therapeutic jurisprudence principles (see Research Question 3: this chapter) is praiseworthy. Despite the limited training in the area, the court clearly boasted a rehabilitative court culture led by magistrates, even if only piecemeal. It is interesting to consider the origins of this culture in the absence of training. I asked Participant I, who commented that:

> It might well be lip service. Everyone knows the underlying fact is that review about rehabilitation ... it is an underlying feeling that I think everybody in that room has.[98]

If the problem is insufficient resources to train the full and expanding pool of DRR magistrates, perhaps a realistic solution is to comprehensively train just one individual to a high standard to oversee all DRR reviews at Manchester Review Court to comply with the international evidence base both in terms of

---

94 Ibid [19].
95 Ibid [21].
96 Ministry of Justice, 'Government response to the Justice Committee's eighteenth report of session 2017–19: the role of the magistracy' (2019) Ministry of Justice. Retrieved from: https://assets.publishing.service.gov.uk/government/uploads/system/uploads/attac hment_data/file/843110/role-magistracy-govt-response.pdf [40].
97 Judicial College, 'Strategy of the Judicial College 2018–2020' (2017). Retrieved from: https ://www.judiciary.uk/wp-content/uploads/2017/12/judicial-college-strategy-2018-20 20.pdf
98 Participant I, interview data, collected by Anna Kawałek (file held with author).

consistency (Component 7) and training (Component 9). For frugal ministers keen to adopt durable solutions to the revolving-door phenomena, training would take up resources in the shorter term, but it could save costs in the longer term by enabling the running of an effective court that can reduce bottom-line problems with recidivism, victimisation, and austerity. If the UK is serious about tackling these issues at their roots, it must fully invest in the models by mirroring international best practice and should have the patience and endurance to watch the benefits play out over the longer term. The Justice Innovation Charity, who were founded to support and oversee British problem-solving, may be willing to host some bespoke seminars and training for magistrates if Manchester through the local mayor were to request help.

There are inherent limitations to the suggestion that a single magistrate should preside over all DRR hearings, but these are not unique to Manchester Review Court. It would require the court to be 'chaired by a judge who "buys in" to the therapeutic jurisprudence model'.[99] In other words, it relies heavily upon a magistrate with a therapeutic-jurisprudence–aligned personality, style, and approach. International problem-solving court expert, Professor Michael Perlin, has posited that 'the success of the courts is overly-dependent on the personal charisma of the presiding judge',[100] but suggests that this could be enhanced through judicial training to instil and crystallise therapeutic jurisprudence values.

Previously, England and Wales' (now-closed) Liverpool Community Justice Centre demonstrated early successes when Judge David Fletcher presided over all hearings.[101] Judge Fletcher's approach, character, and attitude was reported to mimic the gold standard, and was comparable to famous therapeutic jurisprudence champions, such as: Pauline Spencer and Greg Connellan (magistrates), Judge Michael King, and Judge Ginger Wren.[102] UK judge, Michael Baker, who set up a problem-solving court called Choices and Consequences ('C2') as part of an offender management programme in Hertfordshire, England, was reportedly of a similar ilk, valuing the importance of rehabilitation and deterrence over punitivism, and he was

99 Michael Perlin, 'There are no trials inside the gates of Eden'Mental Health Courts, the convention on the rights of persons with disabilities, dignity, and the promise of therapeutic jurisprudence' in Bernadette McSherry & Ian Freckelton (eds.) *Coercive care* (UK: Routledge/Taylor & Francis 2012).

100 Perlin (n 84) [214].

101 Center for Court Innovation, 'Judge David Fletcher, North Liverpool Community Justice Centre' (Center for Court Innovation, November 2005) <https://www.courtinnovation.org/publications/judge-david-fletcher-north-liverpool-community-justice-centre> (Accessed 1 July 2020); George Mair and Matthew Millings, 'Doing justice locally: the North Liverpool Community Justice Centre' Centre for Crime and Justice Studies. Retrieved from: https://www.crimeandjustice.org.uk/sites/crimeandjustice.org.uk/files/Doing%20justice%20locally.pdf.

102 Mair and Millings (ibid.); Liverpool Echo, 'Judge David Fletcher made a difference at the North Liverpool Community Justice Centre in Kirkdale' (Liverpool Echo, 21 December 2012) <https://www.liverpoolecho.co.uk/news/liverpool-news/judge-david-fletcher-made-difference-3327912> (Accessed 1 July 2020).

shown to foster therapeutic relationships with addicted burglars in court.[103] Recent research evaluated C2 and a similar programme in Bedfordshire ('PI'), reporting that the two judges now presiding, Judge Mensah and Judge Grey, had behavioural styles and values that encapsulated the therapeutic jurisprudence ideal.[104] Service-users placed great emphasis on their relationship with the judges, and interestingly, these UK problem-solving courts did respond to the international evidence base by adhering to Component 7. This is undoubtedly easier to coordinate when utilising a single district judge rather than panels of lay magistrates.

The charisma of UK judges, Judge Fletcher, Judge Baker, Judge Mensah, Judge Grey, and many of the Manchester Review Court magistrates, offer great hope that therapeutic jurisprudence personalities do exist within UK judiciaries, if only in small pockets, and despite deep-seated punitive sentiments characteris-ing the broader UK criminal justice milieu. We should capitalise on these talents. Though it is preferable, I am not suggesting sourcing a single district judge for the DRR role at Manchester Review Court, given they are expensive and due to the lack of funding for the area, but I do suggest making available a single magis-trate (who already sits in DRR reviews) each fortnight that the court runs to over-see the reviews, selecting this individual carefully, and training him or her to a high level. If a fresh suite of problem-solving courts is on the UK agenda,[105] then the collapse of the original drug courts is made even more pertinent to prevent any forthcoming UK problem-solving courts from suffering that same ill fate. Successful delivery will rely on authenticity and investment in key areas, including Components 7 and 9. Reductions to the DRR panel to just one magistrate (or at most two to include a reserve) sit with broader objectives for England and Wales seeking to curtail expenditure in training, and to reduce the overall quantity of magistrates over the longer term.[106] It is also worth noting that in the drug court context it is not necessary for magistrates to form a bench representative of a cross-section of society to serve as a mini-jury since magistrates are not sentencing offenders currently (cf. Chapter 4).

To summarise the findings from this section, the data shows that the breach of Component 7 resulted in inconsistent application of therapeutic jurisprudence approaches across benches, and that male magistrates could impact therapeutic responses in a positive direction. This finding contradicts the stereotype that dic-tates that females are more emphatic than men. However, it was speculated that the nature of the court, dealing exclusively with male clientele, could have caused male magistrates to perform more therapeutically when interacting with this

---

103 Michael Baker, 'Choices and consequences – an account of an experimental sentences pro-gramme' (2014). Crim. L.R. Issue 1 Thomson Reuters (Professionals) UK Limited; Sam King, Matt Hopkins, & Neil Cornish, 'Hertfordshire choices and consequences (C2) and Bedfordshire prolific intensive offender management (PI) evaluation' [unpublished].
104 Jake Phillips, Anna Kawałek, & Anne-Marie Greenslade, 'An evaluation of the choice and consequences and PI programmes in Bedfordshire and Hertfordshire' (2020) Ministry of Justice.
105 Ministry of Justice, 'A smarter approach to sentencing' (2020) White Paper.
106 House of Commons Justice Committee (n 92).

demographic. As the analysis developed, it was conjectured that inconsistencies across benches are more likely to be linked to the limited training opportunities offered to magistrates, rather than gender. I have therefore suggested that training a single magistrate, highly skilled in therapeutic approaches, should preside over all hearings to overcome these issues and would increase compliance to both Component 7 and Component 9. Importantly, it is worth noting that emerging from the wine analyses, so far, are systemic issues that are thwarting authentic operation of English and Welsh problem-solving court practice. To develop these arguments further, it is important to learn more about the therapeutic quality of magistrates' wine through a discussion of findings for Research Question 2.

3.4 Research Question 2 ('wine')

Having now established that Manchester Review Court's non-adherence to Drug Court Component 7 impacted the consistency of magistrates' approaches, and that inconsistency was exacerbated by non-adherence to Component 9 by lack of training standardising judicial behaviours, this section seeks to explore the broad therapeutic quality of magistrates' interactional and behavioural styles to answer Research Question 2 ('wine'). The answers to this question has already been touched upon with the previous discussions; however, a more explicit analysis of the quality this court facet would provide useful detail before examining the interrelationship between the wine and bottle components in the next chapter.

Therapeutic jurisprudence research into problem-solving court 'wine' has paid close attention to how judiciaries recast their role to a social worker by developing specialised interactional styles and proactive judicial leadership. Nuanced and consolidated by the key text 'Judging in a Therapeutic Key',[107] these techniques are often contextualised by the psychology of procedural justice. Procedural justice is concerned with how judiciaries 'apply procedures that fully respect the individual's participatory and dignitary interests'.[108] Elsewhere, other key interactional styles have been cited as: empathy, acceptance, warmth and self-expression, hope and expectancy, a future focus, and empowerment and possibility.[109] In American research, Petrucci[110] demonstrated that respect cornerstones a therapeutic court communication. Other styles of engagement are referenced as: neutrality, respect, participation, and trustworthiness[111] and voice, validation, and voluntariness.[112] Goldberg's Canadian judicial training manual[113]

107 Winick & Wexler (n 4).
108 Ibid. (129).
109 Michael Clark, 'A changed-focused approach for judges' (2001) in Winick & Wexler (eds.) (n 3).
110 Petrucci (n 4).
111 Roger Warren, 'Public trust and procedural justice' (2002) in Winick & Wexler (eds.) (n 3).
112 Alison Lynch & Michael Perlin, '"Life's hurried tangled road": a therapeutic jurisprudence analysis of why dedicated counsel must be assigned to represent persons with mental disabilities in community settings' (2016) NYLS Legal Studies Research Paper No. 2833365.
113 Susan Goldberg, 'Problem-solving in Canada's courtrooms: a guide to therapeutic justice' (2011). National Judicial Institute.

identifies key techniques as: empathy, respect, active listening, a positive focus, non-coercion, non-paternalism, clarity. Thus, whilst 'therapeutic jurisprudence wine' offers somewhat of an elastic concept, it is characterised by a therapeutic spirit and energy operationalised by judiciaries during court conversations with service-users.

I found that the feedback given to magistrates was overwhelmingly positive in this respect, especially amongst service-users, who valued the problem-solving style driven by the bench. This finding is made even more impressive considering how little training we know that magistrates received. The positive feedback is too extensive to report in its entirety, but is illuminated by the sampled quotations below.

> I was impressed and that's why I gave a very high score on that questionnaire you gave me. I don't usually give a high score; I'm usually always like a zero to three or four out of ten. But they [the magistrates] are in the sevens and tens.[114]
>
> I think they're [magistrates] very approachable.[115]
>
> I think to have the court, it's like an anchor. It's incredibly necessary and important – not only to society but also to the individual. It's positive to see magistrates in a different way.[116]
>
> I think they [magistrates] have been chosen well, they must've been for them to do this DRR review court.[117]
>
> I think these magistrates deserve respect.[118]
>
> They're doing everything that it says on the tin.[119]
>
> I'm very, very, very impressed. Everyone has been really down to earth.[120]
>
> I'm impressed – they're very manageable and very understanding. And they show a lot of empathy.[121]
>
> They [offenders] begin to view this court in a different way and they start to see the magistrate as people that want to encourage them to change.[122]

Although the quotations qualitatively depict magistrates applying wine therapeutically, the upcoming sections involve a deeper quantitative investigation into the indicators used to measure the therapeutic interpersonal skills and behavioural styles to identify specific areas of excellence and weakness (cf. Chapter 2, Table 2.1).[123] The rationale for breaking them down in such a nuanced way is to allow findings to feed into practice more easily through a detailed evaluation

114 Participant V, interview data, collected by Anna Kawałek (file held with author).
115 Participant III, interview data, collected by Anna Kawałek (file held with author).
116 Participant I, interview data, collected by Anna Kawałek (file held with author).
117 Participant V, interview data, collected by Anna Kawałek (file held with author).
118 Participant IV, interview data, collected by Anna Kawałek (file held with author).
119 Participant V, interview data, collected by Anna Kawałek (file held with author).
120 Participant V, interview data, collected by Anna Kawałek (file held with author).
121 Participant IV, interview data, collected by Anna Kawałek (file held with author).
122 Participant II, interview data, collected by Anna Kawałek (file held with author).
123 Kawałek (n 1).

Table 3.5 Means (M) and Average Means (AM) for Therapeutic Support, Dialogue, and Change

	TS	TD	TC
P1 (m)	3.38	3.78	3.24
P2 (m)	3.05	3.33	3.1
Average (m)	3.22	3.56	3.17

of where and how magistrates could improve, and also what worked well. As such, the broader skills (harnessing therapeutic support, engaging therapeutic dialogue, and inspiring therapeutic change), and the substituting skills, will be examined to answer Research Question 2 ('wine'). As in the previous analyses, Phases 1 and 2 will be analysed together as they were measured quantitatively using the same categories. Analyses will be carried out using means and bivariate correlations. Findings will then be further ratified by qualitative data.

Table 3.5 was generated to demonstrate Phase 1 and Phase 2 means for each of the three main skills. The average mean of each skill (rather than the substantiating variables) was calculated first to allow for a broader comparison within and across phases. Table 3.5 shows that magistrates were most proficient at engaging therapeutic dialogue according to both phase 1 (m=3.8) and phase 2 (m=3.33) data.

The results therefore converge to indicate that therapeutic dialogue was magistrates' strongest skill. The Phase 1 and Phase 2 data differed on the second most therapeutic skill. In Phase 1, magistrates were intermediately proficient at therapeutic support (TS), but in Phase 2, therapeutic change (TC) was intermediate, and vice versa. Although results on this point seem dissonant, in reality there was such little difference (.05) between the Phase 2 proficiency of support and change; within a triangulation rationale, the findings became complementary through means testing.[124] Using an average mean of each phase, therapeutic change was found to be magistrates' least therapeutic skill overall (m=3.17), and therapeutic support was intermediate overall (3.22).

The cause of therapeutic change scoring least proficiently might be explained by the findings from Research Question 1a ('wine'), in which descriptive findings indicated that female magistrates applied this skill non-therapeutically according to both datasets, which could mean that females bring down the average score. Nevertheless, the qualitative indicators also suggest that every skill was operated to a 'good' (therapeutic) standard.[125] In other words, regardless of the skill rankings (first, second, or third), they were all applied therapeutically overall. This heavily suggests that magistrates were pouring therapeutic-jurisprudence–friendly

124   Udo Kelle & Christian Erzberger, 'Making inferences in mixed methods: the rules of integration in Abbas Tashakkori & Charles Teddlie (eds.) *Handbook of mixed methods in social & behavioural research* (Thousand Oaks, CA: Sage, 2003).
125   Vagias (n 19).

Table 3.6 Means of Magistrates' Support Scores Phases 1 and 2[a]

	Interest/ compassion	Understand alcohol and other drugs	Reiterating goals	Personable	Faith/hope in progress	Giving praise	Motivate
p1	3.7(T)	**2.9(NT)**	3(T)	3.5(T)	3(T)	3.5(T)	3.6(T)
p2	3.1(T)	3(T)	**2.9(NT)**	3.1(T)	3.1(T)	3.1(T)	**2.7(NT)**
AM	3.4	3	3	3.3	3.1	3.3	3.2

[a] For full names of the variables see Table 2.1, Chapter 2 (this book).

wine at Manchester Review Court, although this could be improved to an average of 'very good' or 'excellent' through training.

To nuance these findings, the forthcoming sections will examine the scores of the variables comprising each principal construct (support, dialogue, change) using the means of both Phase 1 and Phase 2 values individually, and then complementarily through the use of average means (AM), and qualitative data will then substantiate the findings. Using deductive thematic analysis,[126] four themes, or skills, emerged as key tenets to the interpersonal and behavioural styles of the Manchester Review Court magistrates from the qualitative data, operated to differing degrees of strength. They will be discussed under the heading of the broader skill from which they are derived:

1. Understanding the complexity of alcohol and other drugs recovery (therapeutic support);
2. Motivating the individual (therapeutic support);
3. Giving the offender a voice (therapeutic dialogue); and
4. Setting realistic goals (therapeutic change).

3.4.1 *Harnessing therapeutic support*

The average mean (AM) in Table 3.6 shows that magistrates applied 'interest/compassion' most therapeutically (m=3.4) and applied 'personability' and ' praise' (m=3.3) jointly second. Although the AM in the bottom row each indicate a good and (therapeutic) score for all subskills between the Phases 1 and 2 scores, the figures in bold fall below the therapeutic threshold within independent data collection phases, namely: 'understanding the complexity of alcohol and other drugs recovery' (Phase 1), 'reiterating goals' (Phase 2), and 'motivating the individual' (Phase 2), suggesting that these skills could be improved. The former two subskills were on the border (2.9) for a therapeutic score, meaning that just

126 Virginia Braun & Victoria Clarke, 'Using thematic analysis in psychology' (2006). Qualitative Research in Psychology, 3(2), 77–101.

a little improvement would take it into the therapeutic realm. Training in these specific areas should thus be prioritised.

Analyses previously suggested that harnessing therapeutic support was broadly poured in a therapeutic-jurisprudence–friendly fashion (magistrates scored 3.22), but it could be improved. This analysis has nuanced this finding by elucidating the facets of harnessing therapeutic support that could bolster its application, as above. In addition to this, it was gleaned from the qualitative data that two subskills were key techniques for Manchester Review Court's operation: 'understanding the complexity of alcohol and other drugs recovery' and 'motivating the individual'. These will be discussed in more depth next.

3.4.1.1 *Understanding the complexity of alcohol and other drugs recovery*

Magistrates scored 3 for this variant, which represents a therapeutic score, although it is on the threshold. This was the least therapeutic skill of the four skills that emerged thematically from the qualitative data. This variable intended to measure how well magistrates understood the recovery process both practically and theoretically, including expected relapse, barriers, and opportunities for success, co-existing addiction issues (medical, physical, social), and knowledge of the wraparound treatment services. The qualitative data showed that magistrates at Manchester Review Court were mostly proficient at this skill:

> Even though I'm not providing a negative, but providing a few days clean, they can see that I'm trying.[127]
>
> Magistrates tended to be empathetic towards relapses.[128]
>
> Magistrates took a kind and realistic approach to positive drug test results.[129]
>
> The magistrate said: 'it's great that you have produced one (of three) negative tests, how about you produce two for next time?'[130]
>
> Magistrates tend to say: 'Okay, you've not done great, you've not got any negatives but you've reduced your drug use significantly; you're only using half of what you were doing, that's a positive step, you've got to look at that going forwards'.[131]

However, on Date 6, I reported:

> These magistrates were much harsher than usual, especially in relation to positive drug tests; they were telling off the service-users in a paternalistic manner for results; service-users were leaving the courtroom irritated.[132]

---

127 Participant III, interview data, collected by Anna Kawałek (file held with author).
128 Ethnographic data (various dates) collected by Anna Kawałek (file held with author).
129 Ethnographic data (Date 6) collected by Anna Kawałek (file held with author).
130 Ethnographic data (Date 10) collected by Anna Kawałek (file held with author).
131 Participant II, interview data, collected by Anna Kawałek (file held with author).
132 Ethnographic data (Date 6) collected by Anna Kawałek (file held with author).

Magistrates did not have much empathy for the difficulties and complexity of the recovery process today. Staff members also commented on this after the hearings.[133]

A service-user today had according to other staff made vast improvements to the number of positive tests submitted, but magistrates today clearly didn't understand that just a few negative tests are to be expected this early on in a recovery journey.[134]

The Date 6 findings are inconsistent with recent scholarly work from the recovery and desistance field, highlighting the psychosocial challenges associated with building and sustaining recovery and desistance narratives.[135] Maruna has posited that this journey involves reversing intractable social patterns into those more productive, pro-social, and coherent-with-desistance narratives.[136] Similarly, empirical research suggests that sustaining long-term recovery entails overcoming engrained chaotic lifestyles, and establishing stability in even basic areas, like sleep, eating, and daytime routine.[137] However, both of these can be a long, albeit frustrating, processes. This sentiment is echoed by the National Association of Drug Court Professionals, who state that:

> a pattern of decreasing frequency of use before sustained abstinence from alcohol and other drugs is common. Becoming sober or drug free is a learning experience, and each relapse to alcohol and other drugs use may teach something about the recovery process'.[138]

Drug courts must thus understand that sobriety for entrenched service-users involves some expectation of early relapse, and this takes time to achieve.[139]

Most of the quotations demonstrate that magistrates embedded these principles into judicial craftsmanship. However, on Date 6, the sampled data run contrary to these findings. This Date-6 data also contradicts therapeutic jurisprudence literature, which emphasises the value of a non-paternalistic, encouraging, and non-hierarchical communication style during court conversations,[140]

---

133 Ibid.
134 Ibid.
135 William Cloud & Robert Granfield, 'Conceptualizing recovery capital: expansion of a theoretical construct' (2008) Substance Use and Misuse, 43(12–13), 1971–1986. doi: 10.1080/10826080802289762; Shadd Maruna, *Making good: how ex-convicts reform and rebuild their lives.* (Washington, DC: American Psychological Association, 2011). doi:10.1037/10430-000
136 Maruna (ibid).
137 William Cloud & Robert Granfield, 'Social context and "natural recovery": the role of social capital in the resolution of drug-associated problems' (2001). Substance Use and Misuse, 36(11), 1543–1570.
138 Ashcroft (n 2) [13].
139 Ibid.
140 Winick & Wexler (n 4).

and further contravenes the drug court literature suggesting that the courts recognise the graduality of achieving stability. Revisiting the Phase 1 quantitative
data to contextualise Date 6 finding showed that magistrates were 50% either
very negative or negative for this variable and neutral for the remaining 50%; this
averaged out as a non-therapeutic score of m=2.2. Results were then compared
to measurements from the same variable from Phase 2 on the same date.[141] Just
one service-user had responded on Date 6, but he disagreed that 'magistrates
understand what it's like to have drug and alcohol problems' (Question 25).
Therefore, the results from all phases corroborate the suggestion that magistrates
on Date 6 were practising this skill ineffectively, and this fell out of line with
the expected principles, values, and ideals posited by the literature. However,
since the previous analyses found that Date 6 was the least therapeutic panel of
the ten investigated, and that magistrates were generally non-therapeutic on this
date, this points to a broader problem with the wine beyond this single variable.
This could be due to gender, as Date 6 was an all-female panel. However, it is
more likely to be attributable to other idiosyncrasies of the bench, including the
amount of training received. On a broader level, this finding augments the previous finding: that a changing bench impacts the consistency in application of wine
at Manchester Review Court under Research Question 1.

Examining this variable more holistically, and in a different light, could offer
a different viewpoint. Wexler has posited that tighter definitions of 'therapeutic'
should be avoided by research communities, as it might 'eclipse' broader issues
or disguise other therapeutic reactions.[142] One could argue that although harsh
interactions about positive drug tests from Date 6 magistrates were intrinsically
anti-therapeutic, the punitive undertones from the interaction may help offenders
produce negative tests for the next session in fear of breaching the court order,
thereby enhancing rehabilitative outcomes. This hypothesis corresponds to a
comment by participants below who stated that sometimes a harsher response is
necessary:

> Sometimes the court needs to say, 'Look, enough is enough'.[143]
> I say get the big stick out. Seriously, seriously, because that's the only
> way you're going to get these DRRs to be f**king reductive if you know I
> mean.[144]

This sits in line with another of the National Association of Drug Court
Professional's observations, stating that: 'although drug courts recognize that

---

141 Question 25: 'Magistrates understand what it's like to have drug and alcohol problems' on
     survey collected by Anna Kawałek (file held with author).
142 Carrie Petrucci, Bruce Winick, & David Wexler, 'Therapeutic jurisprudence: an invitation
     for social sciences' in David Carson & Ray Bull (eds.) *Handbook of psychology in legal con-
     texts*, 2nd ed. (Chichester: Wiley & Sons, 2003) [584].
143 Participant II, interview data, collected by Anna Kawałek (file held with author).
144 Participant V, interview data, collected by Anna Kawałek (file held with author).

Table 3.7 Understanding the Complexity of Alcohol and Other Drugs Recovery: Panel Analysis (Phase 1)

Date group	Mean
1	2.43
2	2.33
3	2.67
4	3.00
5	3.33
6	2.17
7	4.00
8	3.00
9	3.00
10	4.00
Total	2.90

individuals have a tendency to relapse, continuing alcohol and other drug use is not condoned'.[145] In other words, a harsher response could, somewhat counterintuitively, abet therapeutic and productive reactions, although this is likely to depend on the personality of the recipient.

A broader panel analysis in Table 3.7 was run to explore the consistency of panels further. Unlike the previous panel analyses, this table explores the skill in question singlehandedly, rather than grouping all variables into the same means-testing analysis.

The table shows that magistrates were very inconsistent at this skill; whereas they applied it non-therapeutically on Dates 1, 2, 3, and 6, they did so therapeutically on Dates 4, 5, 7, 8, 9, and 10. This is highly indicative of discrepancy in its application across panels. The Phase 3 data confirmed that magistrates had different approaches to relapse:

> Some magistrates approach things differently, and they're not prepared to allow such leeway and they might well think, 'You know what? There is general relapse, and there is pulling the wool'.[146]

The participant in the sampled data confirms that some magistrates are more lenient than others when approaching service-users' test results. A scattered approach to drug test results would be problematic for service-users who are then required to navigate ever-changing expectations across review sessions when they are already living in worlds that are so chaotic.[147] If the recovery and desistence

145 Ashcroft et al. (n 2) [13].
146 Participant I, interview data, collected by Anna Kawałek (file held with author).
147 Peggy F. Hora, William G. Schma, & John T.A. Rosenthal, 'The importance of timing' in (eds.) Winick & Wexler (n 4).

literature strongly indicates that stability, coherency, and routine is of the essence for rehabilitating this cohort,[148] how can the setup of a changing bench, with changing expectations within this variable, possibly lend itself to fruitful rehabilitative outcomes? This belies the purpose of a therapeutic court that requires a joined-up approach by cross-fertilising insights, such as constancy of therapist or social worker, from the social sciences. Although this issue once again pertains to the lack of fidelity to drug court Component 7, the problem with infidelity is highlighted by this variable, as it means attitudes to test results vary according to the bench.

Lack of understanding regarding alcohol and other drugs recovery within magistrates' knowledge bases is not a fault of the magistrates themselves and is certainly no reflection of some reluctance to engage on their part. We already know that magistrates' expertise was instilled exclusively by their reading of leaflets for nearby recovery centres or services, which were left in the staffroom. It is therefore commendable that they scored as highly as they did, and for this, magistrates' efforts should be celebrated. However, clearly, training magistrates in this area would be beneficial to the court, and this could be achieved through better partnership working with the drug services and/or more general theoretical and practical training, delivered by experts. Attending conferences paid hosted by the Judicial College or more bespoke training sessions presented in-house by the Centre for Justice Innovation are some examples for to enhance this skill. This is a dynamic field where there is currently a lot going on in the UK, which magistrates should be supported and encouraged to tap into.

In addition to those issues already raised with the training at the Judicial College under the Constitutional Reform Act 2005, other explanations also appear to be systemic, and link to the changes overseen by the court centralisation reform under the Courts Act 2003, section 6.[149] We have already seen that the UK has undergone significant centralisation reforms to its court systems, broadening the geographical remit in which the lay magistracy can preside. From a drug court perspective, this undermines England and Wales' ability to adhere to Component 7. However, critics have also argued that court centralisation initiatives have curtailed local justice, and repressed magistrates' autonomy by boycotting independent decision-making powers.[150] Magistrates' courts were once part-funded by local councils (20%) and part-funded by the central government (80%), but finances are now administered wholesale by the central body.[151] The local aspect of the previous structure allowed budgets to be controlled by the

---

148 Cloud & Granfield (n 135) and Maruna (n 135).
149 Courts Act 2003, section 6.
150 Phil Bowen & Jane Donoghue, 'Digging up the grassroots? The impact of marketisation and managerialism on local justice, 1997 to 2013' (2013) British Journal of Community Justice, 9–21; Justice Select Committee (n 92).
151 Penelope Gibbs, 'Return magistrates' courts to local control' (The Law Society Gazette, 3 June 2013) <https://www.lawgazette.co.uk/analysis/return-magistrates-courts-to-local-control/71223.article> Accessed 1 July 2020.

Magistrates Committee. As the Magistrates Committee comprised of magistrates themselves, this gave magistrates real power over the jurisdiction of their presiding court, and over the broader administration of justice. A side effect of the 2003 restructure was also to abolish the Magistrates Committees, and centralise powers to an HMCTS board; places are reserved for judges only, which means that magistrates no longer have the same voice, or certainly none with real meaning or impact, as they did pre-2003.[152]

This has been reported to have adverse consequences on the morale and mood of magistrates, who have felt disempowered, underappreciated, and sidelined.[153] Penelope Gibbs, a former magistrate who is also a key writer in this area, has stated that: 'now magistrates have no influence over the running of the courts, despite having many ideas on how they could be run more efficiently'.[154] David Simpson, erstwhile West London magistrates' court clerk, characterised the courts within the old system as being like close-knit families; however, the community spirit, teamwork, and loyalty was soon expunged as the centralisation remodel began to take effect.[155] A 2015 report by Rob Allen, an independent researcher and cofounder of Justice and Prisons,[156] carried out a comparative analysis between the United States (where most of the international drug courts are located) and the UK, paying heed to the structural differences between the jurisdictions.[157] It was reported that, through Justice Reinvestment schemes, America tends to rely on a devolved justice structure where powers are given to counties, rather than being centralised to the state.[158] Allen asserts that: 'the involvement of local counties in criminal justice is one of the distinguishing features of the system in USA'.[159] By way of comparison, 'in England and Wales, local government plays a very limited role in criminal justice'.[160] Therefore, the UK uses a centralised model to govern the court systems, whereas the United States applies a decentralised justice framework. According to key writers,[161] a devolved structure underscores, bolsters, and empowers effective drug court practice as it allows community and local justice to ensue. However, the centralised structure will only continue to gain momentum under the Courts Act 2003.[162] It has been suggested that re-establishment of local power, which began

152 Ibid.
153 Ibid.
154 Ibid.
155 Ibid.
156 Justice and Prisons (2011) <justiceandprisons.org> Accessed 1 July 2021.
157 Rob Allen, 'Rehabilitation devolution – how localising justice can reduce crime and imprisonment' (2015) *Transform Justice*. Retrieved from: http://www.transformjustice.org.uk/wp-content/uploads/2015/12/TRANSFORM-JUSTICE-REHABILITATION-DEVOLUTION.pdf.
158 Ibid.
159 Ibid [15].
160 Ibid [15].
161 Ibid; Bowen & Donoghue (n 150).
162 Allen (n 157).

to dissolve under Blair's Labour Government then was continued under the Coalition Government, is too much of a radical idea. Whilst some areas of criminal justice have been offered local options (most predominantly, youth justice), arguably there is little hope for devolving central powers due to ongoing centralisation and privatisation goals.[163]

Donoghue and Bowen have argued that 'this process of centralised administration made it all but impossible for magistrates to introduce new and effective practices into their own courts'.[164] Greater Manchester is a big county, and magistrates often travel far to work. Those coming to the court from further areas become unable to embed local issues into their craftsmanship through a local justice philosophy. From the perspective of judicial expertise, this is problematic because as magistrates attend work from wider areas of Greater Manchester, this makes it difficult for them to craft tailor-made responses to alcohol and drug issues in their work because the prevalence and trends of these issues, and the available treatment services, change according to region. However, although this impacts the therapeutic jurisprudence friendliness of the wine, ultimately, the centralisation initiative activated by the Courts Act 2003 creates a bottle-level quandary, where a centralised system is inconducive to good problem-solving practice in house.

This might not be the only cause of the low scoring of 'understanding the complexity of alcohol and other drug recovery'. It is worth also noting that the shortcomings found within magistrates' knowledge bases for this variable may also be attributable to fragmentation of stakeholders. Manchester Review Court also failed to comply with Drug Court Component 10, under which the National Association of Drug Court Professionals states that: 'forging partnerships among drug courts, public agencies, and community-based organisations generates local support and enhances drug court programme effectiveness.[165] Although this is explored in greater depth in the next chapter, the main point is that this component emphasises the importance of a multidisciplinary approach amongst partners, with the court at the centre of the model.

At Manchester Review Court, linking service-users to the appropriate drug services was exclusively the job of probation officers, and this occurred outside of the courtroom. In other words, the important process of linking service-users to drug treatment occurred out of ear and eyeshot of magistrates. Probation officers assess the ongoing needs of individual service-users, coordinate with the treatment services, and liaise with relevant organisations to initiate and maintain appropriate support for a myriad of areas beyond drug treatment services, such as: housing, finance, counselling, domestic violence, and so on. Any progress or change was communicated back to the court in a written report before review. This not only meant that magistrates did not assume the same pivotal leadership

163 Bowen & Donoghue (n 150).
164 Bowen & Donoghue (n 150) [13].
165 Ashcroft (n 2).

role as they would in a traditional drug court by connecting and coordinating the programme, but it also meant limited expose to the issues and goings-on outside of the court sphere. This undoubtedly compromised their understanding of alcohol and other drugs under this variable.

I noted:

> When offenders asked magistrates questions about treatment or services, they reverted to the probation officer for answers because this simply was not deemed to be their remit.[166]

In addition, this configuration gave a strange sense that the court was not the centrepiece of the model but was merely an ancillary component to the main probationary aspect; this contravenes any interpretation of the drug court archetype derived by the international literature. This point will be revisited in the next chapter; however, for the purposes of this analysis, the court's circumscribed role in the full process meant that magistrates' understanding of the linked services, and related alcohol and drug recovery knowledge, was invariably limited. This is again a systemic bottle problem, relating to the provisions of the DRR set out in the Criminal Justice Act 2003,[167] rather than one solely concerning magistrates' administration of the wine.

Gaps in magistrates' alcohol and other drugs knowledge may be further catalysed by the constantly changing wraparound services supporting the DRR. Manchester Integrated Drug and Alcohol Services (MIDAS) were, at the time of this study, the umbrella treatment service for Manchester Review Court, embedding and overseeing support areas thematically. However, my participant told me that the service providers regularly changed as they are put out to tender on a three-year rotation.[168] This meant that the service providers, and their idiosyncratic systems, were constantly alternating. This rendered it even more challenging for magistrates keep on top of their understanding of the area.

> With every new provider you get different ways of doing things.[169]

Consider that the changing bench meant that magistrates might on average sit thrice on the DRR panel per year. This is only nine sessions before the services become uprooted and are replaced by a new provision. This makes it very difficult to upkeep up-to-date knowledge.

Although this does put up a hurdle for well-informed practice, it is perhaps not insurmountable. With some passion and dedication for good craftsmanship, magistrates could educate themselves through voluntary visits to the service providers

---

166 Ethnographic data collected by Anna Kawałek (file held with author).
167 Criminal Justice Act, 2003.
168 Participant II, interview data, collected by Anna Kawałek (file held with author).
169 Ibid.

and probation offices to enhance their knowledge bases. Time out of other court sessions could be given to allow for this. That England and Wales' magistrates are unpaid volunteers, Justices of the Peace intended to represent a mini jury, mean that they are willingly giving their time to administer justice, and more specifically opt to take part in the DRR court reviews. This might indicate a passion for the area, which should be capitalised upon. Of course, prioritising continuity under Component 7 would also help to create a more educated knowledgeable bench, and the preference would be to implement a single presiding magistrate with a toolkit of specialised knowledge. However, currently, magistrates might be amenable to visit the sites of the wraparound services, and should be supported to do this.

Overall, this section has shown that the variable 'understanding the complexity of alcohol and drugs recovery', as part of the harnessing therapeutic support skill, was applied inconsistently, and with room for improvement. As the analyses of the wine have progressed, what has emerged is a UK bottle that continues to tighten in therapeutic jurisprudence unfriendliness; training opportunities have depreciated, there have been chronic and ongoing court centralisation initiatives, and the UK has abandoned a devolved power structure, all of which make good practice difficult. However, I have made suggestions for change to overcome these issues throughout the discussions. The next section will explore the second skill that emerged thematically from the qualitative data: motivating the individual.

3.4.1.2 Motivating the individual

As part of harnessing therapeutic support, this variable measured the motivational quality of panels' interactional and behavioural styles. The importance of motivation during problem-solving court conversations is captured by Bruce Winick, co-founding father of therapeutic jurisprudence: 'problem solving courts are all characterized [*sic*] by active judicial involvement and the explicit use of judicial authority to motivate individuals to accept needed services and to monitor their compliance and progress'.[170] As such, instilling motivation is a crucial aspect of the judicial role in the international examples. This variable was embedded into the measurement system because, like the international prototype, DRR reviews intend to boost offender outcomes by spurring service-users to stay clean from drug use and compliant with their court order, in part through motivation.[171]

Motivating the individual is clearly a key principle for keeping offenders on track, and one that was done especially well in the Hertfordshire problem-solving court by Judge Grey; service-users have reported feeling excited and inspired after the court reviews due to the motivational sentiments offered by Judge Grey.[172] In

---

170 Bruce Winick, 'Therapeutic jurisprudence and problem solving courts' (2003) 30 Fordham Urb. L.J. 1055. Available at: https://ir.lawnet.fordham.edu/ulj/vol30/iss3/14 [1060].
171 Kerr et al. (n 4).
172 Phillips et al. (n 104).

previous analyses, I found that magistrates scored an average m=3.2 for 'motivating the individual', thus indicating that it was practised therapeutically (good). The qualitative data brought fresh life to this insight and highlighted its sheer importance to Manchester Review Court's functioning, where every interviewed participant identified it as fundamental. In the following two examples, participants were asked what they perceived to be the purpose of the DRR reviews:

> [The purpose is] motivating them and to try and reduce the drug use, just generally motivating them to do things positive in their life.[173]
>
> [The purpose is] to provide visible motivation and encouragement in review, support, and a rock-like feature.[174]

This shows that both participants identified motivation, imparted by magistrates, as a forefront objective of Manchester Review Court. This confirms the importance of this facet to the model and consolidates existing England and Wales drug court research, in which Kerr et al. established 'motivational' as one of five core styles of judicial engagement within the old models.[175] In other words, in closely related research, motivation was also viewed as key for leveraging key outputs. In that project, researchers lifted the following quote from their data to exemplify this sentiment: 'if you want it to work, it will work, we see an awful lot of successes'.[176] A similar example from my data is:

> We know you can do this – you have done it before, and you can do it again. It is in your power now.[177]

The fact that this aspect of the wine was/is critical to the DNA of both models, and that there are fundamental similarities between the data samples, could hint that Manchester Review Court is the ghost of its predecessor, Salford drug court; this discussion is extended in the next chapter.

The object of motivation was most commonly identified as to decrease drug use and increase law compliance and obedience with the court order;[178] this is in line with traditional drug court goals under Component 1.[179] However, other purposes included motivation to attend treatment appointments, probation meetings, drug testing, and any relevant out-of-court disposals, such as community service provision, picking up methadone scripts, and obtaining help for

---

173 Participant II, interview data, collected by Anna Kawałek (file held with author).
174 Participant I, interview data, collected by Anna Kawałek (file held with author).
175 Kerr et al. (n 4) [26].
176 Ibid [25].
177 Ethnographic data collected by Anna Kawałek (file held with author).
178 Participant I, interview data, collected by Anna Kawałek (file held with author); Participant II, interview data, collected by Anna Kawałek (file held with author).
179 Ashcroft et al. (n 2).

physical and medical issues, as well as for psychological treatment with the GP.[180] This links to international theory, where Winick writes that 'the use of motivational interviewing and related psychological strategies for sparking and maintaining motivation to accept needed treatment can sustainably increase the potential that problem solving courts may have to help the individual to solve his or her problems'.[181]

It was apparent when interviewing service-users shortly after review that they had internalised, activated, and absorbed magistrates' motivational remarks:

> I'll be drug-free for the next time; I am sure.[182]
>> I am buzzing after the review; I want to proove I can do this.[183]
>> He makes me feel like it is possible.[184]

Another participant stated that the motivational styles offered by magistrates distinguished Manchester Review Court from the regular courts:

> They [magistrates] are very much more encouraging of the defendant's progress, even if there is very little.[185]

Other examples of magistrates motivating participants are seen in the following quotations:

> We believe in you, the court believes in you, it's now in your power to change.[186]
>> You have done exceptionally well this month, and we are proud of you.[187]
>> Two negative tests in one month, wow, so do you think we could add a third for next month?[188]

Within a triangulation rationale, the quotations calibrate the statistical data to suggest that motivation was operationalised therapeutically by magistrates. To build upon Research Question 2 ('wine'), a panel analysis was carried out to explore consistencies within magistrates' application of this variable.

Table 3.7 shows much variety in the motivational quality across panels, where scores ranged from very good (therapeutic) to poor (non-therapeutic); whereas

---

180 Participant V, interview data, collected by Anna Kawałek (file held with author).
181 Bruce Winick, 'The judge's role in encouraging motivation for change' in (eds.) Winick & Wexler (n 4) [188].
182 Participant III, interview data, collected by Anna Kawałek (file held with author).
183 Participant V, interview data, collected by Anna Kawałek (file held with author).
184 Participant III, interview data, collected by Anna Kawałek (file held with author).
185 Participant I, interview data, collected by Anna Kawałek (file held with author).
186 Ethnographic data collected by Anna Kawałek (file held with author).
187 Ethnographic data collected by Anna Kawałek (file held with author).
188 Ethnographic data collected by Anna Kawałek (file held with author).

Table 3.8 Motivating the Individual: Panel Analysis (Phase 1)

Date group	Mean
1	3.00
2	4.50
3	3.83
4	3.60
5	3.67
6	2.67
7	5.00
8	4.33
9	1.25
10	4.60
Total	3.59

on Dates 6 and 9, panels applied motivation non-therapeutically, it was applied therapeutically on the remaining six dates, and most therapeutically on Date 10 (4.6). This not only implies that non-compliance to Component 7 resulted in inconsistent application of motivation, but the wide spread of scores could flag it as a key impactor on the more general trend finding inconsistencies across benches (Research Question 1 ('wine')). Changes in therapeutic quality across dates further reflect scores within prior analyses, where 6 and 9 (all-female panels) were less therapeutic than 10 (mixed), and there appears to be a gender influence. However, that this is a fundamental judicial style, with the capacity to significantly bolster participant outcomes and marshal positive reactions, makes it especially troublesome that some benches were less motivational than others.

This inconsistency was echoed in the interview data, where participants identified a similar theme:

> I think it is motivational depends on the magistrates, different ones have different ways of doing things.[189]
>
> I think the main man is motivational, but other times I leave court feeling sh*t for fu**ing up a few tests. That doesn't make me want to do well.[190]
>
> I think the benefit of just one magistrate would also be for motivation. It makes them [service-users] more accountable if they went to see the same individual every time.[191]

This crystallises points already drawn out; activation of Component 7 (consistency) would stabilise motivation levels and Component 9 (training) would

189 Participant II, interview data, collected by Anna Kawałek (file held with author).
190 Participant V, interview data, collected by Anna Kawałek (file held with author).
191 Participant II, interview data, collected by Anna Kawałek (file held with author).

increase its quality to ensure that it was practised at a continually high level. Importantly, this would enhance the power of the court across key and authentic outcomes. Findings around consistency of motivation again ties into the research by Kerr, et al.,[192] where it was stipulated that 'continuity of judiciary could help improve offenders' motivation to stay in treatment and complete their sentence, leading to reduced drug use and related offending'. As such, motivation could be more pronounced through adherence to Component 7 in both models. Given the significance of motivational styles to the English and Welsh courts, rejecting the international blueprint in this area is most unsettling; this should remain at a persistently high level for the court to reach optimal performance.

If motivation is a central tenet of Manchester Review Court, the good news is that magistrates were applying it therapeutically. However, there was room for improvement, and in Phase 2 they scored a non-therapeutic score of m=2.9 overall, though this did stabilise at a therapeutic level when combined with data from other vantage points (m=3.2) (see Table 3.5). If therapeutic jurisprudence draws upon the fruits of the social sciences, magistrates could train in psychosocial techniques such as: motivational interviewing, cognitive behavioural therapy, stages of change,[193] and other positive psychology methods,[194] which are therapeutic-jurisprudence–approved approaches proven to increase continuation, progression, and compliance within intervention programme by enhancing motivation.

A key training area could be motivational interviewing. Michael Clark stipulates that this technique comprises two theoretical modalities: first, expectancy (internal motivation) and; second, self-efficacy (external motivation). The first is expectancy theory, encompassing acceptance and self-choice, in which early-stage participants ask themselves whether and why they should accept treatment and the benefits of engaging in self-change in order to instil internal motivation. In the drug court context, this means that the participant must first accept their recovery and desistance journey. A similar idea is put forward by Winick, who states that 'to succeed, treatment of rehabilitation will require a degree of intrinsic motivation on the part of the individual'.[195] Judicial officers can help participants realise this by asking questions around why the programme will be beneficial, or '*why* should I change?' questions.

The second theory, self-efficacy, is aligned with more traditional motivation methods, and involves devising strategies for achieving obtainable goals through goal setting, by engaging with '*how* should I change?' questions. This can be aided by benches giving external encouragement through 'you can do it'-type

192 Ashcroft et al. (n 2).
193 Michael Clark, 'Influencing positive behavior change: increasing the therapeutic approach of juvenile courts' (2001) Federal Probation, 65(1), 18–27.
194 Astrid Birgden & Tony Ward, 'Pragmatic psychology through a therapeutic jurisprudence lens: psycholegal soft spots in the criminal justice system' (2003) Psychology, Public Policy, and Law, 9(3/4), 334–360; William Miller & Stephen Rollnick, *Motivational interviewing: helping people change* (3rd ed.) (New York: Guilford Press, 2003).
195 Winick (n 181).

statements. These motivation efforts are futile before inner motivation has been realised. Indeed, according to Miller and Rollnick,[196] the first element must be procured before participants can move on to the second step to avoid overburdening them with prescriptive and value-laden advice. Winick has also positioned the notion of motivation within a personal autonomy genre, positing that problem-solving courts should endeavour to make individuals feel as though their treatment choices are independent, through 'central route persuasion'.[197] This will instil commitment to the goal and can 'increase the intrinsic motivation to accomplish it'.[198] One of the quotations from Manchester Review Court already exhibits this concept ('we believe in you, the court believes in you, it's now in your power to change').

This two-tiered theoretical approach to motivational interviewing has in many ways already been subscribed to by AA/NA practitioners, who encourage members to use 12 steps to guide recovery from drug or alcohol addiction. Like the motivational interviewing model, the earlier steps involve acceptance and the latter ones involve strategic planning and devising goals. For example, see Steps 1 and 3:

- We admitted we were powerless over alcohol – that our lives had become unmanageable (Step 1);
- We made a decision to turn our will and our lives over to the care of God as we understood Him (Step 2).

Step 1 ignites the recovery process through a process of recognition, and Step 2, aside from the religious connotations whereby atheists substitute God with a family member, involves actively choosing a recovery journey through mastery, control, and personal ownership. Later steps move away from acceptance towards implementation of targets. Most later steps from the 12-step model demonstrate this notion, but take Step 8 as an example:

- Made a list of all persons we had harmed, and became willing to make amends to them all (Step 8).

As such, motivational interviewing theory alongside practical recovery models dovetail with one another. By transposing these frameworks into the problem-solving court domain, clearly jurisdictions must be carefully attuned to these stages to have great affect on service-users' motivation. If they are still in the first stage, judiciaries should ask questions about why change would be beneficial through some form of Socratic dialogue. If service-users are in the second stage, goal setting, and more traditional motivational statements are apt. If service-users

196 Ibid.
197 Winick (n 181) [186].
198 Ibid [186].

are persistently producing positive drug tests and not making progress, magistrates should review whether the participant has graduated from the internal motivation stage, and, if not, seek to encourage this shift through engaging in Tier 1. This is, of course, a highly nuanced approach that would be nearly impossible to do well, or even on a basic level, without specific training in the area. It therefore illuminates problems already identified relating to Manchester Review Court's non-compliance to Drug Court Component 9, stipulating the importance of judicial training.

Certainly, during my observations, I never encountered magistrates asking Tier 1 questions; they tended rather to focus on Tier 2 exchanges. However, in other ways, Manchester Review Court respects this staged theory. According to the National Offender Management Service, the final criterion for accepting offenders onto the DRR programme requires that they 'the offender expresses his or her willingness to comply with the requirement'.[199] One would therefore expect that by the time participants arrive in the courtroom, they have moved through Stage 1, with internal motivation is intact. This suggests that there was no need for magistrates to engage in Tier 1, and that the external motivation offered was in line with the above-mentioned theoretical frameworks. However, the accuracy of assessing this when admitting participants onto the DRR, and the complexity arising from offenders' accepting the order because it is a perceived softer option, complicates this stipulation.

Beyond breach of Component 9, other elements of Manchester Review Court created barriers to implementing a credible motivational interviewing strategy. First, in many cases it would mean overseeing gradual change from acceptance to application if ascribing to this theory. Aside from this being nearly impossible with a changing bench, it would require a long-term intervention. This is problematic given that DRR provisions tend to last around six months, which averages at around four to six court sessions per participant (whilst other areas of the suspended sentence or community order continue for longer). In light of the recovery and desistance literature indicating that completion of these processes takes many years, especially for entrenched users,[200] how could the court review sessions make much real impact on a long-term motivation and change when the reviews are, and could only ever be, short-sighted? In the next chapter, I will argue that this window should be extended.

Second, the review court was operated fortnightly on a single afternoon in the main magistrates' court, unlike a traditional drug court which is typically its own entity, operating throughout the working week. This meant that each service-users' contact with the court was restricted to a five- to ten-minute slot, fortnightly at most. When translating motivational interviewing theory into practice, Clark advised that participants could graduate through the two phases in a single

---

199 National Offender Management Service, 'Supporting community order treatment requirements' (2014) Commissioning Group [3]; (n 167) section 209.
200 Granfield & Cloud (n 135); Maruna (n 135).

day, by asking service-users 'why should I change?' questions in a morning session and 'how to change?' questions in an afternoon session. Participants' limited contact with Manchester Review Court, and the restrictions with it being housed in the main court on just one afternoon, would render this suggestion all but impossible to implement. If the review court was its own body, busy with many clients on a daily basis, this would be easier to achieve as it would allow available slots to appear more regularly. Again we are seeing structural-level problems creating hurdles for good practice.

It seems fair to conclude this section by reporting that motivation was a fundamental canon for the operation of Manchester Review Court, which if done well could significantly enhance the power of the court. We can therefore propose that it is the most important variable of the four skills that emerged thematically from the qualitative data. Results suggest that it was applied therapeutically, although there could be some improvement through training in key therapeutic-jurisprudence–endorsed psychological techniques, a key area being motivational interviewing to improve magistrates' mastery of this technique. However, the discussion also made clear that this is a niche and complex area. It would thus require high-quality judicial training through adherence to Component 9. Given this, a more detailed analysis into its effect on court outputs would be useful, which could be achieved through a quantitative analysis using regression models. Throughout this section, I have made suggestions to enhance practice in this area, which interlace with systemic factors (bottle).

3.4.2 Engaging therapeutic dialogue

Having now analysed the therapeutic quality of harnessing therapeutic support (see Table 3.5) and its most crucial variables ('understanding the complexity of alcohol and other drugs' and 'motivating the individual'), it is time to return to the second skill: engaging therapeutic dialogue. This section seeks to undertake a similar analysis to that for support by investigating the therapeutic quality of dialogue more broadly, before discussing the variable that emerged thematically from this skill: 'giving the offender a voice'.

Table 3.5 already exposed engaging therapeutic dialogue as magistrates' strongest skill of the three. Of these, the average mean (AM) of Phase 1 and 2 data

Table 3.9 Means of Magistrates' Engaging Therapeutic Dialogue Scores: Phases 1 and 2

	Sincerity/ honesty	Without pity/ disdain	Not interrupting	Slow, clear, and loud speech	Attentiveness	Giving the offender a voice
1	4.1	3.7	3.6	4	4.1	3.7
2	3.4	3.1	3.4	3.6	3	3.5
AM	3.8	3.4	3.5	3.8	3.6	3.6

triangulated in Table 3.8 shows that magistrates applied: 'sincerity' (m=3.8) and 'slow, clear, and loud speech' (m=3.8) most therapeutically within convergent results. These were therefore the most therapeutically applied subskills within dialogue, and across all variables measured. As such, they are the strongest of magistrates' subskills.

Scores of very good are presented in bold; high scores like these were not achieved for variables from therapeutic support or therapeutic change skills. The average mean of each variant for dialogue was either higher or on a par with scores for support and change, which is indicative of engaging therapeutic dialogue being a well-practised skill. The fact that the lowest dialogue score was the same as the highest support score (m=3.4) confirms its strength, and no variables were non-therapeutic. All these points together allow me to conclude with confidence that this skill was exercised therapeutically. As such, there were no significant areas of improvement, although skills could be bettered to excellent or very good.

Where this analysis had already confirmed that 'giving the offender a voice' was applied with firm therapeutic jurisprudence, the qualitative data verified its significant to the dialogue skill because it emerged thematically, discussed below.

3.4.2.1 Giving the offender a voice

'Giving the offender a voice' sought to measure magistrates' proficiency at allowing service-users to express themselves in the courtroom, submit their own goals and strategies for change, and the extent to which magistrates encouraged them to take an active role during the review hearings. It was embedded into the measurement system based on the work of Michael King, key writer in the area, who has postulated that judiciaries should enlist a turn-taking dialogue that affords service-users the space to effectively communicate their viewpoint.[201] In an empirical study of a domestic violence court, Petrucci found that judges' listening techniques, which allowed the offender to have a voice, were a key part of a respectful court conversation.[202]

Furthermore, giving litigants a voice in court is a well-established principle from procedural justice. Whilst they are exclusive paradigms, it is not uncommon for therapeutic jurisprudence to borrow the insights brokered by procedural justice, especially during the theorisation, practice, and/or analysis of the problem-solving court wine.[203] Experts Burke and Lebel have posited that giving service-users a voice is one of the four fundamental precepts of procedural justice.[204]

201   Michael King, 'Enhancing judicial communication' [TJ in the mainstream blog, 3 June] [Blog post]. Retrieved from https://mainstreamtj.wordpress.com/2016/06/03/enhancing-judicial-communication-tj-court-craft-series-1/ Accessed 1 July 2020.
202   Petrucci (n 6).
203   Winick & Wexler (n 4).
204   Kevin Burke & Steven Leben, 'Court review: volume 44, issue 1/2 – procedural fairness: a key ingredient in public satisfaction' (2007) A White Paper of the American Judges Association the Voice of the Judiciary.

Lynch and Perlin have also famously stated that therapeutic jurisprudence is a 'legal theory that seeks to reshape legal rules, procedures, and lawyer roles to enhance their therapeutic potential … in accordance with the key principles of voice, validation and voluntariness', and scholars have consistently shown the importance of 'the three Vs' to the effective operation of American mental health courts.[205] A similar conceptualisation is offered within the scholarly work of Judge Roger Warren who posits that the key tenets of procedural justice are: neutrality, respect, participation, and trustworthiness.[206] For participation, Warren defines this as 'the extent to which the judicial officer allows the litigants to have an active voice in the decision-making process'.[207]

Although procedural justice is defined differently according to the scholar, whatever approach to procedural justice from which one chooses to extrapolate key principles, a close reading would show the definitions are equal; each is concerned with how to diffuse feelings of fairness in the courtroom, by giving the litigant a voice. Notably, this variable is also linked to discussions already presented on motivation because offender voice, including goal setting, is theorised to help instil motivation.[208]

In more local research, McIvor examined the Scottish drug courts, and emphasised that procedural justice was a key feature of the judiciary–service-user interaction. She found that when the judicial dialogue was perceived as fair, primary outputs were strengthened.[209] This links to the work of Warren, who observed that procedural justice facilitates trust and confidence in the court system,[210] and Gottfredson, et al. demonstrated replicable results in the US context.[211] Work by procedural justice experts Tyler and Bies[212] have deepened this theory, finding that perceived levels of legitimate treatment, induced by a therapeutic interactional style, increases compliance with a problem-solving court order by strengthening confidence in the process. The literature indicates that actual decisions reached by judges are insignificant compared to perceived levels of fair treatment during process; by infusing procedural justice, individuals become willing to comply with outcomes even if opposed to the decision due to greater trust in the decision-making process.[213]

---

205 Alison Lynch & Michael Perlin, '"Life's hurried tangled road": a therapeutic jurisprudence analysis of why dedicated counsel must be assigned to represent persons with mental disabilities in community settings' (2016) NYLS Legal Studies Research Paper No. 2833365. doi:10.2139/ssrn.2833365 [4].

206 Warren (n 111).

207 Ibid. [134].

208 Winick (n 3) [181].

209 Gill McIvor, (n 11).

210 Warren (n 11).

211 Denise Gottfredson, Brook Kearley, Stacey Najaka, & Carlos Rocha, 'How drug treatment courts work: an analysis of mediators' (2007) Journal of Research in Crime and Delinquency, 44(1), 3–35.

212 Tom Tyler & Robert Bies, 'Beyond formal procedures: the interpersonal context of procedural justice' (1990) Applied Social Psychology and Organizational Settings, 77, 98.

213 Ibid.

Table 3.8 already demonstrated that magistrates scored an average mean of 3.6 for 'giving the offender a voice' through convergent results from Phases 1 and 2. The score not only shows that as a successful therapeutic interaction, but is also the most therapeutic of the four leading skills, which emerged thematically, at Manchester Review Court. It is worth mentioning that a survey item from Phase 2 tapping into procedural justice, which stated 'the review process is fair' caused 85% of participants to either strongly agree or agree. Since surveys were handed to participants after review, this is likely to be linked to the previous finding that 'giving the offender a voice' was applied well in the courtroom. This statistic can be compared to a survey by the American Justice Innovations Center gathering public perceptions around mainstream court proceedings, finding that 60% of defendants 'strongly agreed' or 'agreed' that that court outcomes were fair.[214] Although there are obvious disparities between this study and my study, including the jurisdictions, sample sizes, and measurement systems, the differences between the statistics are still telling of the impact of increased procedural justice on offender perceptions;. Manchester Review Court, exampling a problem-solving court, increases the feelings of procedural justice by nearly 25% compared to a mainstream court.

> It's a lot less daunting. Instead of having to speak through a solicitor you actually get to talk to them yourself, which is obviously better because you're getting your voice heard. This is good, fairer.[215]
>
> Instead of trying to put you down all the time, at least he'll listen, know what I mean?[216]
>
> I think, in the main, they give them the chance to talk ... I think sometimes people don't get asked questions. Or they don't feel that they can talk to a complete bunch of strangers ... I think people want to talk and magistrates usually give them the opportunity to do that.[217]
>
> You can have a conversation with them, and when I talk, they are interested.[218]
>
> Magistrates would often ask open ended questions to encourage participants to speak.[219]

The sampled quotations highlight that participants felt that this variable yielded a uniquely therapeutic, democratic, and non-adversarial court culture compared to

214 Rachel Swaner, Cassandra Ramdath, Andrew Martinez, Josephine Hahn, & Sienna Walker, 'What do defendants really think? Procedural justice and legitimacy in the criminal justice system' (Centre for Court Innovation, 2016). Retrieved from: https://www.courtinnovati on.org/sites/default/files/media/documents/2018-09/what_do_defendants_really_thi nk.pdf.
215 Participant III, interview data, collected by Anna Kawałek (file held with author).
216 Ibid.
217 Participant II, interview data, collected by Anna Kawałek (file held with author).
218 Participant IV, interview data, collected by Anna Kawałek (file held with author).
219 Ethnographic data (various dates) collected by Anna Kawałek (file held with author).

Table 3.10 Giving the Offender a Voice, Panel Analysis

Date group	Mean
1	3.14
2	3.67
3	3.67
4	3.80
5	4.17
6	2.67
7	3.67
8	3.67
9	4.50
10	4.60
Total	3.71

the mainstream courts, and this is something that service-users appreciated. 'You actually get to talk to them'[220] implies that participants not only felt that having his voice heard was a real privilege, but also that these conversations were invaluable for engendering feelings of fairness, hence: 'this is good, fairer'.[221] The comparisons between the mainstream courts and Manchester Review Court made by participants signals increased faith and assurance in the court: for instance, 'instead of having to speak through a solicitor you actually get to talk to them yourself'. The advantages of the well-applied nature of this variable were explored further by participants.

> Helps give them a better understanding of what kind of person you are.[222]
> They start to see the magistrates as people.[223]
> You actually get your voice heard, rather than someone else mediating it, which can be quite frustrating.[224]
> I do feel listened to.[225]

The benefits are manifold: it allowed magistrates to ascertain a more holistic understanding of service-users and their circumstances; it humanised the law within a therapeutic jurisprudence ethos; enabled fairer and more equal correspondence; and it allowed stakeholders to undertake more direct forms of communication.

220 Participant III, interview data, collected by Anna Kawałek (file held with author).
221 Ibid.
222 Participant IV, interview data, collected by Anna Kawałek (file held with author).
223 Participant II, interview data, collected by Anna Kawałek (file held with author).
224 Participant IV, interview data, collected by Anna Kawałek (file held with author).
225 Participant III, interview data, collected by Anna Kawałek (file held with author).

In predecessor drug court research, Kerr et al.[226] reported that one critical area of judicial engagement was 'interactive'. Researchers did not elaborate on the meaning of this insight, but if we transpose the orthodox definition of 'interactive' offered by the *Cambridge Dictionary*, it means 'involving communication between people'.[227] This resembles the turn-taking discourse presented by King,[228] inclusive of offender voice, thus revealing further similarities across findings from the predecessor drug courts and Manchester Review Court, an important point that is developed in the next chapter.

A panel analysis for this variable was run to explicitly explore consistencies in its application (Table 3.9), linking to Research Question 1 ('wine'),

The statistics demonstrate that panels operated this skill to differing degrees of skilful therapeutic jurisprudence. There was no tailor-made training designed to enhance this area (Component 9), but despite this, most panels practised it well (therapeutically, above 3). All-female Panel 6 applied it non-therapeutically (m=2.7); this had already been regarded as a weaker bench composition, perhaps due to a gender bias. Although the overall score is regarded as strong (m=3.7) in broad terms, magistrates could improve it to very good or excellent by drawing upon best-practice principles of international magistrates and judges to improve its administration. Undertaking some self-reflection exercises could be key; Judge King, a well-versed practitioner in this field, suggests that judiciaries could review their own behaviours following a hearing by asking themselves questions such as:

- 'Did you find ways to engage in two-way communication?'; and
- 'Can you identify examples of good two-way communication with features of turn-taking?'.

Given the lack of training at Manchester Review Court, King's recommendation could be conducive for improving this variable for amenable magistrates with the will.[229] Aside from the usual recommendation pertaining to adherence to Components 7 and 9, this judicial engagement style broadly raised fewer concerns than those analysed previously.

3.4.3 Inspiring therapeutic change

Having now analysed the therapeutic quality of harnessing therapeutic support and engaging therapeutic dialogue and their most crucial variables respectively, I shall now analyse the final skill: inspiring therapeutic change. This section seeks to

---

226 Kerr et al. (n 4).
227 This is referenced as: Interactive (2018) in *Cambridge advanced learner's dictionary and thesaurus* (Cambridge: Cambridge University Press). Available at: https://dictionary.cambridge.org/dictionary/english/interactive.
228 King (n 201).
229 Ibid.

Table 3.11 Means of Magistrates' 'Change' Scores: Phases 1 and 2

	Setting realistic goals	Asking questions	Building upon strengths	Positive future
P1	3.7 (T)	3.8 (T)	**2.6 (NT)**	**2.9 (NT)**
P2	3.1 (T)	3.2 (T)	3 (T)	**2.9 (NT)**
AM	3.4 (T)	3.5 (T)	**2.8 (NT)**	**2.9 (NT)**

undertake a similar analysis to those in previous sections by examining the quality of inspiring therapeutic change more broadly, before discussing the variant that emerged thematically from the qualitative data, 'setting realistic goals'. I will also speculate on where and how it can be improved (Table 3.11).

Inspiring therapeutic change was previously identified in Table 3.5 as the weakest of the measured skills at Manchester Review Court (m=3.1). Considering this skill's constituent variables in Table 3.12 shows that magistrates most therapeutically administered: 'asking questions' (m=3.5) and 'setting realistic goals' (m=3.5); these were both practised at a good therapeutic level.[230] Comparatively, 'building upon strengths' and 'focusing on the future' were non-therapeutically operated, scoring fair, and the former was the most weakly practised of all variables. These areas should be reviewed, and could be enhanced through training.

It is interesting that both 'focusing on the future' scores were the same across both datasets (m=2.9, non-therapeutic); this indicates a perfect correlation within a triangulation rationale. Non-convergent is the 'building upon strengths' variable across data collection stages, one result being therapeutic (Phase 2), the other non-therapeutic (Phase 1). However, the difference in scores were minor (.4 of a point), and results became complementarily through means scoring suggesting it was applied non-therapeutically score (m=2.8). Overall, these observations suggest that inspiring therapeutic change was operated well in some areas; however, improvement of 'building upon strengths' and 'focusing on the future' would yield more therapeutic results.

3.4.3.1 Setting realistic goals

This is a well-renowned technique for tracking attainment of problem-solving court participants, where 'research suggests achievement is promoted through the setting of goals'.[231] Duffy describes goal setting as a form of 'behavioural contracting' derived from clinical practice as it provides positive targets and a firm

---

230 Vagias (n 19).

231 Michael King, 'A judicial officer assists offenders to set rehabilitation goals and strategies' [Blog post] (28 February 2017). Retrieved from https://mainstreamtj.wordpress.com/2017/02/28/a-judicial-officer-assists-offenders-to-set-rehabilitation-goals-strategies-tj-court-craft-series-8/, Accessed 1 July 2020.

set of meetable criteria to guidepost performance, which is agreed to by all stake-holders.[232] Building sustainable goals can help to stabilise the chaos and compulsiveness that often characterises the lives of this cohort, and garners positive responses when approached incrementally by providing a structured approaches to recovery.[233] According to King, it is an essential part of a judicial officer's role in this context; by becoming effective problem-solvers, it empowers practitioners to carry out 'transformational leadership' by inspiring and supervising positive change, thus building feelings of satisfaction.[234]

This variable sought to measure how sensibly magistrates set goals, and the extent to which they reflected authentic recovery journeys. It is a clear constituent component of inspiring therapeutic change is an explicit method for helping to apply this area. Measurements for this variable were based on the idiosyncrasies of each case, rather a blanket approach to progress and results, and I was able to read the written reports for service-users during data collection to help nuance my approach when taking measurement. Effective goal setting is highly interlaced with other variables from the measurement system; it helps to cultivate offender motivation (and is thus linked to 'motivation'), it must be practised under the auspices of a court perceived to be working in the best interests of the participant (thus linking to 'giving the offender a voice'), and it relies upon satisfactory practical and theoretical knowledge of recovery (thus linking to 'understanding the complexities of alcohol and other drug recovery'). For each of these variables, we have already seen that they were operated therapeutically, although systemic issues, particularly in the area of training, impeded magistrates' ability to reach optimal levels of very good or excellent. As such, the same bottle-level critiques from previous discussions are relevant here.

At Manchester Review Court, a typical service-user would attend DRR court reviews at four to six-week intervals depending on progress. During sessions, magistrates would review change and usually set three goals to achieve before the next hearing. In light of the court's breach of Component 7, to communicate goals across inconsistent benches, magistrates would record goals in writing through notetaking, which they would pass to the next panel, although they sometimes encountered difficulties retrieving records, and not every panel made these notes.[235] Note-passing between benches was an intuitive approach from magistrates, which clearly sought to make the best of an uncompromising system relating to Component 7, and it represented the only attempt to provide coherency and linkage across and between changing review panels. It hints that magistrates themselves understood the difficulties associated with non-compliance to Component 7.

232 James Duffy, 'Problem-solving courts, therapeutic jurisprudence and the constitution: if two is company, is three a crowd?' (2011) Melbourne University Law Review 35(2), 394–425 [401].
233 Ashcroft et al. (n 2).
234 Michael King, Arie Freiberg, Becky Batagol, & Ross Hyams, *Non-adversarial justice* (2nd ed.) (Alexandria, NSW: The Federation Press, 2014).
235 Ethnographic data (various dates) collected by Anna Kawałek (file held with author).

Usually the goals related to service-users increasing the numbers of negative drug test results produced monthly, but could also relate to improvement of other domains, such as: attending appointments, finding permanent or short-term housing, seeking financial help, improving family relationships and/or relinquishing ties with drug-using networks, finding work, or even attending more gym sessions![236] The importance of goal setting was highlighted by participants:

> You want something firm for the defendant to understand – 'this is what's expected of you' – to provide attainable objectives.[237]
> It does help keep on track of stuff.[238]
> It helps them to know what they need to do.[239]

Although appropriate application of this variable would require expert knowledge beyond intuition, which we have already seen had gaps and shortcomings due to systematic barriers, the statistical data suggested magistrates broadly operated this variable therapeutically (m=3.4). This sentiment was reflected by the qualitative data, which captured a positive, progressive, and forward-thinking approach from magistrates.

> They (magistrates) realise if you've been taking drugs for 20 years, you're not going to stop overnight so they're looking at small steps and ways to reduce your drug use. So I think most deal with it very well.[240]
> Even though I'm not providing a negative, well, providing a few days clean, they can see that I'm trying.[241]
> They are looking at more positive steps rather than focusing on 'you're still using every day, that's very bad'.[242]
> They are okay when you sometimes don't do well. You've got to show you are trying though.[243]

These findings compound the predecessor drug court research, which reported that the original models helped to firm up goals through structured reduction plans.[244] One of the five styles of judicial interaction was identified as 'personalised'.[245] Although its meaning was left somewhat unclear, it appears to span an individually tailored approach to goal setting within a similar measurement, as well as a

236 Ibid.
237 Participant I, interview data, collected by Anna Kawałek (file held with author).
238 Participant III, interview data, collected by Anna Kawałek (file held with author).
239 Participant II, interview data, collected by Anna Kawałek (file held with author).
240 Participant II, interview data, collected by Anna Kawałek (file held with author).
241 Participant III, interview data, collected by Anna Kawałek (file held with author).
242 Participant I, interview data, collected by Anna Kawałek (file held with author).
243 Participant III, interview data, collected by Anna Kawałek (file held with author).
244 Kerr et al. (n 4).
245 Ibid.

personable approach in the courtroom. Again, similarities between the operation of the old and new models are apparent.

To substantiate a court behavioural contract, Winick has suggested that goals are amalgamated with a rewards and sanctioning system, which is applied periodically or intermediately depending on progress.[246] Rewards and sanctioning is a key facet of the international gold standard under Drug Court Component 6. However, in the next chapter, during analysis of the 'bottle', I will discuss magistrates' lack of powers under the Criminal Justice Act 2003[247] to incentivise progress by applying positive or negative consequences to reward and punish behaviours under Component 6, hence another example of infidelity. Under the current structure, discretion to breach DRR offenders fell entirely in the hands of probation officers, which meant that there were no real ramifications for service-users failing to meet objectives set in court. This means that Manchester falls out of kilter with the international examples, which famously dovetail recovery progress with criminal justice efforts through a carrot-and-stick style approach. We can assume that non-compliance to Component 6 eroded participant motivational levels based on the international evidence. However, it was explicitly reported to disempower magistrates by undermining many of the efforts that they made during review. Whether participants adhered to court-set goals or not made no real difference to their court order, so from the perspective of this variable, goal setting was nothing more than ideological. And whilst it was theoretically important, the fact that the goals had very little meaning in practical terms brings into question the purpose of review, in which the idea is to touch base with a legal body, where the threat of criminal sanction aids compliance.[248] It is difficult not to question how seriously service-users took goal setting when there were no real criminal justice consequences for failing to comply and meet court expectations.

That being said, drug and alcohol recovery centres dealing exclusively with addicts (rather than addicted criminals), tend to use goal setting as a distinguished method for aiding progress, without the threat of criminal effects for violating targets. As goals at Manchester Review Court tended to relate to recovery as opposed to desistance progress, there is no reason to believe that failing to recover had to be entangled with criminal consequences, and it is in some ways more therapeutic than those courts adhering to the international blueprint under Component 6. Nonetheless, it raises fidelity questions, and by falling short of the ideal presented by the gold standard, the impact on outcomes remains questionable.

A further issue with the Criminal Justice Act 2003[249] is fragmentation; I have already stated that Component 10 is concerned with partnership forging, and I

---

246 Bruce Winick, 'How judges can use behavioral contracting' (2002) in (eds.) Winick & Wexler (n 3) [227].
247 (n 167).
248 Ashcroft et al. (n 2).
249 (n 167).

will discuss this in greater depth in the next chapter. For this discussion, in-house goals were limited to the court and did not collide with those of probation and drug treatment agencies. Moreover, the powers to breach service-users for failing to meet goals took place outside of court, at the probation services, unlike in a traditional drug court, where this is carried out by Judicial Officers in court. This was a wholly disintegrated strategy; achieving authentic communication across parties is made much easier when all stakeholders are present, but this was made impossible due to the absence of individual probation officers sitting in court (they instead used a point-of-contact officer to oversee all cases after private probation companies lost their right of audience).[250] This meant that court goals were mediated through the officer, and whilst they did this honestly, it risks a Chinese whispers effect.

If the treatment and probation services are affixing their own goals to the order, without direct collaboration with the court, this risks individual service-users having to navigate a far-ranging and conflicting series of objectives, complicating an order designed to bring stability to chaotic lifestyles. The lack of alliance between bodies, through no fault of their own, meant that the full DRR was a disconcerted effort, with the court feeling particularly isolated, insular, and disjointed, and the goings-on outside of court almost mysterious. For the purpose of this analysis, these systemic factors impeded the adept application of the 'setting realistic goals' variable.

I will return to these issues shortly, but for the purpose of this discussion, a panel analysis was run to explore consistency to build on findings for Research Question 1 ('wine').

Although most therapeutic panels were Panels 6, 8, and 9, each scoring 4 (good), it is interesting that all-female Panels 6 and 9 had previously been identified as the weakest panels. Their high scores for this variable therefore contradict previous findings by suggesting that a female influence on the panel increases therapeutic quality of appropriate goal setting (although Panel 8 was mixed gender). This variable is very much linked to problem-solving, which is the ability to solve issues proactively as they arise, and so the finding that females were better at this skill could be explained by the already presented research, suggesting that women's brains are more proficient at administering this skill empathetically by connecting the left and right hemispheres of their brains.[251]

Interestingly, Table 3.12 shows that every panel applied this skill therapeutically and it was therefore executed with more consistency than the previous three variables. This is likely to be because it was the only area where coherency across benches was attempted through magistrates note taking and passing goals between benches, thus affirming the effectiveness of this approach. It also could suggest that more detailed note taking, recording peripheral data, such as

250 Ministry of Justice, 'Transforming rehabilitation A strategy for reform' (2013). Retrieved from https://consult.justice.gov.uk/digital-communications/transforming-rehabilitatio n/results/transforming-rehabilitation-response.pdf.
251 Ingalhalikar et al. (n 65) [68].

Table 3.12 Appropriate Goal Setting, Panel Analysis

Date group	Mean
1	3.57
2	3.17
3	4.17
4	3.20
5	3.83
6	4.00
7	3.00
8	4.00
9	4.00
10	3.80
Total	3.69

offender demeanour or attitude, specific conversations, or anything else deemed important, should be rolled out to improve coherency in a system that discarded Component 7. Although positive impacts could be induced by this method, it is unlikely to have serious effects on therapist-style relationships in court, as authentic application of Component 7 would. Since the averages within Table 3.12 showed that magistrates did not score good or excellent for this variable, there was room for some improvement. As it is clearly related to the 'understanding of alcohol and other drugs recovery' variable, this variable might also be improved through training in alcohol and other drug issues. Notably, in the predecessor drug court report, it was also disclosed that continuity of the bench was a key for provision for goal setting to improve accountability and to make goals more concrete.[252] Hence there are further similarities between the findings of my study and for the predecessor drug courts.

It is also key to draw upon international best therapeutic jurisprudence practice for handling drug addiction cases. I propose that magistrates write goals down for service-users to take home in order to increase their clarity and as an ongoing reminder of objectives between reviews. This is not my own suggestion; Participant III said that he did this after every review and kept the piece of paper in his front pocket as a reminder to stay on track in-between judicial contact; written goals could be made standard practice. Writing goals down for service-users would also act as a motivation strategy to keep offenders on track in between reviews. Moreover, the related variable 'reiterating goals' is a technique that is unique to the review process, but unfortunately it was not practised therapeutically; I noticed that some, but not all, magistrates would recap the goals set during review before the individual left the courtroom to ensure that

252 Kerr et al. (n 4).

service-users were clear about progress expectations. Reiteration should be rolled out further to ensure goals are met. International magistrates Pauline Spencer and Michael King offer strategies for helping articulate offender goals; I particularly like Australian Spencer's[253] suggestion of using a staircase diagram where each step represents incremental movement towards the overall goal at the top. Building upon Service-user 1's suggestion of writing goals down, Manchester Review Court magistrates might use a written staircase diagram that benches readdress and work with alongside service-users every session to improve consistency in absence of Component 7, to help them meet their goals. It is essential that they draw upon international best practice to find new and creative ways to apply therapeutic court-craft.

3.4.4 Short summary of the four key skills in the courtroom

Four variables emerged thematically as key to the therapeutic application of the Manchester Review Court wine. Each of these could be improved through high-quality bespoke training, consistency of benches, and alliance between parties. However, awareness on a more basic level of the key strategies that garner court outcomes is important, as is the key therapeutic jurisprudence principles governing the area. Collaboration with international bodies would enhance application by borrowing renowned and well-researched best-practice principles. Browsing the International Society for Therapeutic Jurisprudence's website or the Therapeutic Jurisprudence in the Mainstream blog (assembled by an Australian magistrate) and/or reading the key text *Judging in a Therapeutic Key*,[254] could be a good starting point for magistrates who possess the impetus. Since training opportunities are circumspect due to resources, providing copies of the aforementioned text could be a more economical starting point.

At the time that I was carrying out this research, Manchester came across as insular, and practitioners were often unclear on the court's purpose, origins, and international roots, and at times could appear to lack morale. Anchoring the court in an international dimension might spark interest, enthusiasm, and understanding, as well as strengthen performance across key areas. A bench book clarifying aims, objectives, and crucial facets of good practice areas could be beneficial for the court. Founding father of therapeutic jurisprudence, David Wexler, has recently called for Amicus Justitia Briefs, which are a 'new type of legal writing', designed to raise the profile of practices across the globe that incorporate a therapeutic jurisprudence orientation.[255] Briefs may take the form of longer or

---

253 Pauline Spencer, 'Steps towards change – a tool for judges working with persons with substance abuse disorders' (2018, 8 May). Retrieved from: https://mainstreamtj.wordpress .com/2018/05/08/steps-towards-change-a-tool-for-judges-working-with-persons-with -substance-abuse-disorders-tj-court-craft-series-12/, Accessed 1 July 2020.

254 Winick & Wexler (n 4).

255 David Wexler, 'The therapeutic application of the law and the need for amicus justitia briefs' (2018) Arizona Legal Studies Discussion Paper, 18–18 [1].

shorter blogs, articles, or manuals, but are intended to be snappy, accessible, and succinct.[256] In the case of Manchester Review Court, I propose that the court engages in these briefs to create global outreach. This goal should incorporate a three-pronged structure:

i. Create the first brief that draws attention to the therapeutic jurisprudence aspect of the review court (particularly magistrates' skills-base) to initiate international dialogue and to spark interest (this could include findings from this book);

ii. Then exchange briefs with personnel from the classic drug courts, or similar models with a problem-solving rationale;[257]

iii. Continue to moderate and edit the original briefs to incorporate the best practice of others whilst monitoring the changing local issues and finetuning practice of the wine.

Amicus Justitia Briefs could be the starting point for developing a Manchester Review Court handbook that includes the goals, objectives, and philosophy of the court, nature of drug abuse and treatment including local issues, practice protocol, overview of the broader legal requirements, as well as global best practice and the historical origins and international backdrop. This bench book would also standardise approaches in court if Component 7 continues to be breached. Developing this manual would also comply with Component 1, where it is stated that: 'documents defining the drug court's mission, goals, eligibility criteria, operating procedures, and performance measures are collaboratively developed, reviewed, and agreed upon'.[258]

Forging links with the broader society, and the exchanging of these briefs, could be mediated by the UK Centre for Therapeutic Jurisprudence, an arm of the international body. The purpose of the UK Chapter is to intensify relations within the UK and across the global society between academics, practitioners, institutions, organisations, and students with an interest in the area, to create a hub for discussion and a mechanism for knowledge sharing. It is thought that this project might spark interest and excitement amongst the Manchester magistrates, who are welcome members of both societies. Next steps could be development of the first Amicus Justitia brief, and the UK Chapter will help to foster international relations by sharing the second brief with the international body, hopefully with the Manchester Review Court magistrates on board. Tying local research back into practice will also be key, including findings from this book, from the Hertfordshire and Bedfordshire problem-solving court study, as well as those from the broad international evidence base.

256 Ibid.
257 Bartels (2016, 2017, 2018) (n 14); Snell (n 13); Shannon et al. (n 12); Judicial College (n 11); Carns & Martin (n 15).
258 Ashcroft et al. (n 2) [1].

3.5 Bivariate analyses

Where possible, a repeat measures design was used; within this, a sample of surveys were given to service-users straight after their review, and participant responses were based on their experience of the review that they had just completed (Phase 2). The quality of this review had already been measured during a court observation (Phase 1). The same variables had been tested at both stages. From a data collection perspective, I would watch a review hearing and take measurements (Phase 1), then once it was completed, service-users would complete a questionnaire (Phase 2). This meant that results of this cohort could be directly correlated on a single review basis for every variable measured.

The purpose of this method was to validate results from both vantage points and compare convergencies of scores on the same variables. This was not always possible because it would risk disrupting the sessions if I was continually moving in and out of the courtroom, and some individuals wanted to rush straight off. However, I obtained a sample of 16 for this analysis. This forthcoming section will examine *only* material gathered using the repeat measures design. It will use bivariate correlations to compare the scores of the variables from each respective construct on a single review hearing (or service-user) basis. A line from the 0 point is added to help interpret the graphs.

3.5.1 *Harnessing therapeutic support* (refer to Graph A, p. 104)

- X Axis: Phase 1
- Y Axis: Phase 2

3.5.2 *Engaging therapeutic dialogue* (refer to Graph B, p. 106)

- X Axis: Phase 1
- Y Axis: Phase 2

3.5.3 *Inspiring therapeutic change* (refer to Graph C, p. 107)

- X Axis: Phase 1
- Y Axis: Phase 2

3.5.3.1 *Scatter graphs: analysis and findings*

The darker circles show more than one variable positioned at that single point on the chart. The variables broadly gather at the higher end of each graph, this confirms that magistrates applied skills therapeutically, reflecting the better end of the Likert scale. Each bivariate correlation shows that the scores for Phases 1 and 2 largely correlate on the same variables as they gather close to or onto the line, which indicates a perfect correlation, showing that the results correspond with each other within a triangulation rationale. The bivariate correlations also confirm that the Phase 1 scores were marginally more generous than those for Phase 2 as was reported earlier. However, as this was so minor, convergent results were found for the same variables using different methods, which adds accuracy to findings from the full chapter; it gives confidence to the measurements taken for the full dataset by auditing a smaller portion of it through a repeat measures design.

The charts show two outliers. One was for therapeutic support and the other for therapeutic change. For each, participants (Phase 2) gave significantly lower results compared to both the observations (Phase 1) and other participants on the same variables (Phase 2). Contextualising these results into additional information from datasets demonstrated that the two anomalies were caused by the same service-user. This individual's details were extrapolated and analysed below to consider the cause.

3.5.3.1.1 REVIEW DETAILS

When invited, unfortunately, this participant did not want to be interviewed, limiting the amount of qualitative information that could be ascertained to substantiate this discussion point. However, we do know that he gave these scores on Date 4, which was a therapeutic panel of a mixed gender, but this shows no resonation to findings from previous sections (Table 3.13).

However, on the survey, the anomaly for the support skill may be contextualised by the final open-ended question ('any other comments?'), where he gave breadth to his negative feedback stating: 'magistrates should have more drug knowledge and about individuals and their lives, etc.' This qualitative feedback can be coded under the 'understanding complexity of alcohol and other drugs recovery' variable as part of the therapeutic support skill, for which he also gave a low score on the questionnaire. As such, his low scores seem to be caused by a poor perception of the bench's understanding of the complexities of drug and alcohol recovery. The panel from this date scored 3 for this variable, which although a therapeutic score, was on the threshold; this indicates that some improvement could be made. This not only explains the abnormality on Graph A but corroborates this being the least therapeutically applied of those that arose thematically.

The anomaly on the change scale is harder to explain due to lack of qualitative evidence, but it could be due to the obvious inter-relatability between this variable and 'setting realistic goals', causing one other to be dragged down, thus explaining the outlying data in both graphs. Other contextual details could be derived from the ethnographic data; this indicated that this participant was in poor spirits on the day due to a bad report from his probation officer, rendering

Table 3.13 Review Context

Date group	4
Panel gender	Mixed

him at risk of breach. Although this should not have affected the scores he gave to magistrates, it may explain why he rated them poorly on this date, for these subskills.

Overall, the bivariate correlations suggest that the results triangulate, other than two outliers. When contextualising the abnormalities, the reason appears to be low feedback for the 'understanding the complexity of alcohol and other drugs recovery' variable. This serves to uphold the discussions sustained throughout this chapter; although the wine at Manchester was poured therapeutically, there were gaps in application. However, the gaps do not indicate lack of flair on the part of magistrates, but rather boil down to structural issues stifling fully efficacious operation of the wine, namely: lack of rota system or consistent panel, limited training, centralised systems, and fragmentation of parties . This concluding point lends itself to the next chapter, which seeks to discuss the therapeutic jurisprudence readiness of the bottle.

3.6 Concluding remarks for Chapter 3

This concluding section sums up the findings presented throughout this chapter, which sought to answer Research Questions 1, 1a, and 2 ('wine'). To reiterate, these are:

1. What impact does an inconsistent bench have on the therapeutic application of magistrates' interpersonal skills and behavioural styles at Manchester Review Court?
a. Does proficiency in these approaches change according to magistrates' gender?
2. What is the broad therapeutic quality of these styles?

To answer these questions, for the statistical data, a cut-off point was used to explore the numbers, where below 3 represented a non-therapeutic score, and above 3 (including 3) represented a therapeutic score; this qualitative coding was translated from the indicators on the Likert scale (excellent to poor). Measurements for the statistical analyses of the wine were taken by examining three skills (harnessing therapeutic support, engaging therapeutic dialogue, and inspiring therapeutic change), comprising substituting variables; these measurement structures have been validated in my work elsewhere.[259] However, some qualitative data was relevant to this discussion, and the same variables were used to code this data through deductive thematic analysis to build a coherent strand of analysis for this chapter. This data was used to clarify the insights from the quantitative data.

The wine data from all phases were knitted together, where findings could be understood as dissonant, complementary, or convergent, within a triangulation

259 Kawałek (n 1).

analysis.[260] Data across phases demonstrated convergency. Furthermore, bivariate analyses were carried out on a smaller data sample within a repeat measures design. This involved comparing scores for the same variables on a single review basis to understand similarities between Phase 1 and Phase 2 scores, and Graphs A, B, and C again confirmed data convergency. Overall, this indicates valid results.

A fidelity analysis considered how the discussion points mapped onto the international framework, and three main areas of the drug court gold standard were flagged for undermining authentic operation: Component 7, Component 9, and Component 10.[261] What also began to emerge were crucial similarities between the wine at Manchester and that reported for the original English and Welsh drug courts, including areas of infidelity. It is worth expressly recapitulating some of the main discoveries from within these areas, before progressing this argument in the next chapter.

3.6.1 Drug Court Component 7

Under Component 7, the National Association of Drug Court Professionals report that 'ongoing judicial interaction is essential'.[262] This is traditionally achieved by implementing a single judge to preside over all hearings. The therapeutic jurisprudence literature is pregnant with examples of how this structure benefits problem-solving court users, including how cross-fertilising a therapist–client style relationship from clinical practice enhances the service-users' relationship with the judge, amplifies personability of sessions, and heightens offender accountability, thus strengthening key outcomes, including recidivism and rehabilitation.[263] Manchester Review Court relied on a changing bench of magistrates instead of one judge/magistrate and, in the absence of a rota system, this left a changing panel; therefore, every time service-users encountered the court, they would see a new panel. That no efforts were made to ensure fidelity to this crucial area shone suspicious light on the efficacy of the court.

Research Question 1 ('wine') sought to understand how the non-compliance to this component impacted the administration of the wine. Panels were coded into dates to reflect the fact that several cases would be seen on one day with the same bench, with each date therefore representing a different composition. The Phase 1 and Phase 2 analyses both showed differences in the therapeutic quality of interpersonal skills and behavioural styles according to the bench. As such, infidelity to Component 7 led to inconsistencies in styles beyond what was expected, ranging significantly across therapeutic to non-therapeutic scores. The variable that was most affected was 'setting realistic goals' as it meant that participants were having to constantly change and adapt their recovery journeys according to the changing

260 Kelle & Erzberger (n 124).
261 Ashcroft et al. (n 2).
262 Ibid [15].
263 Winick & Wexler (n 4); Hora 2002 (n 5).

expectations of panels. The Phase 3 data ratified this insight, where participants agreed that different benches had different approaches, methods, and styles, and this undermined court impact, including goal setting. Participants advised that this should be made consistent to enhance the court experience and in turn, impact.

Findings from this question built upon predecessor research by Kerr et al.,[264] where the researchers found difficulties implementing consistent benches in the original drug court models. Although partial continuity (where one magistrate would sit for at least two consecutive hearings) was achieved 90% of the time, the researchers revealed some non-adherence to Component 7, and the difficulties implementing this area.[265] Whilst these issues were nascent, the researchers predicted declination in Component 7 over the long term, a trajectory has been confirmed by data from this book.

My data illustrated that this issue is underpinned by court centralisation reforms under the section 6 of Courts Act 2003 activated by Blair's Labour administration.[266] Under this legislation, the ramifications for courts across the country have been profound. By closing courts, the geographical catchment area has expanded, and the lay magistracy travel further to work. From the perspective of problem-solving courts, it has made consistency harder to achieve because the pool of magistrates, from which a bench is formed, has become bigger. This means that a consistent panel would be difficult to achieve without legislative change reversing the reforms and reimplementing a localised model. However, this suggestion is far-fetched; it would undermine current managerial, quality assurance, and regulatory priorities that currently define the justice sector as well as goals seeking to pare back on the overall quantity of magistrates. I have therefore argued that a more realistic, and ideal, scenario would be implementing a single magistrate to deal with all DRR reviews, if not a rota system to reinstate some partial continuity. A single magistrate seems like a plausible suggestion, given the irregularity of Manchester Review Court review hearings (one afternoon, fortnightly), and would simply require one individual to be available for the DRR role each session. However, such individuals must possess a therapeutic jurisprudence spirit, approach, and personality, have a toolkit of specialised knowledge, and should be on board with justice innovation, which can be all be enhanced through good quality training.

As this seems remarkably straightforward, perhaps the real issue is stimulating political will, appetite, and aegis to support the measures that allow these types of practice to function successfully. The 2003 court reforms were on the agenda for some time before the original drug court models were deployed.[267] We already

---

264 Kerr et al. (n 4).
265 Ibid.
266 Salford was integrated into Manchester Magistrates' Court in 2012, Bury in 2017, and further anticipated integration of Bolton in the near future – Participant I, interview data, collected by Anna Kawałek (file held with author); Participant II, interview data, collected by Anna Kawałek (file held with author).
267 (n 43), section 6.

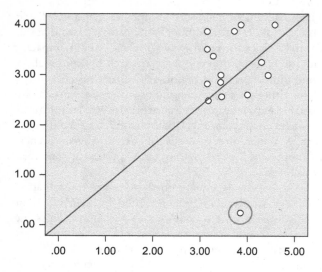

Graph A A Scatter Graph Demonstrating 'Therapeutic Support' Variables for Phase 1 and 2 Data

know from the previous research that the drug courts were struggling with this area despite them being at only a very early point in their (short) lifespan.[268] This suggests that the old courts were incepted based upon a poorly thought-out conceptual model, which failed to account for policy and legislation that would undermine fidelity to crucial areas. If UK ministers are serious about revolutionising justice, as current policy suggests,[269] attempts must be made to mirror international best practice, including the plethora of data that evidences that compliance to Component 7 enhances problem-solving court outcomes. Ongoing infidelity to this area illuminates of some of the causes of the failures in this area pertaining to onset implementation and priorities.

During this discussion, panels were contextualised into bench demographics, and a gender discrepancy emerged. Added inductively as Research Question 1a, the impact of magistrates' gender was analysed through a confirmatory analysis. The descriptive statistical data for the given sample evidenced that female magistrates were weaker than males. Through parametric analysis, namely a one-way ANOVA combined with Tukey corrections, a statistically significant difference arose between mixed panels of magistrates who were more therapeutic than all-female panels at harnessing therapeutic support, meaning that this finding would be found again in another study. This finding was then ratified by qualitative data, in which participants suggested that a male panel caused therapeutic responses. I speculated that this could be linked to the male-only court clientele. However,

268 Kerr et al. (n 4); Matrix Knowledge Group (n 4).
269 Cf. Chapter 2; Ministry of Justice (n 105).

the qualitative data also suggests that other judicial qualities were more plausible impactors on consistency, namely: age and life experience, personality, attitudes to addiction, and most importantly, training. With all things considered, inconsistencies in therapeutic jurisprudence are likely to be rooted in something deeper seated than gender, most likely, lack of training standardising practice. It is also important to emphasise that the purpose of this analysis was not to accuse certain magistrates of being less therapeutic, but rather to comment on the impact of non-compliance to Component 7, and to explore causes. What is of real importance to this discussion is that infidelity to a crucial drug court component had significant repercussions on the functioning of the court, and the previous report suggests that this problem is chronic.

3.6.2 Drug Court Component 9

During analysis of Component 7, training emerged as a problematic area. Specifically, under Component 9, the international body states that effective drug court practice involves 'continuing interdisciplinary education which promotes effective drug court planning, implementation, and operations'.[270] Manchester Review Court was in breach of Component 9 due to the limited training provided to magistrates; the last session was given in 2010, excluding some of the current magistrates because the pool had naturally changed with time, catalysed and broadened by court centralisation efforts expanding the judicial circle.

Under the Constitutional Reform Act 2005, the Lord Chief Justice leading the Judicial College is responsible for training UK judiciaries, and they work closely with the Magistrates Association to develop relevant courses. However, due to austerity, judicial training opportunities in recent years have been reduced for the lay magistracy more generally, let alone those specialising in the field of problem solving. The raw figures suggest that spending in this area has been reduced by a third. This goes hand in hand with the ongoing initiatives to reduce the overall quantity of court staff in this area, including judicial officers.[271] The lack of training meant that some magistrates were operating Manchester Review Court blind, without any training. If certain panels are weaker in therapeutic jurisprudence proficiency, how can we blame them? Moreover, since the previous drug court research also identified that a lack of training put up barriers for good practice, does this explain their chequered history?

This point leads on to analysis of the broad therapeutic quality of the wine to answer Research Question 2 ('wine'). The data complementarily showed that engaging in therapeutic dialogue was magistrates' strongest skill, harnessing therapeutic support was intermediate, and inspiring therapeutic change was the least therapeutic. Whilst differences in quality did manifest themselves, they were unsubstantial, and magistrates scored good (therapeutic) for each skill; this shows that the wine at Manchester Review Court was being poured in a therapeutic

---

270 Ashcroft et al. (n 2) [21].
271 House of Commons (n 92); Constitutional Reform Act 2005.

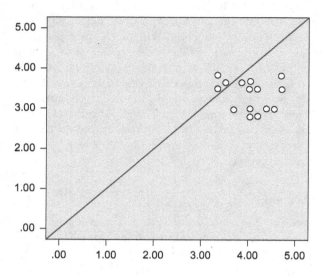

Graph B A Scatter Graph Demonstrating 'Therapeutic Dialogue' Variables for Phase
1 and 2 Data

fashion. When considering the little or non-existent training given to magistrates,
this finding is quite remarkable, and magistrates should be rewarded for their
good efforts and positive impacts.

A nuanced analysis, breaking down the main skills into their substituting variables, helped to identify specific areas of excellence and weakness. There was
some room for improvement for certain variables, but when taking the average
mean, only two variables were practised non-therapeutically; these were 'helping
the individuals build upon their strengths' and 'retaining a positive focus on the
future'. However, most variables could be improved to good or very good levels.
Moreover, through thematic analysis of the qualitative data, four skills emerged
as central tenets to the application of the wine, although they were implemented
within differing degrees of strength. These were:

1. Understanding the complexity of alcohol and other drugs recovery;
2. Motivating the individual;
3. Giving the offender a voice;
4. Setting realistic goals.

These findings built upon the report for the predecessor drug courts, in which
the judicial interactional styles were reported as: 'motivational; personalised;
interactive; authoritarian and challenging'.[272] Key elements of this interaction

272 Kerr et al. (n 4) [25].

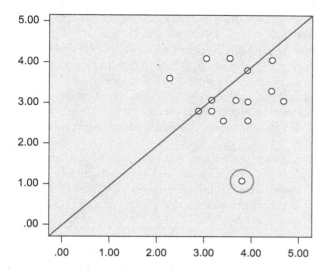

Graph C A Scatter Graph Demonstrating 'Therapeutic Change' Variables for Phase 1 and 2 Data

in the original models were reported to be an interested approach, listening to offenders, engaging with them genuinely and non-judgementally, and encouraging them to want to do well.[273] This demonstrates fundamental similarities between the wine aspects of both models, and hints that Manchester is the ghost of Salford drug court.

Of these skills, the data from this book suggested that 'motivating the individual' was the most crucial interpersonal style because motivating service-users was also a forefront objective of the court. The most therapeutically applied skill was: 'giving the offender a voice', which is a facet of procedural justice. 'Understanding the complexity of alcohol and other drugs recovery' was magistrates' weakest skill, and most explicitly links to insufficient training. 'Setting realistic goals' was practised with the most consistency; however, goals were likely to be incongruent with those set by partnership agencies (such as the probation and drug services) due to problems building alliance under Component 10.

Despite it being more significant to certain areas, training could enhance every one of these key variables, enabling them to reach good and excellent strengths. If Judicial College funding is tightening and the bottle intensifying in unfriendliness, it may be up to Manchester Review Court itself, and the magistrates within it, to carve out creative solutions for training through extra-curricular methods, including and most crucially, linkage with the international

273 Ibid.

body of therapeutic jurisprudence, which could be facilitated by the UK Chapter for Therapeutic Jurisprudence. That UK magistrates are unpaid Justices of the Peace, choosing to volunteer their time to DRR court work, indicates a passion for rehabilitation that should be capitalised upon. Of course, the ideal solution would be one highly knowledgeable and skilful DRR magistrate presiding over all hearings through fidelity to both Component 7 and Component 9 to mirror successful international and national models. A decentralised court model would also increase magistrates' understanding of local issues through a local justice philosophy, but this would mean reversing the court centralisation reforms, activated by the Courts Act 2003, which is unrealistic.

Although these discussion points have intended to critique the quality of the wine, adherence to Component 9 clearly rests on unfriendly structural factors, and most expressly links to problems with judicial training administered by the Judicial College under the Constitutional Reform Act 2005[274] as well as centralisation court reforms under the Courts Act.[275]

3.6.3 Drug Court Component 10 (and Component 6)

The final area from the international framework that was problematic from a wine perspective was Component 10. Under this component, the National Association of Drug Court Professionals state that: 'forging partnerships among drug courts, public agencies, and community-based organisations generates local support and enhances drug court program effectiveness'.[276] Gaps within magistrates' knowledge bases could be linked to fragmentation of stakeholders. Under the Criminal Justice Act 2003,[277] the court review aspect of the DRR is in many ways nothing more than an ancillary component to the probationary-led order (which is unlike a traditional drug court). This meant that breaches and sanctioning fell exclusively into the hands of probation workers, and this occurred at the probation offices, outside of the courtroom. Not only did these factors mean that magistrates were unable to assume the same pivotal role as they do in the international examples, but this also limited exposure to the issues and advice given to service-users outside of court, thus circumscribing magistrates' understanding of key activities and areas.

In the context of the wine, this indubitably compromised magistrates' contextual knowledge of offender progress, their personal circumstances, and the available support services. Furthermore, goals set outside of the courtroom, at the probation and drugs services, did not necessarily collude with those set within court, due to lack of alliance and authentic communication that would be expected under Component 10. This is potentially confusing for drug users who often possess chaotic lifestyles, who are then required to navigate a wide-ranging

274 (n 271).
275 (n 43), section 6.
276 Ashcroft et al. (n 2) [23].
277 (n 167).

series of objectives. Relatedly, under the Criminal Justice Act 2003, magistrates' power breach and sanction met a lacuna, and were instead given wholesale to probation workers, thus limiting magistrates' powers in court.

However, although these issues undermined the quality of the wine, they ultimately critique the nuts and bolts, and the policy and legislation governing Manchester Review Court, and are therefore, rooted in problems that are systemic, rather than a lack of motivation, capability, or talent, on the part of ground level practitioners.

3.6.4 Concluding remarks for Chapter 3

This chapter has demonstrated that the wine at Manchester Review Court was poured in a therapeutic-jurisprudence–friendly manner. An analysis that mapped onto the international framework could disclose and contextualise areas of strength and weakness. To create fidelity to the international drug court, changes to the following areas should be made to enhance the wine:

- A consistent bench should be implemented to comply with Component 7. This currently looks unlikely due to the reforms centralising courts across England and Wales. A single presiding magistrate is preferable, is perhaps more realistic given these structures, and sits with UK goals to reduce the quantities of court staff.
- Regardless of whether Component 7 is adhered to, enhanced judicial training through the Judicial College is key for adherence to Component 9. Due to austerity measures curtailing expenditure in this area, it might be up to magistrates to find new and creative ways to train themselves. Drawing upon international best practice is crucial, and this could be initiated through Amicus Justitia briefs and alignment to the UK therapeutic jurisprudence Chapter and the international society. Reducing the bench to just one magistrate would require less training expenditure and would initiate the effects associated with compliance to Component 7.
- Increasing alliance through partnership working would increase knowledge bases of key areas through adherence to Component 10 through more collusion with the probation services. Better communication in this area would also allow goal setting to become more effective, including encouraging individual probation officers to attend and support court sessions. Increasing magistrates' powers to reward and sanction progress would further incentivise progress and would comply with Component 6.

Even though these discussions pertain to application of the wine, it has been difficult to maintain a focus on this aspect without venturing into the terrains of the bottle. As the above bullet points elucidate, the jurisdiction of England and Wales fails to support the full application of therapeutic jurisprudence because it withholds a friendly bottle for good wine. Many of these issues are long-standing, and similarities to the original drug courts can be drawn by scrutinising the predecessor report.

What this analysis has shown is that magistrates were working well under difficult structures, and despite these hurdles, the wine that they administrated was therapeutic-jurisprudence–friendly. Although the wine was operated in accordance with therapeutic-jurisprudence philosophy, where the current UK criminal justice system is emphasising managerialism, centralisation, and austerity measures, the bottle remains unfriendly. It is perhaps those in the judiciary that hold the power and enthusiasm to effect change, to make legitimate recommendations to improve the system, and to find creative ways to maximise therapeutic jurisprudence. Empowering these voices should be encouraged if the UK wants to initiate a successful rehabilitation revolution, and the national and international bodies could provide a crucial mouthpiece. Manchester Review Court holds significant potential, and this is because of the talents that lie within the practising at the frontline.

The next chapter extends the investigation to a broader, structural, and systemic evaluation of the bottle. It will conclude that there is still great hope for successful problem-solving courts in England and Wales if a specialist matrix is adhered to.

Bibliography

Ashcroft J., Daniels D. and Herriaz D., 'Defining drug courts: the key components. U.S. department of justice' (2004). https://www.ncjrs.gov/pdffiles1/bja/205621.pdf

Baker M., 'Choices and consequences – an account of an experimental sentences programme' (2014) (1) Criminal Law Review. Thomson Reuters (Professionals) UK Limited.

Bar-On R., Tranel D., Denburg N.L. and Bechara A., 'Exploring the neurological substrate of emotional and social intelligence' (2003) 126(8) Brain, 1790–1800, doi:10.1093/brain/awg177.

Bartels L., 'Looking at Hawaii's opportunity with probation enforcement (HOPE) program through a therapeutic jurisprudence lens' (2016) 16 QUT Law Review, 30.

Bartels L., *Swift, certain and fair: does project HOPE provide a therapeutic paradigm for managing offenders?* (Springer, 2017).

Bartels L., 'HOPE-ful bottles: examining the potential for Hawaii's opportunity probation with enforcement (HOPE) to help mainstream therapeutic jurisprudence' (2019) 63 International Journal of Law and Psychiatry, 26–34.

Birgden A. and Ward T., 'Pragmatic psychology through a therapeutic jurisprudence lens psycholegal soft spots' (2003) 9(3/4) Criminal Justice System Psychology, Public Policy, and Law, 334–360.

Bowen P. and Donoghue D., 'Digging up the grassroots? The impact of marketisation and managerialism on local justice, 1997 to 2013' (2013) 11(2) British Journal of Community Justice, 9–21.

Boyd C.L., Epstein L. and Martin A.D., 'Untangling the causal effects of sex on judging' (2010) 54(2) American Journal of Political Science, 389–411.

Braun V., and Clarke V., 'Using thematic analysis in psychology' (2006) 3(2) Qualitative Research in Psychology, 77–101.

Burke K. and Leben S., 'Court review: volume 44, issue 1/2 – procedural fairness: a key ingredient in public satisfaction' (2007) A White Paper of the American Judges Association the Voice of the Judiciary.

Cambridge Advanced Learner's Dictionary and Thesaurus, Cambridge University Press. https://dictionary.cambridge.org/dictionary/english/interactive, Accessed 2 July 2020.

Carns T. and Martin S., 'Probation accountability with certain enforcement a preliminary evaluation of the anchorage pilot PACE project' (2011) Alaska Judicial Council.

Center for Court Innovation, 'Judge David Fletcher, North Liverpool community justice centre' *Center for Court Innovation* (November 2005). https://www.cou rtinnovation.org/publications/judge-david-fletcher-north-liverpool-communit y-justice-centre, Accessed 1 July 2020.

Clark M., 'Influencing positive behavior change: increasing the therapeutic approach of juvenile courts' (2001) 65(1) Federal Probation, 18–27.

Clark M., 'A changed-focused approach for judges' in D.B. Wexler and B.J. Winick (eds.) *Judging in a therapeutic key: therapeutic jurisprudence and the courts* (Durham, NC: Carolina Academic Press, 2003).

Cloud W. and Granfield R., 'Social context and 'natural recovery': the role of social capital in the resolution of drug-associated problems' (2001) 36(11) Substance Use and Misuse, 1543–1570.

Cloud W. and Granfield R., 'Conceptualizing recovery capital: expansion of a theoretical construct' (2008) 43(12–13) Substance Use and Misuse, 1971–1986. doi:10.1080/10826080802289762.

Collins E., 'Status courts' (2017) 105 Geo. Law Journal, 1481–1528.

Demack S., 'Tests of statistical significance – their (ab)use in the social sciences – a comment' (2007). https://www.jiscmail.ac.uk/cgi-bin/webadmin?A3=ind 0809&L=RADSTATS&E=base64&P=103048&B=------_%3D_NextPart_001 _01C914DB.62AED010&T=application%2Fpdf;%20name=%22(ab)use%20of%2 0Significance%20Testing.pdf%22&N=(ab)use%20of%20Significance%20Testing. pdf&attachment=q.

Duffy J., 'Problem-solving courts, therapeutic jurisprudence and the constitution: if two is company, is three a crowd?' (2011) 35(2) Melbourne University Law Review, 394–425.

Estep B., 'Better courts case-study: West London drug court' (2014) Centre for Justice Innovation. https://b.3cdn.net/nefoundation/c5d489a84bc7c9aa59 _cym6idhsz.pdf.

Field A., *Discovering statistics using IBM SPSS statistics* (London: SAGE, 2013).

Freiberg A., 'Problem-oriented courts: innovative solutions to intractable problems?' (2001) 11(8) Journal of Judicial Administration, 7–23.

Frederick J.G. and Larry B.W., *Essentials of statistics for the behavioral sciences* (Wadsworth: Cengage Learning, 2014).

George D. and Mallery P., *IBM SPSS statistics 23 step by step: a simple guide and reference* (Routledge, 2016). doi:10.4324/9781315545899.

Gilligan C., *In a different voice: psychological theory and women's development* (Cambridge, MA: Harvard University Press, 1982).

Gottfredson D., Brooke K., Najaka S. and Rocha C., 'How drug treatment courts work: an analysis of mediators' (2007) 44(1) Journal of Research in Crime and Delinquency, 3–3.

Greenberga D.M., Warriera V., Allisona C., and Baron-Cohen S., 'Testing the empathizing–systemizing theory of sex differences and the extreme male brain theory of autism in half a million people' (2018) 115(48) PNAS, 12152–12157.

Harwin J., Ryan M., Tunnard J., Pokhrel S., Alrouh B., Matias C. and Schneider M., 'The family drug & alcohol court (FDAC), evaluation project final report' (2011) Nuffield Foundation, Brunel University.

Hora H., 'A dozen years of drug treatment courts: uncovering our theoretical foundation and the construction of a mainstream paradigm' (2002) 37 Substance Use and Misuse, 12 & 13, 1469–1488.

Hora P.F., Schma W.G. and Rosenthal J.T., 'Therapeutic jurisprudence and the drug treatment court movement: revolutionizing the criminal justice system's response to drug abuse and crime in America' (1999) 74 Notre Dame Law Review, 439. http://scholarship.law.nd.edu/ndlr/vol74/iss2/4.

House of Commons Justice Committee, 'The role of the magistracy sixth report of session 2016–17' (2016) House of Commons. https://publications.parliament.uk/pa/cm201617/cmselect/cmjust/165/165.pdf.

House of Commons Justice Committee, 'The role of the magistracy: follow-up eighteenth report of session 2017–19' (2019) House of Commons. https://publications.parliament.uk/pa/cm201719/cmselect/cmjust/1654/1654.pdf.

Ingalhalikar M., Smith A., Parker D., Satterthwaite T.D., Elliott M.A., Ruparel K., Hakonarson H., Gur R.E., Gur R.C. and Verma R., 'Sex differences in the structural connectome of the human brain' (2014) 111(2) PNAS, 823–828. doi:10.1073/pnas.1316909110.

Judicial College, 'Strategy of the judicial college 2018–2020' (2017). https://www.judiciary.uk/wp-content/uploads/2017/12/judicial-college-strategy-2018-2020.pdf.

Judicial College, 'Judicial monitoring condition' (2015). http://www.judicialcollege.vic.edu.au/eManuals/VSM/7157.htm.

Kawałek A., 'A tool for measuring therapeutic jurisprudence values during empirical research' (2020) 71C International Journal of Law and Psychiatry, 101581.

Kelle U. and Erzberger C., 'Making inferences in mixed methods: the rules of integration' in A. Tashakkori and C. Teddlie (eds.) *Handbook of mixed methods in social & behavioural research* (Thousand Oaks, CA: SAGE, 2003).

Kerr J., Tompkins C., Tomaszewski W., Dickens S., Grimshaw R., Wright N. and Barnard, M., 'The dedicated drug courts pilot evaluation process study' (2011) Ministry of Justice Research Series, 1. Ministry of Justice, London.

King M., 'A judicial officer assists offenders to set rehabilitation goals and strategies' *Blog Post* (28 February 2017). https://mainstreamtj.wordpress.com/2017/02/28/a-judicial-officer-assists-offenders-to-set-rehabilitation-goals-strategies-tj-court-craft-series-8/, Accessed 1 July 2020.

King M., 'Enhancing judicial communication' [TJ in the mainstream blog, June 3] *Blog Post*. https://mainstreamtj.wordpress.com/2016/06/03/enhancing-judicial-communication-tj-court-craft-series-1/, Accessed 1 July 2020.

King M., Freiberg A., Batagol B. and Hyams R., *Non-adversarial justice*, 2nd ed. (Alexandria, NSW: Federation Press, 2014).

King S., Hopkins M. and Cornish N., *Hertfordshire choices and consequences (C2) and Bedfordshire prolific intensive offender management (PI) evaluation* (Leicester University, unpublished).

KPMG Consulting, 'Evaluation of the drug court of Victoria. Government advisory services. Final report.' (2014) Magistrates' Court of Victoria, 18.

Liverpool Echo, 'Judge David Fletcher made a difference at the North Liverpool community justice centre in Kirkdale' *Liverpool Echo* (21 December 2012). https ://www.liverpoolecho.co.uk/news/liverpool-news/judge-david-fletcher-ma de-difference-3327912, Accessed 1 July 2020.

Lundqvist L.O., 'Facial EMG reactions to facial expressions: a case of facial emotional contagion?' (1996) 36(2) Scandinavian Journal of Psychology, 130–141. doi:10.1 111/j.1467-9450.1995.tb00974.x.

Lynch A. and Perlin M.L., "Life's hurried tangled road': a therapeutic jurisprudence analysis of why dedicated counsel must be assigned to represent persons with mental disabilities in community settings' (2016) NYLS Legal Studies Research Paper No. 2833365. doi:10.2139/ssrn.2833365.

Mair G. and Millings M., 'Doing justice locally: the north Liverpool community justice centre' Centre for Crime and Justice Studies, 2011. https://www.crimeandjusti ce.org.uk/sites/crimeandjustice.org.uk/files/Doing%20justice%20locally.pdf.

Maruna S., *Making good: how ex-convicts reform and rebuild their lives* (Washington, DC: American Psychological Association, 2011). doi:10.1037/10430-000.

McDonald R., *Factor analysis and related methods* (Hove: Psychology Press, 2014).

McIvor G., Therapeutic jurisprudence and procedural justice in Scottish drug courts' (2009) 9(1) Criminology and Criminal Justice, 5–25.

McIvor G., Barnsdale L., Eley S., Malloch M., Yates R. and Brown A., 'An evaluation of the Glasgow and Fife drug courts and their aim to reduce drug use and drug related reoffending' (2006) 9 Criminology and Criminal Justice 2009, 29.

Mestre M., Samper P., Frias M. and Tur A., 'Are women more empathetic than men? A longitudinal study in adolescence' (2009) 12(1) Spanish Journal of Psychology, 76–83. doi:10.1017/S1138741600001499.

Miller W. and Rollnick S., *Motivational interviewing: helping people change*, 3rd ed. (New York: Guilford Press, 2003).

Ministry of Justice, 'Transforming rehabilitation a strategy for reform' (2013). https ://consult.justice.gov.uk/digital-communications/transforming-rehabilitation/ results/transforming-rehabilitation-response.pdf.

Ministry of Justice, 'Government response to the justice committee's eighteenth report of session 2017–19: the role of the magistracy' (2019) Ministry of Justice. https://assets.publishing.service.gov.uk/government/uploads/system/upl oads/attachment_data/file/843110/role-magistracy-govt-response.pdf.

Ministry of Justice, 'A smarter approach to sentencing' (2020) White Paper.

National Offender Management Service, 'Supporting community order treatment requirements' (2014) Commissioning Group.

Pauline Spencer, 'Steps towards change – a tool for judges working with persons with substance abuse disorders' (8 May 2018). https://mainstreamtj.wordpress.com/ 2018/05/08/steps-towards-change-a-tool-for-judges-working-with-persons -with-substance-abuse-disorders-tj-court-craft-series-12/, Accessed 1 July 2020.

Peggy F.H., William G.S. and John T.A.R., 'The importance of timing' in D.B. Wexler and B.J. Winick (eds.) *Judging in a therapeutic key: therapeutic jurisprudence and the courts* (Durham, NC: Carolina Academic Press, 2003).

Perlin P., 'Mental health courts, dignity, and human rights', on page 193 in B. McSherry and I. Freckelton (eds.) *Coercive care: law and policy* (Abingdon: Routledge, 2013), 212.

Petrucci C., 'Respect as a component in the judge-defendant interaction in a specialized domestic violence court that utilizes therapeutic jurisprudence' (2002) Criminal Law Bulletin, 38.

Petrucci C., Winick B. and Wexler D., 'Therapeutic jurisprudence: an invitation for social sciences' in D. Carson and R. Bull (eds.) *Handbook of psychology in legal context*, 2nd ed. (Chichester: Wiley & Sons, 2003).

Phillips P., Kawalek A. and Greenslade A.M., 'An evaluation of the choice and consequences and PI programmes in Bedfordshire and Hertfordshire' (2020) Ministry of Justice.

Rob A., 'Rehabilitation devolution – how localising justice can reduce crime and imprisonment' (2015) *Transform Justice*. http://www.transformjustice.org.uk/wp-content/uploads/2015/12/TRANSFORM-JUSTICE-REHABILITATION-DEVOLUTION.pdf.

Roger W., 'Public trust and procedural justice' in D.B. Wexler and B.J. Winick (eds.) *Judging in a therapeutic key: therapeutic jurisprudence and the courts* (Durham, NC: Carolina Academic Press, 2003).

Ruiz V., *The role of women judges and a gender perspective in ensuring judicial independence and integrity* (UNODC). https://www.unodc.org/dohadeclaration/en/news/2019/01/the-role-of-women-judges-and-a-gender-perspective-in-ensuring-judicial-independence-and-integrity.html, Accessed 01 July 2020.

Seppälä E., 'Are women really more compassionate?' *Psychology Today* (20 June 2013). https://www.psychologytoday.com/gb/blog/feeling-it/201306/are-women-really-more-compassionate, Accessed 1 July 2020.

Shannon L., Hulbig S., Birdswhistell S., Newell K. and Neal C., 'Implementation of an enhanced probation program: evaluating process and preliminary outcomes' (2015) 49 Evaluation and Programme Planning, 50–62.

Snell C., 'Fort Bend county community supervision and corrections special sanctions court program evaluation report' (2007) University of Houston.

Stimler K., 'Best practices for drug court: how drug court judges influence positive outcomes' (2013) (Master's Thesis), Minnesota State University-Mankato, Mankato, MN.

Susan G., 'Problem-solving in Canada's courtrooms: a guide to therapeutic justice' (2011). National Judicial Institute.

Swaner R., Ramdath C., Martinez A., Hahn J. and Walker S., 'What do defendants really think? Procedural justice and legitimacy in the criminal justice system' *Centre for Court Innovation* (2016). https://www.courtinnovation.org/sites/default/files/media/documents/2018-09/what_do_defendants_really_think.pdf.

Tyler T. and Bies R., 'Beyond formal procedures: the interpersonal context of procedural justice' (1990) 77 Applied Social Psychology and Organizational Settings, 98.

Vagias W., 'Likert-type scale response anchors. Clemson international institute for tourism and research development' (2006) Department of Parks, Recreation and Tourism Management, Clemson University.

Verma R., 'Sex differences in the structural connectome of the human brain' (2014) 111(2) PNAS, 823–828. doi:10.1073/pnas.1316909110.

Wexler D.B. and Winick B., Law in a therapeutic key: developments in therapeutic jurisprudence (Durham, NC, Carolina Academic Press, 1999). http://www.austlii.edu.au/au/journals/CICrimJust/1997/9.pdf.

Wexler D.B. and Winick B.J., *Judging in a therapeutic key: therapeutic jurisprudence and the courts* (Durham, NC: Carolina Academic Press, 2003).

Winick B., 'Therapeutic jurisprudence and problem solving courts' (2003) 30 Fordham Urban Law Journal, 1055. https://ir.lawnet.fordham.edu/ulj/vol30/iss3/14.

Winick B., 'How judges can use behavioral contracting' in D.B. Wexler and B.J. Winick (eds.) *Judging in a therapeutic key: therapeutic jurisprudence and the courts* (Durham, NC: Carolina Academic Press, 2003).

Winick B., 'The judge's role in encouraging motivation for change' in D.B. Wexler and B.J. Winick (eds.) *Judging in a therapeutic key: therapeutic jurisprudence and the courts* (Durham, NC: Carolina Academic Press, 2003).

4 Analysis and discussion of the 'bottle'

4.1 Introduction

Scholarly work by therapeutic jurisprudence proponents has emphasised the wine part of the seminal wine-bottle analogy, paying heed to the interactional styles of judges within problem-solving court jurisdictions.[1] In that spirit, the last chapter (Chapter 3) analysed the therapeutic quality of the wine at Manchester Review Court using a tool that was statistically validated in my work elsewhere.[2] As Chapter 3 progressed, it became clear that although the wine was good, there is little point pouring proficient wine if the bottle is not conducive to good practice. Therefore, to incur therapeutic responses, good wine must be complemented with something broader, something systemic, something structural – something that lies at bottle level. With that in mind, this chapter will analyse the therapeutic-jurisprudence friendliness of bottle to explore the sustainability of the landscapes surrounding the court. Using the data collected by the bottle vantage points,[3] through triangulation principles it will answer Research Questions 1, 2, and 3 ('bottle') below:

1. Research Question 1 ('bottle'): does the court adhere to the international drug court gold standard?[4]
2. Research Question 2 ('bottle'): is it the remains of the original drug courts?
3. Research Question 3 ('bottle'): what is the therapeutic quality of Manchester Review Court's bottle?

I have reiterated the following mantra throughout this book: there is no track record of Manchester Review Court in the available literature repositories evidencing its existence, no empirical research, not in the media or any policy document,

---

1 Bruce J. Winick & David B. Wexler, *Judging in a therapeutic key: therapeutic jurisprudence and the courts* (Durham, NC: Carolina Academic Press, 2003).
2 Anna Kawałek, 'A tool for measuring therapeutic jurisprudence values during empirical research' (2020) International Journal of Law and Psychiatry, 71C, 101581.
3 See Diagram A, Chapter 2.
4 John Ashcroft, Deborah Daniels, & Domingo Herriaz, 'Defining drug courts: the key components. U.S. Department of Justice' (2004). Retrieved from: https://www.ncjrs.gov/pdf files1/bja/205621.pdf.

and nor is there a court handbook at the site outlining objectives and expected practice. The death of literature made analysis difficult, and since fidelity questions have been raised, the ten key drug court components document was an appropriate mechanism to frame the evaluation. This chapter will systematically deal with each of the ten key components to identify areas of adherence and non-adherence to its principles. Synchronously, it will compare findings of the predecessor drug court research to identify differences and similarities to speculate on the UK's chequered history in this field. In light of the findings, it will end positively by presenting a new fidelity matrix for a fresh generation of British problem solving courts.

4.2 'Bottle': findings and discussion

4.2.1 Drug Court Component 1

Under Component 1, the National Association of Drug Court Professionals are concerned with the basic principles governing drug courts and their key infrastructural pillars, including their mission statements, expectations, visions, objectives, 'goals, eligibility criteria, operating procedures, and performance measures'.[5] I have already suggested that these rudimentary areas should be configured by developing a court bench book to help enrich understanding and standardise practice (Chapter 3).

Given that Manchester Review Court is somewhat of an enigma, it is useful to clarify the extent to which its business objectives sit in line with a traditional drug court. Under this component, the international body states that 'the mission of drug courts is to stop the abuse of alcohol and other drugs and related criminal activity'.[6] In the absence of a bench book or literature (underscored by the mantra[7]), there was no official written outline of Manchester's purpose. The closest guidance is provided for under section 210 of the Criminal Justice Act,[8] but this is remarkably unclear.[9] However, we can extrapolate the broader objectives of the DRR itself

---

5 Ibid [1].
6 Ibid.
7 'There is no track record of Manchester Review Court in the available literature repositories evidencing its existence, no empirical research, not in the media or any policy document, and nor is there a court handbook at the site outlining objectives and expected practice.'
8 Criminal Justice Act, 2003, section 210.
9 A community order or suspended sentence order imposing a drug rehabilitation requirement may (and must if the treatment and testing period is more than 12 months) –
   (a) Provide for the requirement to be reviewed periodically at intervals of not less than one month;
   (b) Provide for each review of the requirement to be made, subject to section 211(6), at a hearing held for the purpose by the court responsible for the order (a 'review hearing');
   (c) Require the offender to attend each review hearing;
   (d) Provide for an officer of a provider of probation services to make to the court responsible for the order, before each review, a report in writing on the offender's progress under the requirement, and;
   (e) Provide for each such report to include the test results communicated to the responsible officer under section 209(6) or otherwise and the views of the treatment provider as to the treatment and testing of the offender.

(aside from the court aspect) from the existing literature. This is stated by the UK National Offender Management Service as 'changing patterns of substance misuse and moving towards a recovery-focused approach to treatment'.[10] Although complete cessation of drug use is a traditional drug court expectation, under the Criminal Justice Act, section 209, the DRR expects that drug use is reduced, but not necessarily ceased.[11]

4.2.1.1 Objectives

Although the purpose of the DRR itself is relatively clear from the literature, objectives of the review court were inexplicit for reasons that I have already outlined. For the DRR ancestors, the Drug Treatment and Testing Orders ('DTTOs'), McSweeney, et al.[12] noted the reviews were designed: 'to enable the courts to better monitor compliance and progress with treatment'. That the DTTOs have now been supplanted by DRRs renders this definition outdated and leaves the purpose of the Manchester Review Court unclear; however, this could be inferred from the data. Participants identified court aims as: rehabilitating drug use as the underlying cause of crime, especially acquisitive,[13] and a mechanism for breaking the broad revolving-door phenomenon.[14] Most markedly:

> (The purpose is) to assess the defendant in reduction of consumption of illegal drugs, which the court has identified as the motivating feature in the defendant committing various offences … The government recognised that individuals commit acquisitive crime to further the drug habit.[15]
>
> The origins come from Miami, and they were designed to tackle the revolving-door crisis[16]

These quotations show that participants perceived Manchester Review Court's instrumental purpose as tantamount to the international drug courts. The latter sample also hints at a telling conflation between the DRR review court and the original UK drug court models. However, participants also tended to identify the aims of the court in the context of intrinsic factors.

> The purpose is to get an idea of where you are, or to review your progress … so they can get an understanding of where you're at and so they can work out how to make a plan that's going to help you.[17]

---

10 National Offender Management Service, 'Supporting community order treatment requirements' (2014) Commissioning Group [2].
11 (n 8) section 209; ibid.
12 Tim McSweeney, Alex Stevens, Neil Hunt, & Paul Turnbull, 'Drug testing and court review hearings: uses and limitations' (2001) Probation Journal, 55(1), 39–53 [40].
13 Participant I, interview data, collected by Anna Kawałek (file held with author).
14 Participant II, interview data, collected by Anna Kawałek (file held with author).
15 Participant I, interview data, collected by Anna Kawałek (file held with author).
16 Ethnographic data collected by Anna Kawałek (file held with author).
17 Participant II, interview data, collected by Anna Kawałek (file held with author).

It is a reminder of where you are. It is a reality check.[18]

To review the progress and how they are getting on, on the order.[19]

To try and help you and motivate you to try and stop taking drugs … get you to do things, keep yourself busy.[20]

Motivating them and to try and reduce the drug use, just generally motivating them to do things positive in their life.[21]

Common to each of these answers is that the purpose of the court to 'review' or 'motivate', but this implies something must *be* reviewed or *be* motivated. Presumably, these are instrumental objectives: drug rehabilitation and law compliance. This means that although the National Association of Drug Court Professional's[22] mission statement was not expressly referred to across participants answers, primary objectives are synonymous with a traditional drug court. With the lack of literature stating as such, we can infer that Manchester Review Court's goals were compliant to the international standard under Component 1. If the evidence base suggests drug courts positively impact what are ultimately core DRR objectives through a fidelity model,[23] this suggests that changing the process at Manchester to align with a traditional drug court, or at least a similar model with well-researched components, could meet help to meet key DRR court outputs.

Notably, the region of Greater Manchester has special problems with drug-fuelled offending compared to other areas of England and Wales. It has been reported that drug misuse accounts for 35% of reoffenders in Greater Manchester.[24] A sustainable model addressing these issues at their roots is therefore important to Manchester as a city. Punitivism might take up fewer short-term human resources,

---

18 Participant V, interview data, collected by Anna Kawałek (file held with author).

19 Participant II, interview data, collected by Anna Kawałek (file held with author).

20 Participant I, interview data, collected by Anna Kawałek (file held with author).

21 Participant II, interview data, collected by Anna Kawałek (file held with author).

22 Ashcroft et al. (n 4).

23 KPMG Consulting, 'Evaluation of the drug court of Victoria. Government Advisory Services. Final report' (2014) Magistrates' Court of Victoria, 18; John Goldkamp, Michael White, & Jennifer Robinson, 'Do drug courts work? Getting inside the drug court black box' (2000) Journal of Drug Issues, 31(1), 27–72; John Goldkamp, 'Challenges for research and innovation: when is a drug court not a drug court?' in W. Clinton Terry (ed.) *The early drug courts: case studies in judicial innovation* (Thousand Oaks, CA: Sage, 1999); Shannon M. Carey, Michael W. Finigan, & Kimberly Pukstas, 'Exploring the key components of drug courts: a comparative study of 18 adult drug courts on practices, outcomes and costs' (2008) NPC Research; Peggy Hora, 'A dozen years of drug treatment courts: uncovering our theoretical foundation and the construction of a mainstream paradigm' (2002) Substance Use and Misuse 37, 12 & 13, 1469–1488; Matthew Hiller, Steven Belenko, Faye Taxman, Douglas Young, Matthew Perdoni, & Christine Saum, 'Measuring drug court structure and operations: key components and beyond' (2010) Criminal Justice and Behaviour; Susan Witkin & Scott Hays, 'Drug court through the eyes of participants' (2017) Criminal Justice Policy Review, 30(7), 971–989. doi:10.1177/0887403417731802.

24 Greater Manchester, 'Greater Manchester drug and alcohol strategy 2019–2021' (2019). Retrieved from: https://www.greatermanchester-ca.gov.uk/media/2507/greater-manchester-drug-and-alcohol-strategy.pdf.

but it only provides immediate results. As such, a problem-solving court could ignite the venture towards longer-term results through rehabilitation and justice innovation. The data showed that 65% of respondents either strongly agreed or agreed that the reviews helped them comply with the law[25] and 85% of respondents either strongly agreed or agreed that the reviews helped them stay on track with their recovery.[26] These are strong results. The qualitative data converged, and service-users and staff agreed that the court had a positive effect upon these areas.

> I've been three days without ... Plus, I'm usually in prison by now.[27]
>
> Sometimes in the week I might think 'oh, I will have a little session but then I am like oh f**k no – I've got me test tomorrow'. And then I leave it ... it makes me comply with the law ... it makes me jump through the hoops.[28]
>
> It does help with my recovery.[29]
>
> It's like an anchor. It's incredibly necessary and important. Not only to society but also to the individual.[30]
>
> I know people I have interviewed about DRRs; they've asked for them again ... they said actually last time that really worked and really helped me.[31]

However, some reservations were also expressed by participants.

> In terms of recovery, the court can provide that assistance. Obviously, it's a limited assistance. Some of that assistance might be the best thing that the defendant has ever had and is all that is necessary, but on some occasions, it might not be enough for the defendant and a lot more is necessary ... the court can only do so much.[32]
>
> Sometimes it works, sometimes it doesn't, and sometimes it may work for a while, it often depends on usage.[33]
>
> It's that individual's responsibility to get off drugs.[34]
>
> These junkies are not going to get off of the ship, and I'm not going to get off the ship, unless I want to.[35]
>
> If you're susceptible to this stuff ... it is horses for courses. [36]

25 Survey Question 10, Phase 2.
26 Survey Question 13, Phase 2.
27 Participant I, interview data, collected by Anna Kawałek (file held with author).
28 Participant V, interview data, collected by Anna Kawałek (file held with author).
29 Participant II, interview data, collected by Anna Kawałek (file held with author).
30 Participant I, interview data, collected by Anna Kawałek (file held with author).
31 Participant II, interview data, collected by Anna Kawałek (file held with author).
32 Participant I, interview data, collected by Anna Kawałek (file held with author).
33 Participant II, interview data, collected by Anna Kawałek (file held with author).
34 Participant I, interview data, collected by Anna Kawałek (file held with author).
35 Participant V, interview data, collected by Anna Kawałek (file held with author).
36 Ibid.

I can't say it's helping me because I'm my own man ... it's up to me at the end of the day.[37]

As such, the data shows that there was a clear perception that effectiveness of the court depended upon the circumstances of the offender, level of drug usage, using-propensity, human personality, and personal motivation. Notably, the latter personal motivation theme was also identified in the report for the English and Welsh predecessor drug courts.[38] This means that the data broadly suggests that Manchester Review Court had positive impacts on instrumental outcomes, namely law compliance and recovery, but these outputs are likely to be realised inconsistently depending upon the idiosyncrasies of the offender. A limitation to these findings was that participants tended to conflate the DRR model, both conceptually and practically, with the separate court aspect when responding to questions. Interestingly, this conflation also presented itself in the predecessor drug court research.[39] Although this is likely to be because the DRR forms the core element of both models, this highlights the court as ancillary to the main DRR. Though this could suggest that Manchester Review Court did not have as much of a positive impact on results as the data initially suggests it is nonetheless a good result for the DRR itself, which has also suffered from little empirical research, especially recent. Research should be undertaken in the future to provide explicit empirical evidence for outcomes.

4.2.1.2 *Eligibility*

Service-user eligibility is specified within the Criminal Justice Act 2003[40] and rephrased by the National Offender Management Service as (the offender must):

  i) Be dependent on or has the propensity to misuse illegal drugs;
 ii) Require and would benefit from treatment and;
iii) Express willingness to comply with the requirement or has a desire to pursue recovery.[41]

Whilst these criteria resemble eligibility for a traditional drug court,[42] the DRR accepts offenders who have committed a broader range of criminal offences. Whereas a drug court restrictively accepts only low-risk offenders committing

---

37 Ibid.
38 Jane Kerr, Charlotte Tompkins, Wojtek Tomaszewski, Sarah Dickens, Roger Grimshaw, Nat Wright, & Matt Barnard, 'The dedicated drug courts pilot evaluation process study' (2011) Ministry of Justice Research Series, 1. London: Ministry of Justice.
39 Ibid.
40 (n 8), section 210.
41 National Offender Management Service (n 10).
42 Ashcroft et al. (n 4).

Table 4.1 Frequency Table Displaying Offence Types for Phase 1 and Phase 2

Offence	Phase 1 %	Phase 2 %
Theft/Stealing	60.9	58.8
Assault/Battery	15.2	23.5
Criminal damage	4.3	5.9
Burglary	6.5	5.9
Breaking restraining order	4.4	0
Blade in public place	4.3	0
Offence against public order	4.4	5.9
Total	100%	100%

non-violent and acquisitive[43] crimes,[44] the DRR accepts participation of these offending groups, spanning the low-, medium-, and high-risk sentencing bands.[45] This was reflected within the demographic information collated for Manchester Review Court extrapolated from service-users' DRR review reports.

4.2.1.2.1 DRUG TYPE

Table 4.1 shows that most cases fell into the theft/stealing bracket according to the Phase 1 and Phase 2 respective datasets (p1 = 61%; p2 = 58.8%). This links to demographic information produced by Kerr, et al.,[46] in which theft was also reported as the most common offence type by accounting for 40% of cases across all six pilot sites. However, as the data in Table 4.1 was sparse, it was

43 Acquisitive are crimes such as burglary, theft, robbery, or handling stolen goods – crimes related to feeding the habit.
44 Michael Perlin, 'Mental health courts, dignity, and human rights', on p. 193 in Bernadette McSherry & Ian Freckelton (eds.) *Coercive care: law and policy* (Abingdon, Oxon: Routledge, 2013); Arica Marlene Burke, 'Would violent offenders benefit from participation in drug court?' (2013) (Master's Thesis, Minnesota). Retrieved from: https://cornerstone.lib.mnsu.edu/cgi/viewcontent.cgi?article=1233&context=etds; Matrix Knowledge Group, 'Dedicated drug court pilots a process report' (2008) Ministry of Justice Research Series 7/08. London: Ministry of Justice; Christine A. Saum & Matthew Hiller, 'Should violent offenders be excluded from drug court participation? An examination of the recidivism of violent and nonviolent drug court participants' (2008) Criminal Justice Review, 33(3), 291–307. Retrieved from: http://www.antoniocasella.eu/archila/saum_2008.pdf; Caroline Cooper & Joseph Trotter, 'Recent developments in drug case management: re-engineering the judicial process' (1994) Justice System Journal, 17(1), 83–96. doi: 10.1080/23277556.1994.10871194; U.S. General Accounting Office, 'Adult drug court evidence indicates recidivism reductions and mixed results for other outcomes' (2005) Report to Congressional Committees. Retrieved from: https://www.gao.gov/new.items/d05219.pdf.
45 National Offender Management Service (n 10).
46 Kerr et al. (n 38).

Table 4.2 Frequency Table Displaying Criminal Offences Recoded into Violent and Non-Violent Offences

Recode 1	Phase 1	Phase 2
	%	%
Non-violent	84.4	76.5
Violent	15.6	23.5
Total	100%	100%

recoded into violent vs. non-violent and acquisitive vs. non-acquisitive typologies to nuance its impact.

First, criminal offences were recoded into violent/non-violent offences because traditional drug courts do not permit participation of the former cohort.[47] Reasons for this have been cited as public safety as well as problems justifying public spending to the community for offenders deemed menacing.[48] Results showing the drug court outcomes for this population are conflicting; whereas some studies have demonstrated that they perform well or are as equally likely to succeed as their non-violent counterparts,[49] other studies have found the opposite effect.[50]

Table 4.2 confirms that most offenders at Manchester Review Court were non-violent (84.4%). As some service-users (15.6%) committed violent offences, there might be lowered effectiveness amongst this demographic in light of research demonstrating this effect.[51] This links to England and Wales' predecessor research, which also reported that violent offenders were unrestricted at the original drug courts, although as at Manchester Review Court, this cohort formed the minority. Offences under this bracket in the old models were cited as: assault occasioning actual bodily harm, threatening behaviour, and possession of an offensive weapon.[52] These are similar to the violent crimes at Manchester cited in Table 4.1. The similarities in eligibility between the original drug courts and Manchester are likely to be linked to the fact that the DRR itself lies at the heart of both models. However, this fact alone makes the UK models unique to their corresponding international drug court counterparts. Their wider inclusion

47 (n 44) (all).
48 Saum & Hiller (ibid).
49 Ibid; Christine A. Saum, Frank R. Scarpitti, & Cynthia A. Robbins, 'Violent offenders in drug court' (2001) *Journal of Drug Issues*, 31(1), 107–128.
50 Ojmarrh Mitchell, David B. Wilson, Amy Eggers, & Doris L. MacKenzie, 'Drug courts' effects on criminal offending for juveniles and adults' (2012) Campbell Systematic Reviews, 8(1), i–87; Deborah Koetzle Shaffer, 'Looking inside the black box of drug courts: a meta-analytic review' (2011) *Justice Quarterly*, 28(3), 493–521. doi: 10.1080/07418825.2010.525222.
51 Saum & Hiller (n 44).
52 Kerr et al. (n 38).

Table 4.3 Frequency Table Displaying Criminal Offences Recoded into Theft and Non-Theft Offences

Recode 2	Phase 1	Phase 2
	%	%
acquisitive	67.4	64.7
non-acquisitive	39.1	35.3
Total	100 %	100%

better parallels looser methods of problem-solving practice, such as Hawaii's Opportunity Probation with Enforcement ('HOPE') programme, which also accepts a wider and violent cohort.[53]

Second, offences were recoded into acquisitive/non-acquisitive offences in line with a traditional drug court's eligibility.[54] For this recode, burglary was understood as an acquisitive crime although some research has shown that drug courts are less effective for property crimes.[55] It was included in this code because according to Manchester City Council,[56] approximately 42% of acquisitive crimes detected in the region of Manchester are linked to drug use, including 42% of robbery offences and 45% of burglaries. As such, the offence of burglary is relevant to the court meeting its objectives in the city of Greater Manchester. Moreover, according to the National Treatment Agency burglary is categorised as an offence that often fuels drug addiction.[57]

Table 4.3 confirms that most service-users fell into the acquisitive category (p1 = 67.4%; p2 = 64.7%). This stacks up with wider regional statistics approximated by Manchester City Council showing high levels of acquisitive crime in Manchester. Although these fairly high percentages indicate that most

53 Lorana Bartels, 'Looking at Hawaii's opportunity with probation enforcement (HOPE) program through a therapeutic jurisprudence lens' (2016) QUT Law Review, 16, 30; Lorana Bartels, 'Swift, certain and fair: does project HOPE provide a therapeutic paradigm for managing offenders?' (Springer, 2017); Lorana Bartels, 'HOPE-ful bottles: examining the potential for Hawaii's opportunity probation with enforcement (HOPE) to help mainstream therapeutic jurisprudence' (2019) *International Journal of Law and Psychiatry*, 63, 26–34.
54 McSweeney et al. (n 12).
55 Shannon Carey, Michael Finigan, & Kimberly Pukstas, 'Exploring the key components of drug courts: a comparative study of 18 adult drug courts on practices, outcomes and costs' (2008) Portland, OR: NPC Research. Retrieved from: https://www.ncjrs.gov/pdffiles1/nij/grants/223853.pdf.
56 Manchester City Council, 'Tackling alcohol and drug related crime. Manchester City Council' (2015). Retrieved from: https://secure.manchester.gov.uk/download/meetings/id/2 0099/6_alcohol_and_drug_related_crime [Accessed 15 August 2017].
57 National Treatment Agency, 'Breaking the link' (2009). Retrieved from: http://www.fead.org.uk/wp-content/uploads/2015/09/nta_criminaljustice_0809.pdf [Accessed 1 July 2020].

participants at Manchester Review Court committed acquisitive crimes, the fact that that some fall within the non-acquisitive bracket again shows broader and less restrictive eligibility compared to a traditional drug court. Similarly to the violence code, court eligibility in this area more expressly parallels looser versions of problem-solving practice, including Fort Worth's (Texas) Supervision With Immediate Enforcement ('SWIFT') court and HOPE (aforementioned). These adaptations of problem-solving courts have higher foci on punitivism and deterrence than a traditional drug court, which arguably justifies a less stringent eligibility spanning violent and non-acquisitive groups. These international models accept offenders from all offence categories, other than sexual.[58] This finding links to Kerr, et al.[59] who also reported that non-acquisitive crime types featured in the predecessor courts, which is again due to the core DRR element predominating in both UK examples.

Notwithstanding points about fidelity, the broader eligibility gives better scope to instil key rehabilitative outcomes across a range of wider individuals with relief from drug court cherry-picking critiques.[60] The same point was noted about HOPE: '[it] has the potential to reach far more participants than drug courts'.[61] Furthermore, the amount and intensity of the drug treatment delivered under the DRR can be tailored to individual needs regardless of its length or the seriousness of offence.[62] This is a well-renowned therapeutic-jurisprudence principle, where a flexible bottle leaves space for rehabilitative therapeutic ideals, the most commonly cited example being the Spanish Juez de Vigilancia Penitenciaria system, which allows conditional release to be granted depending on both the length of time served and offenders' behavioural record, which can enhance wellbeing by motivating rehabilitation and helping to identity and build strengths that encourage pro-social behaviours.[63] As the JVP system offers itself as a friendly bottle, so does the DRR in respect of this versatility.

4.2.1.2.2 SUBSTANCE TYPE

UK policy states that DRR participants can be using substances either single-handedly, in combination, and/or in addition to alcohol to be eligible for the

58 Kelle Stevens-Martin, 'The SWIFT court: tackling the issue of high-risk offenders and chronic probation violators' (2014) Corrections Today. http://www.aca.org/aca_prod_imis/ Docs/Corrections%20Today/2014%20Articles/Sept%20Articles/Martin.pdfn [Accessed 2 July 2020].
59 Kerr et al. (n 38).
60 Tracey Velázquez, 'The verdict on drug courts' (9 December 2010). https://www.thenatio n.com/article/archive/verdict-drug-courts/ [Accessed 2 July 2020].
61 Bartels (2016) (n 53), page 6.
62 National Offender Management Service (n 10).
63 David B. Wexler, 'Moving forward on mainstreaming therapeutic jurisprudence: an ongoing process tofacilitate the therapeutic design and application of the law TJ' (2014). Paper 6. https://papers.ssrn.com/sol3/papers.cfm?abstract_id=2564613 [Accessed 16 August 2018].

Table 4.4 Frequency Table Displaying Main Drug Type for Phase 1 and 2

Drug Type	Phase 1 %	Phase 2 %
Heroin	22.9	17.6
Crack cocaine	10.4	11.8
Cocaine	2.1	5.9
Mix	64.6	64.7
Total	100%	100%

DRR.[64] Table 4.4 discloses the drug typologies for the Manchester Review Court cohort. 'Mix' refers to polysubstance individuals who had problems with more than one main illicit or licit drug type, although tobacco was excluded as it is an underlying cause of criminal activity. Table 4.4 shows that most cases fell within the 'mix' drug type for both phases (p1 = 64.6%; p2 = 64.7%). In a study that compared the frequency and patterns of mono and poly drug abuse, Kedia, et al.[65] stated that: 'the interaction among multiple drugs can heighten the neurological, physiological, and psychological impact on the user as well as potentially increase the negative consequences of poly drug abuse'. This suggests that the addictions of polysubstance users have more complexity than singular users, arguably by enduring a more difficult recovery process combining with other issues. This could indicate that Manchester Review Court is less effective for polysubstance users compared to their single-user counterparts. However, this is not a distinguishing feature from a fidelity perspective, because the same demographic is also accepted by the international models.[66]

The most prevalent single-use drug type at Manchester Review Court was heroin (p1 = 22.9%; p2 = 17.6%), crack cocaine was the second (p1 = 10.4%; p = 11.8%), and cocaine powder the least (p1 = 2.1%; p2 = 5.9%) for both Phases 1 and 2. Other drug types did feature (alcohol, methamphetamine, marijuana, synthetic cannabinoids), although they were always combined with another drug, so were included in the 'mix' code. Prevalence of the former two drug types links to national evidence suggesting that individuals who are dependent on opioids and/or crack cocaine are responsible for an estimated 45% of acquisitive crime (shoplifting, burglary, vehicle crime, and robbery).[67]

---

64 National Offender Management Service (n 10).
65 Satish Kedia, Maria Sell, & George Relyea, 'Mono- versus polydrug abuse patterns among publicly funded clients' (2007) Subst Abuse Treat Prev Policy. doi:10.1186/1747-597X-2-33.
66 Ciska Wittouck, Anne Dekkers, Brice De Ruyver, Wouter Vanderplasschen, & Freya Vander Laenen, 'The impact of drug treatment courts on recovery: a systematic review' (2012) Hindawi Publishing Corporation, *Scientific World Journal*, 2013, Article ID 493679. doi:10.1155/2013/493679.
67 Greater Manchester (n 24).

Empirical research augments that drug use and crime correlate particularly strongly amongst heroin users.[68] A local report by Regan, et al. (carried out around the time that data collection for this book was taking place) estimated that in Manchester there were 4,709 heroin and/or crack cocaine users aged between 15 and 64.[69] This was a rate of 12.97 per 1,000 of the population (1.3%), which is higher than the estimated rate for England (which is 8.40 per 1,000 of the population).[70] Notably, the city of Manchester is reported to have a far bigger problem with drugs and alcohol than other places in England.[71] Indeed, there has been a 74% rise in drug-related deaths in Greater Manchester over the last ten years, which translates to 480 deaths in the latest three-year tracking period (2015–17).[72] According to local documentation, if the figure for Greater Manchester was at the England average, this would equate to 136 fewer deaths per three-year period. Therefore, Manchester's special problem with heroin and crack cocaine substances are likely to explain the prevalence of these drug typologies within my study. These figures sit in line with broader court objectives, seeking to deal with problems with drug-fuelled recidivism, as well as highlighting the special need to tackle these issues at their root due to their prevalence in Greater Manchester.

An international study examining the characteristics of programme and participant population in 69 drug courts found that the average drugs of choice were as follows: methamphetamine (56%), cocaine (17%), heroin (12%), marijuana (26%), and alcohol (20%). This falls largely in line with the drug using typology from this study, confirming similarities between the UK and local models. A further study of two American drug courts in Escambia and Oskaloosa reported that for both courts, the most predominant single drug type was cocaine, followed by marijuana, and then alcohol.[73] The prevalence of the singular drug types (especially, heroin and cocaine) at Manchester Review Court, and the poly substance demographic, matches the international examples. In the previous report by Kerr, et al. (2011) no drug use figures were generated by researchers, making it impossible to comment on changes in service-users since 2011, or similarities between the UK models. However, we could conjecture that there were similarities, given that the DRR is the core element of both.

68 Mark Bryan, Emilia Bono, & Stephen Pudney, 'Drug-related crime' (2013) No. 2013-08 Institute for Social and Economic Research.
69 David Regan, 'Manchester City Council report for information' (2015) Manchester City Council Item 5Health Scrutiny Committee. Retrieved from: https://democracy.manches ter.gov.uk/Data/Health%20Scrutiny%20Committee/20151029/Agenda/5._Reform_of_ Public_Health.pdf [Accessed 2 July 2020].
70 Ibid.
71 Greater Manchester (n 24).
72 Ibid.
73 Roger H. Peters & Mary R. Murrin, 'Effectiveness of treatment-based drug courts in reducing criminal recidivism' (2000) Criminal Justice and Behavior, 27, 72.

Table 4.5 Frequency Table Displaying Age Groups for Phase 1 and Phase 2

Age	Phase 1	Phase 2	Overall
	%	%	%
18–25	13.8	21.4	17.6
26–35	10.3	28.6	19.45
36–45	37.9	21.4	29.65
46–55	37.9	28.6	33.25
Total	100.0	100.0	

4.2.1.2.3 AGE

Table 4.5 shows that most participants were older: 36–45 (second eldest, second highest) and 46–55 (eldest, highest) and fewer participants dominated the lower age brackets: (18–25 and 25–36). This strongly suggests that the non-attendance cohort was populated by a younger demographic (discussed later under Component 1 of this chapter: 'attendance problems'). Demographics collected for the original drug courts showed that just under half (45%) of participants were between 26 and 35 years old across all sites.[74] My study therefore confirms an increase in older participants since 2011.

The older demographic could be explained by a study conducted by Hansten, et al. demonstrating that attrition rates tended to be higher amongst younger drug court participants,[75] although non-attendance of court sessions does not necessarily indicate withdrawal from the DRR. Mendoza, et al.[76] hypothesised that this correlation between age and attrition was because younger individuals had greater problems with substance use compared to older individuals. This could be linked to Maturation Reform Theory, which posits criminality begins to reduce after the age of 25.[77] A 2015 study corroborated this theory by demonstrating that crime levels incline prior to mid-twenties, and then decline afterwards.[78] In the context of the theory, this is when individuals mature and crave stable lifestyles consistent with social and legal norms. Shannon, et al. have also

---

74 Kerr et al. (n 38).

75 Michelle L. Hansten, Lois Downey, David B. Rosengren, & Dennis M. Donovan, 'Relationship between follow-up rates and treatment outcomes in substance abuse research: more is better but when is 'enough' enough?' (2000) Addiction, 95(9), 1403–1416.

76 Natasha S. Mendoza, Jessica V. Linley, Thomas N. Nochajski, & Mark G. Farrell, 'Attrition in drug court research: examining participant characteristics and recommendations for follow-up' (2013) Journal of Forensic Social Work, 3(1), 56–68. doi:10.1080/19369 28X.2013.837418.

77 Sheldon Glueuk & Elenour Gleuk, *Juvenile delinquents grown up* (New York: Commonwealth Fund, 1940).

78 Michael Rocque, Posick Chad, & Hoyle Justin, 'Age and crime' in Wesley G. Jennings, George E. Higgins, Mildred M. Maldonado-Molina, & David N. Khey (eds.) *Encyclopedia of crime and punishment* (1–8) (Hoboken, NJ: John Wiley & Sons), [2015].

shown that older participants are more likely to be successful in community-based criminal justice involvement, presumably due to increased maturity.[79] In line with these principles, it could be that older attendees were able to keep on track of appointments due to higher human recovery capital,[80] higher motivation levels,[81] and/or living in social conducive support.[82] This sits in line with statistics suggesting that there has been a 48% increase in hospital admissions related to substance misuse amongst those aged 15–24 over the last 6 years in Greater Manchester. Moreover, rate of admissions per 100,000 population aged 15–24 years in Greater Manchester is 31% higher than the rate in England. As such, the younger demographic is already complex and troublesome, but particularly so for the city of Manchester. This may contextualise the findings from this study.

However, the figures in Table 4.5 stand in opposition to statistics portrayed by the British Drugs Survey suggesting that although 31% of 16–24-year-olds admitted to having taken drugs, 35–44-year-olds were the biggest users of drugs with nearly half (47%) of this age group having taken them.[83] They also fall out of kilter with large-scale international drug court research that examined 90 participants in a city in Texas, finding that participants of a younger age dominated the sample, and the mean age was 32.3 years.[84] The same study showed that a younger cohort tended to be less successful in drug courts; however, this was by a small margin. Taking these findings and theories as a whole, there is no consistent explanation of why older users dominated the sample in this study; however, it is likely to be linked to maturity and attrition. Although the raw figures at Manchester, which has an older cohort, do not stack up with the inter-

---

doi:10.1002/9781118519639.wbecpx275 isbn: 9781118519639. https://digitalcommons.georgiasouthern.edu/crimjust-criminology-facpubs/120.

79 Lisa Shannon, Afton Jackson, Jennifer Newell, Elizabeth Perkins, & Connie Neal, 'Examining factors associated with treatment completion in a community-based program for individuals with criminal justice involvement' (2015) Addiction Science & Clinical Practice, 10(Suppl 1), A60. doi:10.1186/1940-0640-10-S1-A60.

80 William Cloud & Robert Granfield, 'Conceptualizing recovery capital: expansion of a theoretical construct' (2008) Substance Use and Misuse, 43(12–13), 1971–1986. doi: 10.1080/10826080802289762; William Cloud & Robert Granfield, 'Social context and "natural recovery": the role of social capital in the resolution of drug-associated problems' (2001) Substance Use and Misuse, 36(11), 1543–1570.

81 Center for Substance Abuse Treatment, 'Enhancing motivation for change in substance abuse treatment' (1999) Rockville (MD): Substance Abuse and Mental Health Services Administration (US) (Treatment Improvement Protocol (TIP) Series, No. 35) Chapter 1 – Conceptualizing Motivation and Change. Available from: https://www.ncbi.nlm.nih.gov/books/NBK64972/

82 L.J. Beckman, 'An attributional analysis of alcoholics anonymous' (1980) *Journal of Studies on Alcohol*, 41, 714–772.

83 Home Office National Statistics, 'Drug misuse: findings from the 2013/14 crime survey for England and Wales' (2014). https://www.gov.uk/government/publications/drug-misuse-findings-from-the-2013-to-2014-csew/drug-misuse-findings-from-the-201314-crime-survey-for-england-and-wales [Accessed 2 July 2020].

84 Barbara Smith & John Martyn Chamberlain, 'Completion rates: an analysis of factors related to drug court program completion' (2017) Cogent Social Sciences, 3(1). doi: 10.1080/23311886.2017.1304500.

national evidence base, this is likely to be linked to the acute attendance problem that faced the court (see next heading of this component).

To conclude the analysis of Component 1 so far, the pillars of Manchester Review Court and traditional international models bear a resemblance. Although the strategic objectives of Manchester Review Court were inexplicit in the literature, we could infer that they were on a par with those of a traditional model, namely: to reduce drug-fuelled reoffending. In terms of meeting these goals, Manchester Review Court appeared to demonstrate successes, but this should be clarified through further analysis. If DRR objectives mirror those of a traditional drug court, which have a strong evidence base, this could suggest that an orthodox model aligning with the international gold standard should be attempted, or at least should provide a groundwork of best-practice principles.

When scrutinising the demographics of clients from Manchester Review Court, there were some stark similarities to the international examples, namely, the drug classifications, especially the prevalence of poly substance offenders, and heroin and cocaine within the singular classes. However, there were also differences; these manifested themselves mostly within offence typologies; the UK versions (including the original drug courts) accept a broader range of eligible participants from the violent and non-acquisitive brackets, better reflecting alternative problem-solving methods, like HOPE and SWIFT. There was also a higher proportion of older individuals compared to the original drug courts and internationally, which is most likely linked to Manchester Review Court's attendance problem. Overall, this analysis has unveiled some fidelity to Component 1 (objectives; drug types), though it was inconsistent. Non-compliance to the international drug court blueprint was mostly found in the area of offence demographics (accepting violent and non-acquisitive offenders). Moreover, key aspects of the court, including eligibility and objectives, should be configured within an operating document to comply with Component 1 stating that 'documents defining the drug court's mission, goals, eligibility criteria, operating procedures, and performance measures are collaboratively developed, reviewed, and agreed upon' and to ensure consistent understanding.[85]

What is also emerging are similarities between the findings in this book and those for the predecessor drug courts. Areas of fidelity and infidelity are largely equivalent. Although this is likely to be because the DRR foregrounds both UK models; this very fact alone highlights fundamental similarities, as well as justifying generalisability of the data to all UK problem-solving courts with the DRR at the core. Moreover, it contributes to the developing question: is Manchester Review Court the ghost of Salford drug court?

4.2.1.3 Attendance problems

It would be useful during this early stage of the chapter to disclose the problems that the court faced with service-user attendance, given that this area has already

---

85 Ashcroft et al. (n 4) [1].

been touched upon. This issue first emerged as a problematic area from the ethnographic data, and was brought to light by the adjournment issues that will be documented under Component 10 (this chapter). However, numerical evidence was gleaned by examining court records, which illuminated significant issues in the area. During the time of this study, just over one third of registered DRR participants attended their court review sessions.[86] The socio-demographic profiling that has just been undertaken found that the data sample comprised largely older individuals. This suggests that the non-attendance cohort could be characterised by a younger age demographic. Although this was problematic from an empirical perspective because it limited the number of individuals available for participation, exposing and discussing this issue was an important qualitative bottle-level finding. The reasons for this problem will be explored in this section.

Section 210 (1) (a–e) of the Criminal Justice Act legislates for the DRR requirements.[87] It states that courts

> may (and must if the treatment and testing period is more than 12 months) … provide for each review of the requirement to be made … at a hearing held for the purpose by the court responsible for the order (a 'review hearing'), require the offender to attend each review hearing.

The crucial words here are 'must' and 'may' – the way that the provisions are written means that the court review aspect of any DRR *under* 12 months is technically a non-statutory requirement. Regular court review hearings to substantiate the DRR only become compulsory when the offender is sentenced to a DRR *over* 12 months. However, consider the following:

> I have only ever encountered a few individuals during my work with a longer DRR, most DRRs are between three to six months, whereas the other community order or suspended sentence requirements might continue for longer.[88]
>
> I read the reports from probation and all participants other than one had a DRR of over six months in length.[89]

If it is standard practice for probationers to be sentenced to shorter DRR lengths (of between three to six months), this means that court reviews fall into a legal blackhole for most participants, and technically become a non-legal requirement under section 210 of the Criminal Justice Act 2003.[90] It is probably no coincidence that the Legal Aid, Sentencing and Punishment of Offenders ('LASPO') Act 2012 removed the restriction for a minimum DRR length of 6 months around the time that the England and Wales drug court closures started to become

---

86 Ethnographic data collected by Anna Kawałek (file held with author).
87 (n 8), sections 210, 1a–e.
88 Participant II, interview data, collected by Anna Kawałek (file held with author).
89 Ethnographic data collected by Anna Kawałek (file held with author).
90 (n 8), section 210.

documented (shortly after publication of the 2011 report).[91] This is because from the perspective of UK problem-solving court sustainability, these two pieces of legislation are not congruent; whereas the LASPO Act 2012 removes the requirement for longer DRRs, it creates a vacancy in legal terms for courts to perform the DRR review under the Criminal Justice Act.[92]

This raises questions: was the non-legality of the court review causing the attendance problem? And did this cause the drug courts to peter out? My data showed this was linked to breach proceedings at probation, which are complicated by the fact that the court review is a non-legal requirement. Participants suggested that service-users are allowed three breaches of their broader DRR before the original sentence is reinstated. Non-attendance at court could constitute one breach, but not always – this rested on the discretion of probation officers. There was clear confusion on this topic amongst practitioners.

> At the moment it's up to the offender managers – they can choose to use [non-attendance at court] as one of the appointments towards a breach.[93]
>
> There are more circumstances that might well point to breach proceedings being instigated, rather than simply putting them down to three absences.[94]
>
> That's not to say, you don't miss it three times, then you won't be breached … failure to attend could constitute at some point a breach of the DRR.[95]

As well as demonstrating inconsistency regarding when and in what circumstances breach proceedings should be initiated by officers, these quotes illustrate that there is no fixed rule for whether non-attendance of court reviews constituted a DRR breach. This could mean that the cohort who consistently attended were those in threat of DRR breach by probation officers. This hypothesis stacks up with the data.

> I don't like coming all the time, but that's just part of the punishment. I've got to come to court, know what I mean? That's part of life … I've never missed any.[96]
>
> You have to, yes. I was going to chip today when I didn't see my name on the list.[97]
>
> It's just part of the order.[98]

These samples suggest that participants, all of whom were on DRRs of less than 12 months and who came from different probation companies, believed that the

---

91 National Offender Management Service (n 10).
92 (n 8), section 210.
93 Participant II, interview data, collected by Anna Kawałek (file held with author).
94 Participant I, interview data, collected by Anna Kawałek (file held with author).
95 Participant II, interview data, collected by Anna Kawałek (file held with author).
96 Participant I, interview data, collected by Anna Kawałek (file held with author).
97 Participant V, interview data, collected by Anna Kawałek (file held with author).
98 Participant III, interview data, collected by Anna Kawałek (file held with author).

court reviews were an embedded legal requirement and that not attending could thus warrant breach proceedings. This means that threat of breach improves attendance at court, but does not answer the question: why were only some individuals in threat of breach? The data gleaned that there were inconsistencies at offenders' respective probation services and hesitancy to breach offenders was linked to privatisation reforms brought forth by Chris Grayling's controversial policy, Transforming Rehabilitation,[99] triggered under David Cameron's (Conservative) administration as part of the austerity agenda.[100] With the rehabilitation of criminal offenders allegedly at its heart, this policy sought to reduce reoffending rates by remodelling the UK justice system. A major part of this involved splitting the nationalised probation services (previously run as probation trusts) by privatising 70% to contracted companies. It caused high-risk offenders to become managed by the state-run National Probation Service (public sector) ('NPS'), and low- to medium-risk offenders to be overseen by private contractors, Community Rehabilitation Companies (private sector) ('CRCs'),[101] including: Sodexo, Interserve, MTC Novo, and Working Links.[102] Note that most offenders (though not all) from this study were managed by CRCS given that they were deemed low risk.

The two-tiered split of probation subjected private companies to competitive business overtones whereby a payment-by-results scheme, placing financial decisions at national level,[103] meant that CRCs only received income when displaying visible outputs according to the binary rate (proportion of offenders who reoffend) and the frequency rate (the average number of re-offences per reoffender).[104] Since many Manchester DRRs were managed by CRCs,[105] this could mean that probationary breaches were prone to a relaxed attitude if it was considered a lack of result. The data consolidates this point:

> It's definitely more lenient than it was ... because there's a cost implication now.[106]

> With it being a private company, any breach has a cost implication, so I think they're encouraged not to breach people.[107]

99 Ministry of Justice, 'Transforming rehabilitation: a strategy for reform' (2013). Retrieved from https://consult.justice.gov.uk/digital-communications/transforming-rehabilitation/results/transforming-rehabilitation-response.pdf.
100 Hardeep Matharu, 'Private companies running failing probation services must be made publicly accountable' (Byline, 2013). https://www.byline.com/column/71/article/1827 [Accessed 2 July 2020].
101 Offender Rehabilitation Act, 2015.
102 Matharu (n 100).
103 With Her Majesty's Prison and Probation Service.
104 Phil Bowen & Jane Donoghue, 'Digging up the grassroots? The impact of marketisation and managerialism on local justice, 1997 to 2013' (2013) British Journal of Community Justice, 9–2.
105 Ethnographic data collected by Anna Kawałek (file held with author); Participant II, interview data, collected by Anna Kawałek (file held with author).
106 Participant II, interview data, collected by Anna Kawałek (file held with author).
107 Ibid.

> If it is that privatisation has occurred, the first question to ask would be … is it that profit is an issue for them and how much does that relate to how they administer breaches and whether fees arise as a result?[108]

If shorter DRRs possess no statutory obligation for court review under section 210 of the Criminal Justice Act, it is easy to see why a lenient attitude to this area of the DRR might arise. Although some transparency is provided when financial penalties are made by Her Majesty's Prison and Probation Service, according to Ian Lawrence (the general secretary of the National Association of Probation Officers), accountability was troublesomely low: 'they [CRCs] should not run those contracts. You cannot expect people who are making a profit from justice to take a detached view about what is the right system to use [to supervise offenders]'.[109] He further described the part-privatised probation system as 'chaos' and 'broken'.[110]

This may be overcome by statutory support mandating the review for shorter DRRs. This would mean replacing the current 12-month requirement to a lower threshold, for instance 3 months, under section 210. Whilst suggesting statutory change may seem far-fetched, it sits in line therapeutic jurisprudence goals to reform an unfriendly bottle: 'if the law itself does not seem to permit much use of therapeutic jurisprudence, then the question of the propriety of actual law reform would come to the fore'.[111] This change would give all DRR reviews coverage under the Criminal Justice Act, thereby regulating breaches at probation companies, despite recent renationalisation of the companies. With the limited number of UK courts dedicated to problem-solving, to avoid this new statutory provision overburdening the mainstream courts it is perhaps better qualified with: 'if the offender lives within the jurisdiction of a problem-solving court'. More reviews could be accommodated if current projection plans to roll out problem-solving courts across England and Wales are successful.[112]

Another way to surmount this hurdle could be to lengthen all DRRs; their customarily short length already detracts from the reality of recovery and desistence narratives, which are evidenced to take several years, especially when accounting for early-stage relapse.[113] Perhaps ironically within a therapeutic-jurisprudence rationale, a longer (and therefore more punitive) DRR may incur better responses

---

108 Participant I, interview data, collected by Anna Kawałek (file held with author).
109 Matharu (n 100).
110 Ibid.
111 David B. Wexler, 'New wine in new bottles: the need to sketch a therapeutic jurisprudence "code" of proposed criminal processes and practices' (2014) Arizona Summit Law Review, 7, 463–480 [3].
112 Phil Bowen & Stephen Whitehead, 'Problem-solving courts: a delivery plan' (2016) Justice Innovation Charity; Ministry of Justice, 'A Smarter Approach to Sentencing' (2020) White Paper.
113 Shadd Maruna, *Making good: how ex-convicts reform and rebuild their lives* (Washington, DC: American Psychological Association, 2011).

by allowing the authorities to oversee the full reformation process, as well as providing coverage under current statute. Longer DRRs also sit in line with punitive populism currently characterising UK cultural justice modalities and thus may be easier to justify to the public (cf. Chapter 2). It also mimics the longer sentences given to offenders within more successful UK problem-solving courts, like Prolific Intensive ('PI') and Choices and Consequences ('C2').[114]

Looking elsewhere, poor attendance at Manchester Review Court could be linked to court accessibility made pertinent by the structural changes to magistrates courts across England and Wales directed by the Courts Act 2003 under section 6 (documented in Chapter 3: harnessing therapeutic support).[115] Remember that this key piece of legislation has centralised the courts across Britain, and continues to do so.[116] During the course of this study, Manchester's Central Magistrates' Court had already taken on the work of the Salford (2012) court (including arguably its drug court) and Bury (2017) magistrates' courts, and had forthcoming plans to integrate Bolton.[117] By significantly broadening the court's catchment area from Central Manchester to Greater Manchester, which covers nearly 500 square miles,[118] effects on the DRR are profound. As the ambit of the model expands, individuals must attend appointments (probation, reviews, treatment, and medical) across a significantly broader geographical radius (for more detail see Component 7, Chapter 3). Even after only these early merges, attending court reviews was a clear problem; one individual stated that he had walked *two hours* from home to make a court review.[119] With further court centralisation reforms on the horizon, this issue is likely to worsen. Relief could be given to this issue: it was reported that some DRR service-users were entitled to a free bus pass from the probation services. Not all held this entitlement, which is most likely linked to austerity, but also because DRRs were too short to justify this expenditure – another reason that they should be lengthened. Many participants (i.e. attendees) reported that they were in receipt of a bus pass, suggesting that they encouraged attendance. Given the number of DRR appointments that require attendance across the city, providing bus passes could be a workable

---

114 Michael Baker, 'Choices and consequences – an account of an experimental sentences programme' (2014) Criminal Law Review. Issue 1 Thomson Reuters (Professionals) UK Limited.

115 Courts Act, 2003, section 6.

116 Ibid; Penelope Gibbs, 'Return magistrates' courts to local control' (The Law Society Gazette, 3 June 2013). https://www.lawgazette.co.uk/analysis/return-magistrates-courts-to-local-control/71223.article [Accessed 1 July 2020]; Rob Allen, 'Rehabilitation devolution – how localising justice can reduce crime and imprisonment' (2015) *Transform Justice*. Retrieved from: http://www.transformjustice.org.uk/wp-content/uploads/2015/12/TRANSFORM-JUSTICE-REHABILITATION-DEVOLUTION.pdf ; Bowen & Donoghue (n 105).

117 Ethnographic data collected by Anna Kawałek (file held with author).

118 Participant II, interview data, collected by Anna Kawałek (file held with author); Participant I, interview data, collected by Anna Kawałek (file held with author).

119 Ethnographic data (date 9) collected by Anna Kawałek (file held with author).

solution. There is no point spending public money on the DRR to rehabilitate individuals if participants cannot attend the appointments that are designed to help them. Provisions should be put in place to enable their attendance, including spending on bus passes to enable the project to run better.

Elsewhere, another staff member rationalised that the reason for non-attendance could be:

> The weather, the football, traffic, traffic problems, and road closures ... or it might well be the fact that it is a courthouse and they're expecting a more adversarial hearing, where they're going to be put on the spot, and that's something that nobody wants.[120]

This demonstrates that it was not always clear from the perspective of staff why some individuals persistently failed to attend. Although the data is not conclusive on this matter, the strongest and most plausible explanation is seemingly a combination of bottle problems, including: the privatisation of probation and its payment-by-results model; vacancy in DRR legislation; shortening the standard DRR length and; court centralisation reforms make court accessibility harder. For these reasons, we can conclude that the bottle is not ready for therapeutic jurisprudence and that Manchester Review Court fails to sufficiently support magistrates' good efforts. However, the data under this component also suggests that Manchester had positive impacts on key objectives, and service-users were largely positive about the court and its impact on recovery and reoffending. As such, rectifying these systemic issues would provide fruitful outcomes for England and Wales, and more specifically Manchester, currently face. It is interesting to point out that based upon the 2011 written evidence, the predecessor drug courts did not seem to face the same problems with attendance.[121] Could the reason be that a year after its publication, enactment of the LASPO Act 2012 shortened DRR lengths, creating a black hole for the court review in statute causing them to peter out? If so, this only suggests that they were incepted based on a poorly thought out conceptual model that failed to account for unconducive bottle factors.

4.2.1.4 Drug Court Component 2

Under Component 2, the international drug court body states that: 'to facilitate an individual's progress in treatment, the prosecutor and defence counsel must shed their traditional adversarial courtroom relationship and work together as a team'.[122] As such, the emphasis of this component is on non-adversarial lawyering, and a more general shift in court culture towards teamwork. Figure 4.1

---

120 Participant I, interview data, collected by Anna Kawałek (file held with author); Participant I, interview data, collected by Anna Kawałek (file held with author).
121 Kerr et al. (n 38).
122 Ashcroft et al. (n 4).

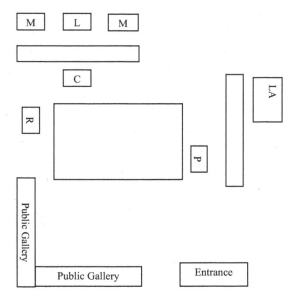

Figure 4.1 The court layout.

displays the composition of the team at Manchester Review Court, where it is worth noting my position ('R') during data collection. The following personnel were present during reviews: probation officer ('P'), legal advisor ('LA'), one or two panel magistrates ('M'), one lead magistrate ('LM'), and the service-user ('C').[123] The team approach was achieved in a weaker design than the international gold standard in light of three notable differences:

- No individual from the treatment team attended court;
- Service-users were consistently represented by one presiding probation officer (otherwise known as a point-of-contact officer) rather than their own officer;
- No defence or prosecuting lawyers took part during the reviews (offenders were instead represented by the probation officer).

Before discussing these bullet points, it is worth noting that the court layout was a unique facet that distinguished Manchester Review Court from the regular courts:

> Its finish and layout are different to the adversarial courtroom ... the court furniture is different ... the tables and chairs can be moved around. It's more of an informal setting rather than fixed benches and a raised platform that the

123 Ethnographic data collected by Anna Kawałek (file held with author).

magistrates sit on. Magistrates do not sit higher up than defendants. There is no dock in the DRR court. There is no witness stand. It is just tables assembled together in a square shape.[124]

As indicated by this quotation and by Figure 4.1, Manchester Review Court was configured to enable close physical proximity between service-users and other stakeholders within a 'square shape'.[125] This was thought to enhance the feeling of support, intimacy, and rapport across parties, and mimicked the substantive structure of a circle of support advanced by many restorative justice practices.[126] Magistrates did not sit on a higher level, thus replacing a traditional hierarchical setup, and sessions were more informal, which was reflected by service-users' mannerism and body language. This can be compared to individuals' first sessions, when they tended to be more formal, which relaxed over time, and advanced participants were open when discussing their life situations with magistrates.[127] My conversations with first-timers after the sessions revealed surprise and gratitude at the friendly reception from magistrates, and service-users commented positively on the court's informality:

Everyone is really down to earth, I'm very impressed. They (magistrates) are very easy-going; very on a level.[128]

Pleasantly surprised.[129]

Many individuals appeared pleasant, contented, and calm when waiting for their review.[130]

First-timers in particular presented as relieved and contented with their experience, and often left the courtroom smiling and thanking magistrates repeatedly.[131]

The roles of all staff at Manchester Review Court had a renewed focus on rehabilitation, and this was reflected in the content of their conversations with participants, which would concern life circumstances, relationships, treatment, appointments, and health, etc., rather than the legal case (cf. Chapter 3). Magistrates possessed therapeutic interpersonal skills with the purpose of motivating and reviewing progress (cf. Chapter 3), the legal advisor performed administrative rather than legal tasks, and the presence of probation, who might not otherwise attend, facilitated multi-agency collaboration as they became a pivot between relevant agencies

124 Participant I, interview data, collected by Anna Kawałek (file held with author).
125 Ibid.
126 Howard Zehr, *The little book of restorative justice* (Intercourse, PA: Good Books, 2002).
127 Ethnographic data (various dates) collected by Anna Kawałek (file held with author).
128 Participant V, interview data, collected by Anna Kawałek (file held with author).
129 Survey data Phase 2 dataset, collected by Anna Kawałek (file held with author).
130 Ethnographic data collected by Anna Kawałek (file held with author).
131 Ethnographic data collected by Anna Kawałek (file held with author).

(such as, drug treatment, housing, and individual probation officers).[132] These properties sit in line with the statement under Component 2; 'once a defendant is accepted into the drug court programme, the team's focus is on the participant's recovery and law-abiding behavior – not on the merits of the pending case'.

Notably, the old UK drug courts' multidisciplinary team operated with more fidelity to this area by inviting the attendance of multiple agencies, including drugs workers.[133] In the earlier parts of this study, I had an interesting interaction with a legal advisor, who sat in Salford drug court prior to the court centralisation initiatives, but had not worked in the review court since the merge. When preparing for the afternoon session, he was confused as to the whereabouts of the multidisciplinary team and asked me if I was the drugs worker whilst I sat in the public gallery data collecting. What is notable about this comment is that, first, it highlights that fidelity was instated more successfully in the old drug court models, thus providing practical endorsement to the findings from Kerr, et al.[134] Second, it suggests that key personnel believed that Manchester Review Court was a centralised version of the old Salford drug court. This is significant as it perhaps gives the clearest original evidence that, from the perspective of key practitioners, the review court was the remains of the original drug courts.[135]

The original UK drug courts operated when Probation Trusts were still in action prior to the activation of Grayling's 2014 policy, Transforming Rehabilitation (already discussed under Component 1). This meant that participants' own probation officers, rather than a single point of contact, could come to court to provide offender support and authentic exchanges of information. However, a part of Transforming Rehabilitation disabled officers from CRCs a right of audience in court during sentencing decisions.[136] As a result, CRC officers were not able to attend; losing this voice in court resulted in Manchester Review Court losing fidelity to the international framework by exacerbating fragmentation. However, since no sentencing took place in this court (cf. discussion of Component 6), there is no reason that CRC officers should not come to court to represent participants. Although there is no point suggesting change to this area given that the probation services have been renationalised, this finding is odd and is perhaps more indicative of high workloads or is a reflection of private officers feeling alienated from this domain following the probation split.

132 Participant I, interview data, collected by Anna Kawałek (file held with author); ethnographic data collected by Anna Kawałek (file held with author); Participant II, interview data, collected by Anna Kawałek (file held with author).

133 Kerr et al. (n 38).

134 Notably they stated that drugs workers sometimes, but not always, attended.

135 Participant I, interview data, collected by Anna Kawałek (file held with author); ethnographic data collected by Anna Kawałek (file held with author).

136 Stephen Whitehead, 'Community sentences case study: embedded CRC presence at Teeside Magistrates Court' (Justice Innovation, 2019). https://justiceinnovation.org/articles/community-sentences-case-study-embedded-crc-presence-teeside-magistrates-court [Accessed 1 July 2020].

Looking at other areas of Component 2, the fact that defence and prosecution solicitors were not present in any of the UK models makes them different from the international drug courts and falls out of line with the guidance under this component. Notwithstanding the points about fidelity, their absence was interpreted positively by service-users:

> It feels different without the lawyers there – less formal.[137]
>
> It's a lot less daunting. Instead of having to speak through a solicitor you actually get to talk to them yourself, which is obviously better because you're getting your voice heard. This is good, fairer.[138]

Compare the latter quotation to a data sample collected by researchers analysing the original drug courts: "'in the drug court they are actually talking to you. They're not interested in your solicitor … . they want to talk to you" (offender)'.[139] The similarities between the quotes for Manchester Review Court and the UK drug courts are palpable. This thus raises questions as to whether they are the same models, only in different guises.

The presence of lawyers was futile because no sentencing took place in the review court; placement onto the programme would occur in the regular courts and breaching for non-compliance of the order would occur at a specialist breach (and mainstream) court, both with the involvement of lawyers. Once the DRR had been accepted, and the individual was placed onto the programme, most of the main DRR work was followed up on at the probation offices (usually by the private Cheshire and Greater Manchester Community Rehabilitation Company although sometimes with the national office), including delivery, linkage, and recommendations to the treatment services, as well as the decision to breach for failure to comply with the order.[140] However, this structure was problematic because it minimalised the involvement of the court in the process.

I have already stated that the review court felt supplementary to the pre-eminent DRR, which is its own probation-led scheme that does not necessarily mandate a court review. Review is in fact an optional inclusion under section 210 of the Criminal Justice Act for DRRs of under twelve months. Each of the above-mentioned factors, including the absence of lawyering, served to make the court feel disjointed, ostracised, and sidelined from the main work. Again, this finding links to the 2011 research for the original drug courts where researchers made the same observation. If we go back even further into UK history, this also links to research for the DRR ancestors (the DTTOs), which noted this same relationship between

---

137 Ethnographic data collected by Anna Kawałek (file held with author).
138 Participant III, interview data, collected by Anna Kawałek (file held with author).
139 Kerr et al. (n 38) [27].
140 Cheshire and Greater Manchester Community Rehabilitation Company (CRC); Private Sector; Participant II, interview data, collected by Anna Kawałek (file held with author); ethnographic data collected by Anna Kawałek (file held with author); Participant I, interview data, collected by Anna Kawałek (file held with author).

the probation services and the courts.[141] For this reason, all UK models contravene the guidance made by the international body, which endorses the drug court as a central hub for multidisciplinary work.[142] This calls into question whether the titles of the original versions, assuming that of 'drug courts', were misnomers.

In this sense, the UK probationary-driven models have parity with the HOPE scheme, which is described throughout the work of Bartels as a supervision programme seeking to rehabilitate probationers from alcohol and other drugs-related offending,[143] like the DRR. By implementing a framework with supervision at the fore, the problem-solving court at HOPE possesses less weight than this aspect of a traditional drug court; Bartels notes that, 'unlike in drug courts, participants are only brought back to court in the event of breach'.[144] As such, though a court features through an introductory warning hearing (in the first instance) and breach proceedings (for breaching), most of the work is executed outside of the courtroom, at the probation services. However, there are also no intermittent review hearings at HOPE, like there are at Manchester. The design of Manchester Review Court thus straddles the original drug court model and HOPE; on the one hand, the court is merely an ancillary component to the main probationary aspect, like HOPE. On the other hand, Manchester features regular court check-ins, like the traditional drug courts (although with a different bench composition each hearing (cf. Chapter 3)). During problem-solving interactions, every version requires judicial officers to operationalise key solution-focused principles by employing a series of therapeutic-infused interpersonal styles to encourage positive behaviour in line with supervision goals.[145] Clearly, they sit within the same problem-solving court family; however, HOPE and Manchester operate with much looser fidelity to the international gold standard through the prominence of the probationary aspect.[146] An interesting contrast is that both international models rely on the presence of lawyers due to the sentencing powers given to judges in court, unlike Manchester Review Court (cf. Component 6: this chapter). Although this means that Manchester is non-compliant to both the HOPE and drug court blueprints, as we will see from the conclusion in this chapter, there is plausibility and integrity in borrowing a hybrid set of best-practice components from both international models when implementing future UK problem-solving courts, but only when they have a realistic delivery plan, are modelled on a well-considered conceptual framework and ascribe to best practice principles.

We can conclude the discussion of Component 2 by reporting that Manchester Review Court was non-compliant in this area. Although review hearings had a

---

141 McSweeney et al. (n 12).
142 Ashcroft et al. (n 4).
143 Bartels (all (n 53)).
144 Bartels (2016) ibid. [34].
145 Bartels (all (n 53)).
146 Ashcroft et al. (n 4).

refreshed focus on rehabilitation, and the physical layout helped to shape a thera-peutic court culture, non-adversarialism in a traditional sense under Component 2 could not be achieved because there were no lawyers present to cornerstone this approach. There were also no individual probation officers or drugs work-ers present in Manchester Review Court. These factors created a physical and metaphorical chasm between the review court and the other crucial elements of the DRR taking place elsewhere. Whilst the lack of lawyers makes Manchester Review Court unique in respect of many of the international efforts, including the authentic drug court and its sister model HOPE, the prevalence of the pro-bationary aspect does bear semblance to HOPE. That the same divide was also prevalent in the original English and Welsh drug courts, and even within their UK forerunners the DTTOs, contributes to the developing argument that there are similarities between all UK models, and hints that Manchester could be the survivor of the original drug courts. However, perhaps more alarming, it shows that all UK models, both past and present lacked fidelity to the international blueprint under Component 2 for similar reasons, which raises suspicions as to their authenticity both now and historically.

4.2.1.5 Drug Court Component 3

This component is concerned with the process by which eligible participants are enrolled onto the drug court programme and linked to the services. Through 'rapid and effective action',[147] promptness is thought to bring about court trans-parency and accountability and increase public confidence. There is little point outlining the process of enrolment at Manchester Review Court because this has not changed since Kerr, et al., whose research presented a diagram providing an 'overview of process from arrest to completion of a DRR within a pilot DDC'.[148] The fact that this process has not changed for Manchester Review Court under-lines similarities between the models. It is difficult to comment accurately on this because it was external to the court, whereas the main body of the empirical work was carried out physically at the courthouse. However, this finding alone serves to highlight the discussion point that the court was sidelined from the core process. Although most of the key performance benchmarks for this component within the international document relate specifically to the DRR itself, rather than the court reviews, this finding alone is telling of the court existing on the border of the main DRR work, and it not possessing the same foothold as the international models.

It is worth reviewing some key areas under the component so far as is possible, despite the fact that data could not be collected due to its externality. First, the international body states that 'eligibility screening is based on established written criteria' and that specialist officials are in place to identify potential participants.[149]

---

147 Kerr et al. (n 38) [2] (figure 1.1).
148 Stands for 'dedicated drug court'.
149 Ashcroft et al. (n 4) [5].

We know that eligibility criteria are outlined in the Criminal Justice Act[150] and repeated throughout policy documentation.[151] Probation officers, who specialise in this area, advise the sentencing courts on the benefits of the DRR, appropriateness, and relevant provisions, and make the final decision regarding programme placement.[152]

Second, the international body states that the participants must be promptly advised about the merits of participating. The Criminal Justice Act states that 'the offender expresses his willingness to comply with the requirement'.[153] This indicates that participant must be aware of the merits of compliance and the rewards for participating in the programme prior to enrolment, in alignment with the international advice.

Third, the international body states that 'trained professionals screen drug court-eligible individuals for alcohol and other drug problems and suitability for treatment'.[154] This drug court provision is again enshrined in the Criminal Justice Act under section 209 (1)[155] – 'specified person having the necessary qualifications or experience with a view to the reduction or elimination of the offender's dependency on or propensity to misuse drugs' – the 'specified person' being a probation officer.

Fourth, the international body states that 'initial appearance before the drug court judge occurs immediately after arrest or apprehension to ensure program participation'.[156] For outlined reasons, it is difficult to comment on the speed of this process. However, a key part involves sentencing by 'the drug court judge'[157]. The predecessor UK drug courts operated this, where it was reported that 'when an individual was sentenced to a DRR, the same district judge or panel of magistrates who sentenced the offender provided continuity in reviewing the offender's progress'.[158] However, we also know that this continuity is no longer implemented at Manchester Review Court due to problems associated with Component 7, including: lack of rota system, centralisation of the courts, and expanding the court's geographical radius (cf. Chapter 3).

Fifth, it is stated that 'the court requires that eligible participants enrol in alcohol and other drugs treatment services immediately'. Under Drug Court Component 4, I will detail that linkage to the services was not always efficient. However, section 209 (2)(b) touches on this by stating: 'a court may not impose

---

150 (n 8).
151 National Offender Management Service (n 10).
152 (n 8) '(a) it is satisfied – (i) that the offender is dependent on, or has a propensity to misuse, drugs, and (ii) that his dependency or propensity is such as requires and may be susceptible to treatment'.
153 (n 8) section 209 (2) (d).
154 Ashcroft et al. (n 4) [5].
155 (n 8) section 209 (1).
156 Ashcroft et al. (n 4) [5].
157 Ibid.
158 Kerr et al. (n 38) [3].

a drug rehabilitation requirement unless ... it is also satisfied that arrangements have been or can be made for the treatment intended to be specified in the order' – and therefore this is a legal requirement.

All of this shows that although direct data to substantiate this discussion could not be gleaned because the enrolment process took place externally to the review court, most of the international guidance under Component 3 was enshrined within the Criminal Justice Act.[159] Regardless of whether it was operated with fidelity, the statute shows that the DRR process, both at the Manchester court and in the original drug courts, at least attempted to mirror that of an international drug court in process. This could suggest that all UK models are/were striving to achieve the gold standard and to 'be' a 'drug court'. The fact that it was difficult to obtain data for this component during court visits illustrates the externality of many of its key elements. This is an important finding because it contributes to the discussion that Manchester Review Court was merely supplementary to the core DRR work and thus operated with infidelity to the international gold standard due to its lack of centrality. That the previous researchers were also quiet on this area, and since the enrolment process has always been the same, alludes to further conceptual, practical, and legal similarities between the UK models, which is likely to boil down to their governance by the Criminal Justice Act[160] and the fact that they each work with the DRR at the core and fore. Although the previous drug courts operated with more fidelity to the area through unification of sentencing and review judges, despite this and with hesitancy, given the limited authentic data to substantiate the discussion, it seems that there has been ongoing fidelity to Component 3, at least theoretically.

4.2.1.6 Drug Court Component 4

Under Component 4, the international body states that 'drug courts provide access to a continuum of alcohol, drug, and other related treatment and rehabilitation services'[161]. Moreover, they state that drug courts should be pillared by accessible, accountable, well-funded, and high-quality providers.[162] Without proper treatment, drug court efforts are fruitless, and the revolving-door cycle of crime is difficult to tackle at its root. However, participants' successful recovery does not rely exclusively on drug rehabilitation treatment and the court must cater for peripheral problems. This is reflected in the international drug court document within the following statement:

> The drug court team also needs to consider co-occurring problems such as mental illness, primary medical problems, HIV and sexually-transmitted diseases, homelessness; basic educational deficits, unemployment and poor job

159 (n 8).
160 Ibid.
161 Ashcroft et al. (n 4) [7].
162 Ibid.

preparation; spouse and family troubles – especially domestic violence – and the long-term effects of childhood physical and sexual abuse.[163]

I have already stated that the region of Greater Manchester has a high prevalence of drug and alcohol problems compared to other areas of England and Wales.[164] Furthermore, recent statistics suggest that upon entering drug and alcohol treatment in Greater Manchester, 22% of adults are in contact with mental health services, 15% of adults identify as having a housing problem, and 73% will not be in regular employment.[165] As such, problems with substances place increased pressure on services for both drug and alcohol treatment and other related domains. The extensiveness of these problems in Manchester makes crucial the successful application of Component 4 and efficient problem-solving courts more generally. I already stated during the discussion of Component 3 (this chapter) that under 209(1)(a) of the Criminal Justice Act, the legislation states that those sentenced to a DRR 'must submit to treatment by or under the direction of a specified person having the necessary qualifications or experience with a view to the reduction or elimination of the offender's dependency on or propensity to misuse drugs'. This suggests that to allow individuals to submit to treatment, as per the requirements of the statute, full and proper treatment support must be in place by law.[166] However, this does not always mean that this was applied well at Manchester Review Court and the upcoming sections seek to explore this sentiment.

4.2.1.6.1 ACCESSIBILITY, COMPREHENSIVENESS, FUNDING, AND ACCOUNTABILITY

Under Component 4, the international body states that; 'treatment facilities are accessible by public transportation, when possible'.[167] At Manchester Review Court, service-users were required to navigate many DRR appointments.[168] These occurred across a broad radius after court centralisation reforms had widened the geographical scope of the model under the Courts Act 2003, section 6. Although the treatment providers were located only two miles away from the court, this short distance does not account for the fact that probationers were coming from peripheral areas of Manchester. As already discussed under Component 1 (attendance), unfortunately only some probationers were supported by a bus pass which, if provided, could have easily alleviated issues with accessibility.[169] Already, therefore, Manchester Review Court is in breach of the international gold standard under this component.

---

163 Ibid.
164 Greater Manchester (n 24).
165 Ibid.
166 (n 8) section 209 (1) (a) 'the offender – must submit to treatment by or under the direction of a specified person having the necessary qualifications or experience with a view to the reduction or elimination of the offender's dependency on or propensity to misuse drugs'.
167 Ashcroft et al. (n 4) [9].
168 Participant I, interview data, collected by Anna Kawałek (file held with author).
169 Participant II, interview data, collected by Anna Kawałek (file held with author).

Elsewhere under this component, the international body states that 'funding for treatment is adequate, stable, and dedicated to the drug court'.[170] Given the UK's recent austerity measures, this area is worthy of particular scrutiny. Through the probation services, Manchester Review Court participants were referred to an umbrella wraparound drug and alcohol treatment service, Manchester Integrated Drug and Alcohol Service ('MIDAS'), who 'offer support to adults, young people, those in the criminal justice system and anyone looking to live a healthier and happier life'.[171] At MIDAS, a number of social interventions and groups are available to support recovery journeys that mostly revolve around addiction treatment. Support options for other life domains, such as housing and homelessness, domestic violence, relationship management, and financial problems, are also available at probation. Leaflets for many of these, and other addiction support groups, including Together Women, Alcohol Anonymous ('AA'), Narcotics Anonymous ('NA'), Shelter, Samaritans, the National Society for the Prevention of Cruelty to Children, Addiction Dependency Solutions, NHS Change for Life, and Barnabus,[172] were advertised on a noticeboard outside of the designated DRR court waiting room. Notably, this amplified the general feeling that the court had a recovery (rather than a legal) orientation, chiming with previous discussions around court culture and non-adversarialism under Component 2.[173] The vastness of support across a number of domains reflected the notion that a successful recovery is far-reaching, as already posited under Component 4.

Because the service providers were external to the review court, it is difficult to comment directly on quality. Paradoxically, drug treatment felt alien to the court and magistrates had little involvement in this aspect, which develops the argument that the court was sidelined from the main work. This contravenes the international advice: 'in a drug court, the treatment experience begins in the courtroom and continues through the participant's drug court involvement'[174]

Although they were external, from the court observations I had a sense that the services insufficiently supported the model. Participants would often complain to magistrates that they were not getting enough help.[175] *En masse*, the interview data stacked up with this observation.

> Probation is not massively useful ... there's not really much available there at all.[176]

> I've asked for help ... It's just not happening.[177]

170 Ashcroft et al. (n 4) [9].
171 MIDAS. https://www.investinmanchester.com/about-us/midas [Accessed 1 July 2020].
172 Participant II, interview data, collected by Anna Kawałek (file held with author); ethnographic data collected by Anna Kawałek (file held with author).
173 Ethnographic data collected by Anna Kawałek (file held with author).
174 Ashcroft et al. (n 4) [7].
175 Ethnographic data (various dates) collected by Anna Kawałek (file held with author).
176 Participant II, interview data, collected by Anna Kawałek (file held with author).
177 Participant V, interview data, collected by Anna Kawałek (file held with author).

In the first quotation, the homeless service-user was having difficulties accessing housing support. However, as his interview took place after his first review, one could speculate that he had not been enrolled long enough to have established the correct support. However, in the second quotation, the participant was struggling to access drug treatment specifically; since he was interviewed after his third review, following a three-month gap since his first court contact, it is unlikely that struggles with access were caused by being in an early stage of the intervention. This links to survey data where the majority (75%) of respondents either strongly agreed or agreed that 'there are enough treatment options available'. Although this seems like a relatively high percentage, it is low compared to other survey responses, especially those relating to the wine, which generally scored above 90%! However, negative feedback was not consistent; another participant gave more positive feedback and appeared to be proactive with attending appointments:

> I have a group every Friday, and then a community order group, the community order, and I'm on licence as well. He comes every week to see me – probation – every week without fail. Then, I go on my groups as well.[178]

An issue here is that he appears to conflate criminal justice appointments with treatment sessions. When asking for clarity, he stated:

> They give you enough [treatment options].[179]

This suggests that he had access to a suitable range of providers and was satisfied by the treatment support available. That some individuals felt that they had had a positive experience was clearly reflected in the statistic (75%). However, interestingly, despite the inconsistencies across service-user feedback, each quoted participant struggled with polysubstance dependence (cf. discussion of Component 1, this chapter), where we might expect similarities in addiction-type to be reflected by consistent feedback. Dissonant results could be linked to the fact that every recovery journey is different and has unique requirements.

> In terms of recovery, the court can provide that assistance. Obviously, it's a limited assistance. Some of that assistance might be the best thing that the defendant has ever had and is all that is necessary, but on some occasions, it might not be enough for the defendant and a lot more is necessary ... the court can only do so much.[180]

Staff agreed that the range of drugs services (particularly follow-up) was insufficient and had worsened with time due to funding cuts.

> The funding has been tough on everything. Things that were there just aren't there anymore. Like they used to have an organisation called 'lifeline'

178 Participant I, interview data, collected by Anna Kawałek (file held with author).
179 Ibid.
180 Ibid.

and they'd do cooking classes with people, they'd do art classes, music and other things, but I don't think that they are going anymore.[181]

This participant also identified that there are now significant delays for obtaining a prescription for methadone, unlike in her earlier working years, when these were instantly available.

> [Scripts] can sometimes take four to six weeks, maybe even eight … Somebody said to me once 'how much am I going to have to go out and steal? … if you'd have put me on the script the week after, I wouldn't have had to go and steal things to get drugs' … it's very different now to how it used to be when I first started. The support is no longer there.[182]

Since this staff member had only been working in this role for three and a half years, this highlights declination within a relatively short space of time. These findings sit in line with UK reforms to Public Health. The legislation of the Health and Social Care Act 2012[183] devolved statutory responsibility for health improvements from the National Health Service ('NHS') to local authorities, supported by a ring-fenced grant from Public Health England (an executive branch of the Department of Health and Social Care in England).[184] In the context of Greater Manchester itself, the Greater Manchester Combined Authority (Public Health Functions) Order 2017[185] deferred powers to the local mayor, who is currently Andy Burnham.[186] This means that the local authority is now responsible for how this money is spent. Part of the restructure has involved reducing spending on public health grants, which were cut by 5% between 2013 and 2018.[187] Further cuts of 3.9% a year will be undertaken until 2020/21; this equates to £3.07 billion in real terms.[188] It has been reported that by 2021 the budget will have been cut by 25% since 2015/16.[189] Cuts to public health funding have been exacerbated by the UK's exit from the European Union ('EU'), which has eliminated grants that would have otherwise been pro-

181 Participant II, interview data, collected by Anna Kawałek (file held with author).

182 Ibid.

183 Health and Social Care Act, 2012.

184 British Medical Association, 'Feeling the squeeze – the local impact of cuts to public health budgets in England' (14 March 2018). https://archive.bma.org.uk/-/media/files/pdfs/collective%20voice/policy%20research/public%20and%20population%20health/public-health-budgets-feeling-the-squeeze-briefing-march-2018.pdf?la=en [Accessed 6 July 2018].

185 The Greater Manchester Combined Authority (Public Health Functions) Order 2017.

186 The Greater Manchester Combined Authority, 'The Mayor'. https://www.greatermanchester-ca.gov.uk/the-mayor/ [Accessed 6 July 2020].

187 British Medical Association (n 184).

188 Ibid.

189 NHS Support Federation, 'Cuts to frontline practitioners' (2020). https://nhsfunding.info/symptoms/10-effects-of-underfunding/cuts-to-frontline-services/ [Accessed 6 July 2020].

vided by Europe to support research for drug and alcohol treatment, such as: the EU Health Programme 2014–2020.[190] Moreover, and worryingly, reports also show that no separate treatment provision was ever commissioned to support DRRs and the like; rather the treatment element of community-led justice disposals were to be sourced from the same supply as the non-criminal population.[191] This means that the wraparound support for DRR participants comes from an already strained area.

This is unlikely to progress on an upward curve; consider the COVID-19 (coronavirus) pandemic, where the pressure on public health resources has (and will continue to be) significant.[192] If economic resources for public health have already diminished at a fast pace since the 2012 devolution, this is only likely to worsen for the foreseeable future. The hard-hit support for the drug and alcohol domain is clearly reflected by the data in this book, but is likely to face an even grimmer reality in future years. An interesting practical feature of the HOPE model, whose successes have been well documented is, controversially, that it utilises *no* support from the treatment providers, and instead relies wholesale on creating and sustaining desistance through a deterrence model that employs swift, certain, and fair justice.[193] As such, as this data shows that the treatment support for Manchester Review Court is sketchy, on face value HOPE offers promise that similar models can be pathfinders to desistance without a treatment provision. However, this would only work if operating with strongly embedded deterrence penological features. It would not be wise to abandon treatment at Manchester Review Court unless there was a significant reworking to align with HOPE almost exactly, though a clear conceptual framework and sustainable delivery plan. I am not advocating this, but rather bringing to light the evidence in the area.

However, the devolved structure has borne some promising fruit. Labour MP and Deputy Mayor for Policing and Crime in Greater Manchester, Baroness Beverley Hughes, recently released a strategy for tackling Manchester's special problem with drug and alcohol addiction.[194] Within this, Hughes and her team do not play down the acute problems that Greater Manchester face in this area.

> In comparison to the rest of the country, drug and alcohol misuse has a disproportionate impact on health and life expectancy in Greater Manchester. The demands that unsafe drug and alcohol consumption are placing on our NHS services are a real cause for concern and we know that our mortality rates and hospital admissions, including those for young people, are significantly higher than the national average.

---

190 European Commission, 'EU health programme 2014–2020'. https://ec.europa.eu/heal th/funding/programme/2014-2020_en [Accessed 6 July 2020].
191 National Offender Management Service (n 10).
192 Office for National Statistics, 'Coronavirus and the impact on output in the UK economy: April 2020' (12 June 2020). https://tinyurl.com/ycxrdxzq [Accessed 6 July 2020].
193 Bartels, 2016, 2017, 2018 (n 53).
194 Greater Manchester (n 24).

From the document, it appears that the restructure allows for a more hands-on approach, enabling ring-fenced local money to be prioritised for drug and alcohol treatment in line with Hughes' priorities and ambitions. Whilst recognising the decline in resources, she sets up a convincing and realistic strategy to pave the way for achieving her benchmarks, involving six priorities for growth. However, this is only enabled by the devolved structure:

> devolution and our history of collaborative working provides a platform for this first ever Greater Manchester Drug and Alcohol Strategy to transform the way we deliver services and prevent and reduce the harms that drug and alcohol use cause within our city region.[195]

Throughout the strategy, it is clear that Hughes sees that drug-fuelled offending should be resolved through problem-solving, community intervention, rehabilitation, remedial solutions, and multidisciplinary work rather than incarceration and punitivism; the document states that 'we will improve public confidence through collaborative problem solving and community based multiagency campaigns'.[196]

I have already addressed the fact that the region of Greater Manchester is a long-standing champion of problem-solving in England (cf. Chapter 2). Many of these more-recent successes are down to the courageous and laudable work of Hugues. Devolution and the appointment of Hughes came about in 2017, during the later parts of the empirical work for this study, which might not only explain the poor (albeit inconsistent) results for Component 4 but could indicate that this area is now on an upward trajectory. That the review court is situated in a region with conducive institutional support could have positive effects. Clearly, Hughes is a keen advocate of therapeutic approaches; this could indicate a strong future for Manchester Review Court, free from institutional headwinds. However, one cannot argue with the curtailing of resources portrayed by the statistics, the UK's exit from the EU, and the COVID-19 pandemic, all of which will have drastic effects on public health funding, not least for drug and alcohol treatment support. And whilst there may be some current and future promise in the region of Greater Manchester as a result of powers being devolved to the local authority comprised of keen figures, as it stands, these factors undermine the sustainability of the review court bottle.

Furthermore, implementation of the reforms to the public health sector stood in alarming paradox to Chris Grayling's policy: Transforming Rehabilitation.[197] The probation split was met by huge resistance on the part of staff and unions.[198] One anticipated problem of the part-denationalised probation model was accountability. The restructuring of the probation services was put in place ostensibly to increase local partnerships by 'bring(ing) together the full range of

---

195 Ibid. [8].
196 Ibid. [19].
197 Transforming Rehabilitation (n 99).
198 Matharu (n 100).

support' across the mental health, housing, employment, and drug treatment services.[199] Acknowledging the UK's problems with this area, the document pledged to rehabilitate repeat offenders.

However, consider that the policy was rolled out in 2013, just one year after devolution under the Health Care Act 2012 had been activated. This opens up important questions; how could ongoing centralisation to the courts (albeit through a continuation of Blairism) be reconciled with privatisation and devolution initiatives otherwise characterising criminal justice strategy? How was increased pressure on the services to support and rehabilitate offenders on the ground anticipated in light of substantial cuts to public health grants and diminishing treatment resources? This at the very least suggests that the nuts and bolts of the UK criminal justice system were operating a series of conflicting models. More specifically, it might also suggest that Transforming Rehabilitation[200] was implemented without proper consideration of existing policy and therefore on a poorly considered conceptual model. Or worse, perhaps ministers were aware of these paradoxes, which would suggest that its true rationale was at odds with its pledges. Was Transforming Rehabilitation[201] a political decision rather than a criminological one? It would seem so.

Problems with the privatised probation model were widely reported from its inception. Not least, it was found that these problems endangered communities, decreased staff morale, limited funding, and diminished accountability.[202] The National Association of Probation Officers ('NAPO'), the trade union for probation staff, reported that:

> our response to this latest 'marketisation' plan is one of total opposition. The Probation Service needs to be reunified and put back under public ownership and accountability. The failures of privatisation has created a fragmented service which is operationally flawed, is fleecing the taxpayer and seriously impacting on community safety.[203]

In 2018, a report by the British Medical Association suggested that Transforming Rehabilitation should be reversed if public health is to be improved. This would include improvement to problems with alcohol and drug addiction. Chief Inspector of Probation Justin Russell commented:

> The Transforming Rehabilitation reforms have severely tested the probation service over the past five years. Fundamental flaws in the original design of

---

199 Transforming Rehabilitation (n 99) [3].
200 Transforming Rehabilitation (n 99).
201 Ibid.
202 Matharu (n 100).
203 National Association of Probation Officers [NATO], 'Napo's online submission to the MoJ consultation – Strengthening probation'. https://www.napo.org.uk/sites/default/files/Napo%20Response%20to%20MOJ%20Consultation_0.pdf [Accessed 1 July 2020].

the contracts, particularly the payment by results mechanism, have starved Community Rehabilitation Companies (CRCs) of essential funding. This has had a significant impact on the quality of supervision many CRCs have been able to deliver.

Transforming Rehabilitation came under serious scrutiny when review of the strategy by the Justice Committee concluded that 'we are unconvinced that the Transforming Rehabilitation model can ever deliver an effective or viable probation service'.[204] The January 2018 cabinet reshuffle under Teresa May's administration led the Justice Secretary to be reassigned from David Lidington to David Gauke (the third and final reassignment of the Justice Secretary under the May government).[205] Just under a year and a half later in May 2019, Mr. Gauke announced that the probation model would be renationalised and all offender management would be brought under the NPS in line with the guidance and in response to the criticism.[206] However, this was not without pressure from key organisations who advised the Ministry of Justice to veer firmly away from any denationalisation despite privatisation being mooted as a retainable feature in some capacity. We are still waiting to see and feel the consequences of this reversal play out. From a problem-solving perspective we can tentatively conjecture that it would mean more organisation (Component 10), more thorough testing and holistic reports (Component 5), better service-user attendance through breaching, and loss of the payment-by-results scheme (Component 1). However, coming back to the main discussion point, under this component, could lead to better funded and more accountable companies to help oversee the treatment provisions of the problem-solving court to comply with Component 4.

The discussion points from this component coalesce around the fact that there has been and will continue to be sustainability implications for Component 4 at Manchester Review Court (and indeed similar models), as the treatment provision of community-driven justice interventions rely so heavily on curtailing public money. Although it was up to the probation services to link service-users to the treatment providers and the split may have thwarted their ability to do this well, clearly there were issues with the economic sufficiency of the treatment providers at a broader level of the British landscapes. As the gulf between policy intention and practice reality widens, the court breaches Component 4 due to: insufficient

204 House of Commons Justice Committee, 'Government should undertake a review of Transforming Rehabilitation reforms' (22 June 2018). https://publications.parliament.uk/pa/cm201719/cmselect/cmjust/482/48202.htm [Accessed 6 July 2020] [74].
205 Marco Cillario, 'Former City solicitor Gauke becomes fourth Justice Secretary in two years amid latest Cabinet reshuffle' (9 January 2018). https://www.legalbusiness.co.uk/blogs/former-city-solicitor-gauke-becomes-fourth-justice-secretary-in-two-years-amid-latest-cabinet-reshuffle/ [Accessed 6 July 2020].
206 Ministry of Justice, 'Justice Secretary announces new model for probation' (16 May 2019). https://www.gov.uk/government/news/justice-secretary-announces-new-model-for-probation [Accessed 6 July 2020].

wraparound services, inaccessibility, a lack of funding to support the treatment provision, and lack of accountability and funding for the probation services shouldering DRR treatment. However, this issue reaches further than a fidelity argument; it is arguable that non-adherence to this component is also a breach of legal requirement under section 209(1)(a) of the Criminal Justice Act 2003, which states that anyone sentenced to a DRR should to submit to treatment.[207] If there are shortages in this area, how can this subsection of the act conceivably be achieved? In the UK, probation companies oversee treatment, however, and, arguably, some probation companies have been unable, due to austerity, to meet this legal requirement to appropriately reduce DRR drug use over recent years.

Although many of these changes occurred after publication of Kerr, et al.,[208] the previous researchers also reported shortages in the original models in this area (and thus indicated breach of Component 4), although this was not expressly linked to funding. The updated data from this book suggests that recent cuts to treatment support were catalytic to an existing problem, and there has been ongoing non-compliance to this key drug court component. However, there is promise; the Justice Innovation Charity has survived the UK turbulence and is still alive and well. Its strategy is to help problem-solving models and other alternative justice interventions improve where required. Part of this involves developing practical tool-kits and legal consultancy to meet local needs. Using her impetus and acting on her desire to pursue problem-solving in Manchester, Baroness Hughes should request help from the UK Centre for Justice Innovation on behalf of the region to help support delivery of Component 4 as a core underpinning pillar of problem-solving court sustainability.

4.2.1.7 Drug Court Component 5

Under Drug Court Component 5, the national association stipulates that 'abstinence is monitored by frequent alcohol and other drug testing'.[209] It continues to suggest that 'an accurate testing program is the most objective and efficient way to establish a framework for accountability and to gauge each participant's progress. Modern technology offers highly reliable testing to determine if an individual has recently used specific drugs'.[210] As such, efficient drug court practice rests upon reliable testing, which increases offender accountability, active participation, and progress monitoring, and can be carried out cost-effectively through urinalysis testing. As such, the drug tests and their effectiveness will be explored throughout this section.

207 (n 8) 209(1)(a).
208 Kerr (n 38).
209 Ashcroft et al. (n 4) [11].
210 Ibid [11].

4.2.1.7.1 THE WRITTEN REPORT

Unremarkably, the testing at Manchester Review Court occurred outside of the courtroom at the probation services. As in the original English and Welsh drug courts models, service-users' progress, including drug test results, were communicated back to the court via a written instrument prepared by probation officers.[211] The written report was technically straightforward; it usually comprised sections documenting progress, both formal (DRR compliance, treatment provider comments, and test results) and co-existing (medical and psychological, relationship and spouse troubles including domestic violence, housing and homelessness, HIV and other sexually transmitted diseases, basic educational deficits, and unemployment/employment).[212] However, because written reports were not standardised across probation companies, quality and information type could be inconsistent.[213] A full (and ideal) report would comment holistically on all aspects of progress and these were best placed to substantiate the review hearing. However, thinner reports with fewer facts were not unusual.[214] There were also several instances when drug test results were incomplete.[215] More astonishing, in 12% of the cases sampled for this study, the report itself was completely missing.[216] Furthermore, quality of test results was problematic.

> Some participants were adamant that the positive test results were wrong leaving magistrates in an awkward and powerless position.[217]

Combine this with magistrates' circumscribed role in the out-of-court happenings and magistrates were left with limited information to ratify the review. Historical UK research for the English and Welsh DTTOs revealed that probation trusts considered generation of reports for the court reviews arduous. This was affirmed in the later 2011 report: probation 'felt that their reporting requirements were already onerous and that they would struggle to fit in more time still for writing reports and attending court'.[218] This could explain occasions when the instrument was populated perfunctorily or the report was absent at Manchester Review Court.[219] A participant further hypothesised that inaccurate results were caused by cut street-drugs, in which the acquired substances are unknowingly permeated with other strands, affecting the testing samples.[220] However, if this is the case, it simply suggests inadequacy in the quality of the

---

211 Ethnographic data (every date) collected by Anna Kawałek (file held with author).
212 Ethnographic data (various dates) collected by Anna Kawałek (file held with author).
213 Ethnographic data collected by Anna Kawałek (file held with author).
214 Ethnographic data (various dates) collected by Anna Kawałek (file held with author).
215 Participant II, interview data, collected by Anna Kawałek (file held with author); Ibid.
216 Court observations, Phase 1 dataset, collected by Anna Kawałek (file held with author).
217 Ethnographic data (various dates) collected by Anna Kawałek (file held with author).
218 Kerr (n 38) [22].
219 Ibid; McSweeney et al. (n 12).
220 Participant II, interview data, collected by Anna Kawałek (file held with author).

testing kits, which should be able to accurately detect these nuances. These findings therefore contravene the advice given under Component 5 stating that 'quality control and quality assurance procedures for ensuring the integrity of the process'.[221] These factors had substantial implications from a court review perspective; it made it tricky for magistrates to expedite them and left the court powerless to effectively review progress;[222] this undermined accountability, responsivity, and, perhaps most crucially, one participant commented that he would be more compliant with the DRR order if the testing results were valid.[223] Perhaps even worse, it made it difficult to take the court reviews seriously and questioned its purpose if the court was unable to 'review' progress.

Coming back to the Criminal Justice Act 2003, section 210 leaves a question mark above the legality of the written report. It states that:

> [the DRR may and must if the treatment and testing period is more than 12 months … (d) provide for an officer of a provider of probation services to make to the court responsible for the order, before each review, a report in writing on the offender's progress under the requirement and; (e) provide for each such report to include the test results'.[224]

Here we run into the same problems as we did under Component 1 with the wording 'must' and 'may'. Where the legislation makes clear that reviews themselves are a legal requirement for DRRs over 12 months along with the remaining provisions in this section, it remains unclear whether subsequent provisions (s1, a–e) are a statutory requirement if a non-compulsory DRR review goes ahead, including supply of a written report with full drug testing history (d) and (e).[225] It is therefore unclear whether these provisions are a statutory requirement for shorter DRRs. If they are, officers were in statutory breach when a report or test result was not provided to the court. The first reading is perhaps more sensical: that the courts 'may' (but not 'must') provide a written report by law if the DRR is under 12 months. However, this unveils the fact that the legislation is another therapeutic-jurisprudence–unfriendly pillar failing to adequately support the operation of Manchester Review Court at bottle level. Making drug tests (and all the provisions in subsection 1(a–e)) a legal requirement for shorter DRRs through legislative reform would improve the power of the review court. Regardless of the legislative provisions, the preferable solution would be lengthening all DRRs to give all service-users coverage under the current legislation as well as a more realistic recovery trajectory, as previously detailed.

221 Participant II, interview data, collected by Anna Kawałek (file held with author).
222 Ethnographic data (various dates) collected by Anna Kawałek (file held with author).
223 Participant V, interview data, collected by Anna Kawałek (file held with author).
224 (n 8), section 210.
225 Ibid.

Notably, although the same issue was not reported in Kerr, et al. for the previous drug courts, the researchers did allude to nascent resource implications for maintaining this area and they projected long-term issues.[226] Clearly there has been a decline over time and Transforming Rehabilitation will have catalysed resource problems. However, resources aside, one must not forget that the LASPO Act shortened the standard length of DRRs in 2012.[227] This left a gap in statutory foothold, and this could have caused declination within all the other legislated areas under section 210 of the Criminal Justice Act (including testing)?[228]

Elsewhere, under the same component, the national body states: 'ideally, test results are available and communicated to the court and the participant within one day. The drug court functions best when it can respond immediately to noncompliance'.[229] The speed of producing and communicating results is also important as it enhances engagement and reactiveness of the court. An area worth considering is electronic alcohol monitoring tags. These are used voluntarily without statutory support at the C2 and PI models and have been reported to be an effective deterrent enabling swift, certain, and fair justice.[230] If tagging were to be adopted at Manchester Review Court, it would increase offender accountability as well as public confidence in the models, and might better sit in line with the eligibility criteria for accepting offenders from violent and non-acquisitive offending brackets. This and other forms of tagging could justify inclusion of an even broader range of service-users from more serious sentencing bands, thereby giving further outreach to an array of offenders in need of rehabilitation in England and Wales. This would move the focus of the model towards deterrence/punitivism though still dovetailing with rehabilitation, fitting with the punitivism populism that still overshadows so many British public conversations. In line with HOPE and Component 4, testing could be administered randomly and more regularly to enhance programme compliance. However, if the court adopts this approach, this could be legislated for under either the Criminal Justice Act or the Bail Act[231] (which currently legislates for electronic tagging in other guises) to avoid complacency.

To conclude this section, this component is concerned with the speed and reliability of drug testing, which at Manchester Review Court was communicated to the court through a written instrument populated by probation officers. Although the old drug courts operated with more fidelity to this area, this has depreciated over time as there are clear problems with the testing kits and

---

226 Kerr (n 38).
227 Legal Aid, Sentencing and Punishment of Offenders ('LASPO') Act 2012.
228 (n 8), section 210.
229 Ashcroft et al. (n 4) [12].
230 Jake Phillips, Anna Kawałek, & Anne-Marie Greenslade, 'An evaluation of the choice and consequences and PI programmes in Bedfordshire and Hertfordshire' (2020) Ministry of Justice.
231 (n 8); The Bail Act, 1976.

the reports. This is likely to be linked to the fact that the old drug courts were in operation before legislation began to mean insufficient statutory support for the area and prior to the LASPO Act.[232] As fidelity to this area has diminished, we can conclude that this is another area that lacks fidelity to the international blueprint.

4.2.1.8 *Drug Court Component 6*

4.2.1.8.1 REWARD AND SANCTIONING POWERS

To respond to service-users' compliance and non-compliance with drug court provisions, the international body advises that judicial officers should impose rewards and sanctions under Component 6.[233] Some international examples of rewards include: praise, dismissal of charges or reduced incarceration or supervision, and graduation from the programme; and sanctions include: demotion to earlier stages, fines, or termination of the programme. This carrot-and-stick approach is arguably the drug courts' most distinguishing feature and has been documented as incurring positive outcomes worldwide.[234]

Manchester Review Court can be distinguished from the classic drug court because magistrates did not execute Component 6 in court. Its operation was restricted to verbal tokens of praise and/or verbal critiques, and although the previous discussions of the wine showed that the interpersonal element was operated well (c.f. Chapter 3), the power of the court was significantly restricted in the absence of Component 6. This is arguably the court's most alarming infraction of the gold standard.[235] Under Component 2 (this chapter), I explained that no sentencing took place in the review court; sanctioning for non-compliance would be induced at the discretion of probation officers where three violations tended to lead to the reinstatement of the original court order. Expulsion from the programme and rescindment of the original order was then formalised at a specialist breach (and mainstream) court.

Although abandoning all punitive sentiments in some ways allowed the court to become wholly therapeutic, it called into question its purpose, which is surely to provide an intersection between therapy and criminal justice. One service-user said that it was difficult to take the review hearings seriously in the absence of sentencing, but that more threat of sentencing alongside rigorous drug-testing rigour would increase compliance.[236] Expanding the number of criminal sanctions might also raise the model's credibility to the public as well as increasing

---

232 (n 227).

233 Ashcroft et al. (n 4).

234 Yih-Ing Hser, Vandana Joshi, Margaret Maglione, Chou Chih-Ping, & Douglas Anglin, 'Effects of program and patient characteristics on retention of drug treatment patients' (2001) Evaluation and Program Planning, 24(4), 331–341.

235 Ethnographic data collected by Anna Kawałek (file held with author).

236 Participant V, interview data, collected by Anna Kawałek (file held with author).

efficiency, accountability, and speed of process. Electronic tagging could help distil Component 6. Alcohol tagging is just one form of a surveillance monitor, which has already been suggested, but this technology also spans curfews and GPS monitoring. Within a rehabilitation rationale, there is no reason these surveillance methods should not be imposed to increase deterrence as part of Component 6. These techniques have been shown to incur good results for the UK's PI and C2 models, where, perhaps surprisingly, the service-users reported that they liked them as they helped to keep them on track with their recovery and law-abiding behaviour.[237] This could be considered as a sanctioning technique or even a reward; ongoing programme compliance dissolves the need for a tag as desistance becomes stabilised; its removal could be carried out symbolically under Component 6, as well as its enforcement.

Staff believed that the lack of adherence to Component 6 was caused by legislative restrictions, in which magistrates lacked sentencing powers under the Criminal Justice Act.[238] However, close reading of the statute, section 211 (1) reveals that 'at a review hearing ... the court may, after considering the officer's report referred to in that subsection amend the community order or suspended sentence order, so far as it relates to the drug rehabilitation requirement'. In other words, if offender progress is deemed to be below or above the expected standard, the court can attach and remove provisions during review if the individual agrees to comply and consents to these changes.[239] Similarly, sections 178 and 192 of the same act give magistrates the power to attach and remove provisions to community orders and suspended sentences, both of which shoulder the DRR.[240] This is significant because it suggests that magistrates have unused powers in line with Component 6 under the Criminal Justice Act. Although it was not entirely clear why magistrates were unaware of these (or at least if they were aware, were not using them), it is mostly likely linked to training under Component 9 and absence of a court handbook outlining rudimentary court standards, expected practice, and regulations (discussed in Chapter 3). Elsewhere, Donoghue has argued that the powers within sections 178 and 192 are rarely used due to ignorance, cost and resources, and availability of magistrates, and fear that it created tension between magistrates and the probation services.[241] These insights may explain their lack of usage at Manchester Review Court.

237 Donna M. Coviello, Dave A. Zanis, Susan A. Wesnoski, Nicole Palman, Arona Gur, Kevin G. Lynch, & James R. McKay, 'Does mandating offenders to treatment improve completion rates?' (2013) Journal of Substance Abuse Treatment, 44(4), 417–425. doi: 10.1016/j.jsat.2012.10.003; Brian Perron & Charlotte Bright, 'The influence of legal coercion on dropout from substance Abuse treatment: results from a national survey' (2008) Drug and Alcohol Dependence, 92(1–3), 123–131. doi:10.1016/j.drugalcdep.2007.07.011; Phillip Bean, *Drugs and crime* (2nd ed.) (Cullompton: Willan Publishing, 2004).
238 (n 8), section 211 (1).
239 Ibid.
240 McSweeney et al. (n 12).
241 Jane Donoghue, *Transforming criminal justice?: problem-solving and court specialization.* (New York: Routledge, 2014).

However, and interestingly, the original drug courts did execute sentencing in-house, where Kerr, et al. stated that 'apart from conducting trials they had the same powers as other magistrates' courts, including being able to give offenders any of the 12 requirements that could be included in community sentences'.[242] One of my participants (an erstwhile Salford drug court practitioner) stated these jettisoned sanctioning powers were the biggest loss when Salford drug court was centralised into Manchester Review Court.[243] Aside from this suggesting that Manchester Review Court was the remains of the original drug courts, this augments Kerr, et al.[244] by showing that the older models benefitted from more fidelity to Component 6.

Despite this, McSweeney, et al. were critical of the 2003 legislation, which also subsumed the DTTOs under the DRR, claiming that it 'restricted the options previously open to the court for responding to non-compliance in a constructive way, by taking no action or imposing a financial penalty in response to a breach of conditions'.[245] This means that both the historical models and Manchester Review Court (both of which operate(d) the later DRR), did not include the same comprehensive range of rewards and sanctions compared to the earlier DTTOs and the international drug courts. However, UK researcher Bean acknowledged that multiple sanctions are crucial to successful drug court delivery.[246] This means that even if magistrates were to spend their unused powers under 178, 192, and 211 of the Criminal Justice Act,[247] this would still fall significantly short of the ideal presented under Component 6. In this respect, neither Manchester Review Court nor the UK 'drug courts' operated with true subscription to this crucial component. Arguably, ongoing infidelity to this aspect of the international blueprint is the most convincing argument for why Manchester Review Court is not and should not be defined a 'drug court'. However, for the same reasons, nor should the original English and Welsh drug courts.

On several occasions, I have pointed out that Manchester Review Court bears a resemblance to HOPE through the prominence of the probationary element. Throughout her evaluative work, Professor Bartels describes a range of (fairly moderate) sanctions available at HOPE to penalise violations of the order (including: cellblock, 2-day, 15-day, or 30-day jail sentences).[248] Bartels details that HOPE has been successful for arousing the same outputs as the classic drug courts (and indeed Manchester Review Court (cf. Component 1, this chapter)) through amplified focus on deterrence and sanctioning. Although there are undoubted parallels between Manchester Review Court and HOPE, the sanctioning powers are perhaps where the biggest discrepancy lies. However, Bartels argues it is precisely this component that facilitates rehabilitative and therapeutic

---

242 Kerr et al. (n 38) [3].
243 Ethnographic data collected by Anna Kawałek (file held with author).
244 Kerr et al. (n 38).
245 McSweeney et al. (n 12) [48].
246 Bean (n 237) cited in ibid.
247 (n 8), sections 178, 192, 211.
248 Bartels 2016, 2017, 2018 (n 53).

outcomes, despite, or perhaps due to, the operationalisation of more punitive swift, certain, and fair justice.[249] Borrowing principles from HOPE could thus provide fruitful responses for Manchester Review Court and its stakeholders. It would involve giving magistrates an assortment of sanctions to accompany progress monitoring, as in HOPE, by extending their powers under the Criminal Justice Act. This systemic change involves altering powers legislated under the Criminal Justice Act, which is ultimately a bottle-level modification. In turn, and perhaps with irony, more punitive sentiments at Manchester could bring about more therapeutic responses and would sit in line with the punitive populism overshadowing current England and Wales' criminal justice (cf. Chapter 2) to align with the international gold standard.

We can conclude the discussion of Component 6 by reporting that Manchester Review Court did not fit the drug court mould as it did not expedite rewards and sanctioning in court to reflect participant behaviour. Although no sanctioning took place in court, there appeared to be some unused powers under the Criminal Justice Act.[250] Through use of the same legislated powers, the predecessor drug court models operated with more fidelity to this key area. However, the powers catalogued within the act do not match the comprehensive assortment recommended by the international blueprint. This means that the original models also lacked fidelity to arguably the most critical drug court component.

4.2.1.9 Drug Court Component 7

See discussion of the wine (Chapter 3) for details of Manchester Review Court's (and the original UK drug courts') fidelity to this component.

4.2.1.10 Drug Court Component 8

Under Component 8, the international body posits that, 'fundamental to the effective operation of drug courts are coordinated management ... program monitoring provides oversight and periodic measurements of the program's performance against its stated goals and objectives'.[251] Therefore, this component is concerned with effective management of crucial information, predominantly research and evaluative data, to help feed and enhance practice.

By repeating the following mantra throughout this book, I have brought attention to the lack of empirical research informing practice at Manchester Review Court: there is no track record of Manchester Review Court in the available literature repositories evidencing its existence, no empirical research, not in the media or any policy document, and nor is there a court handbook at the site outlining objectives and expected practice. Perhaps more alarmingly, there was a distinct

---

249 Ibid (2018).
250 (n 8), sections 178, 192, 211.
251 Ashcroft et al. (n 4) [17].

lack of basic data for areas such as: anticipated attendance, number of active cases, patterns of drug use, programme graduates and terminations, cost–benefit analyses, client demographics, attrition, and reoffending and recovery rates.[252]

Problematically, the paucity of guiding documentation caused confusion amongst practitioners pertaining to the court's definition, some regarding it as a centralised version of the old Salford drug court and others a different method of UK problem-solving practice.[253] This led to ambiguity of the court's purpose, contravening the international guidance: 'the design and operation of an effective drug court program result from thorough initial planning, clearly defined program goals, and inherent flexibility to make modifications as necessary'.[254] Moreover, there were clear information storage issues for the court. For example, upon my request, Cheshire and Greater Manchester CRC ran a report to disclose all DRR service-users who had attended the review over the previous six-month period. This revealed only seven participants. This figure is vastly inaccurate because the court would often see more than seven CRC service-users in a single afternoon.[255] This example discloses some stark problems with the administration of the court systems. I will ensure that the key findings from this book are received by the court, and I am looking to develop further research in this area. However, coordination of basic data is of the essence to comply with Component 6. I have already suggested that a court manual might help to clarify these areas, standardise practice, policy, and procedure, and help manage other key information (cf. Chapter 3). This could be in digital or printed format and should be shard as Amicus Justia Briefs. However it is achieved, running analyses on rudimentary data is key to improving the court.

The original English and Welsh drug courts were luckier in this respect. Through the support of the government, they benefitted from two bespoke process evaluations, one in 2008 and the other in 2011.[256] Although these did not report on all areas (such as outcomes), they provided the court with some invaluable practical information to guide operation. Furthermore, the 2011 researchers stated that 'having a co-ordinator (a legal advisor) with ring-fenced time was considered important by staff in getting the necessary systems and processes in place'. This was deemed to be a critical ingredient for allowing agencies to communicate effectively, to coordinate and manage the systems, and oversee key areas, including: panel rota, referrals, local steering group meetings, as well as liaising with partnership agencies to complete monitoring data, and acting as the main point of contact for receiving queries and overseeing visits.[257] However, despite a court manager ensuring good results, the predecessor researchers uncovered staff resourcing problems, including increased workloads of other legal advisors,

252 Ethnographic data collected by Anna Kawałek (file held with author).
253 Ibid.
254 Ashcroft et al. (n 4) [17].
255 Phase 1 dataset, collected by Anna Kawałek (file held with author).
256 Kerr et al. (n 38); Matrix Group (n 44).
257 Kerr et al. (n 38).

which indicated that there could be problems maintaining this area over the longer term.[258]

The abandonment of a court manager could explain many of the basic problems at Manchester Review Court, including adjournment, non-attendance, the rotating bench, and poor organisation of the key systems although note that I have since been told there is a new person in this role at the court since the merge of Bury magistrates' court. To ensure effective practice, the review court should reinstate this role if it has not been done already; this could be a legal advisor given that their remit in the review court is to provide administrative assistance (cf. Component 2), but it could also be another court person, such as a lead magistrate. I strongly believe that practitioners examined in this study had the bandwidth for good practice, and if the systems allowed it, they could achieve good things. Moreover, there could yet be hope for a blanket increase in the organisation and coordination of all courts across England and Wales. The Ministry of Justice plan to modernise the magistrates' courts by replacing 'outdated IT systems and old-fashioned paper-based processes'.[259] This might enable more fluent communication between parties. However, part of the modernisation anticipates cuts to 10,000 staff members (already ongoing) as the court systems become digitalised.[260] This includes paring back the number of judicial officers and legal advisors.[261] These resourcing strains could help to explain why, since the predecessor drug courts, there was no legal advisor dedicated to this role at the review court during my data collection window[262]. However, if this has catalysed existing problems, then this policy has had conflicting impacts.

In sum, Component 8 ensures that high-quality research informs practice and expects that rudimentary data is collated for key areas. It also oversees effective management of the administrative systems and coordination of relevant information. Due to the lack of literature even acknowledging its existence, there is no currently useful research for Manchester Review Court specifically, although there is some more general research for the DRR. Although this could now be on an upward curve, the court lacks fidelity to this component. No manager to help oversee the key areas during my data collection only exacerbated these issues and could have contributed to many of the court's organisational problems. This

258 Ibid.
259 Ministry of Justice, 'Swift and sure justice: the government's plans for reform of the criminal justice system' (2012). https://assets.publishing.service.gov.uk/government/uploads/system/uploads/attachment_data/file/217328/swift-and-sure-justice.pdf [Accessed 6 July 2020] cited in Jane Croft, 'Court modernisation project "risks missing 2023 deadline"' (9 May 2018). https://www.ft.com/content/1e1542c2-4f93-11e8-9471-a083af05aea7 [Accessed 6 July 2020].
260 House of Commons Justice Committee, 'The role of the magistracy: follow-up eighteenth report of session 2017–19 (2019) House of Commons. Retrieved from: https://publications.parliament.uk/pa/cm201719/cmselect/cmjust/1654/1654.pdf.
261 Ibid.
262 Please note that since the Bury merge, evidence suggests that this role has been reinstated at the Manchester women's problem-solving court and at Manchester's Review Court.

is unlike the original English and Welsh drug court models, which demonstrated early successes when this component was adhered to. More research, as well as recruiting an individual to play a coordinating role, would mobilise compliance to this pillar of success, if it has not been done already.

4.2.1.11 Drug Court Component 9

Please see discussion of the wine (Chapter 3) for details of Manchester Review Court's (and the original UK drug courts') fidelity to this component.

4.2.1.12 Drug Court Component 10

As stated during the wine analysis, under Component 10, the National Association of Drug Court Professionals are concerned with partnership working and building multi-agency alliance, stating that: 'a drug court is especially well suited to develop coalitions among private community-based organizations [*sic*], public criminal justice agencies, and alcohol and other drugs treatment delivery systems'.[263] Although I have already developed some discussion points for this area (cf. discussion of the wine, Chapter 3), this hybrid component also engages some bottle-level analysis.

A holistic approach to cases, achieved through dedicated partnership working, was identified as critical DNA to the practical and conceptual features.

> It's intended to be a multi-strategy approach, tackling the defendant's addiction, but perhaps providing support, in terms of accommodation and debt, health issues and such.[264]

However, my interview data was somewhat inconsistent on the adequacy of Component 10; whereas service-users felt that the full team was well-aligned, staff members thought it could be improved.

> Everything clicks together ok.[265]
> [There is room for improvement] with probation's recording, but also with the court's recording so you know who is coming in.[266]
> I know that on occasion, the flow of information isn't as consistent as it would've been or could've been if it was just one organisation.[267]

The latter two participants linked fragmentation across parties to the chaos created following the probation split under Transforming Rehabilitation.[268] The

---

263 Ashcroft et al. (n 4) [23].
264 Participant I, interview data, collected by Anna Kawałek (file held with author).
265 Participant V, interview data, collected by Anna Kawałek (file held with author).
266 Participant II, interview data, collected by Anna Kawałek (file held with author).
267 Participant I, interview data, collected by Anna Kawałek (file held with author).
268 Transforming Rehabilitation (n 99).

restructure meant that some tasks (such as: producing the review reports, purchasing, economic spending, and decision-making) were required to go through a central hub at national level, causing delays, disorganisation, and dissolution between parties.[269] It is likely that the inconsistent perceptions of staff and service-users is attributed to their different stakes in the process; staff are required to grapple with the internal administrative systems and can thus theoretically provide more first-hand insight into their successes.

Chiming with discussions about the attendance problem (cf. Component 1: attendance, this chapter), one of the most problematic areas for Component 10 was court adjournment, caused seemingly by a lack of coalition between probation officers and the court. Most sessions would review roughly between 5 and 8 individuals; however, on average, 12 to 15 individuals were listed. To deal with non-attendees, the court postponed hearings for around six weeks. The participant would then reappear on the list six weeks later; however, most often, they would then not show up again. This caused the court to then readjourn and become stuck in the same continuous cycle. With the absence of individual probation officers in court (cf. Component 2, this chapter), it was difficult to ascertain why the same cohort of participants were not showing up.[270] However, from an outsider's perspective, it appeared disorganised and clumsy and seemed to undermine staff morale when it was as though the court was not taken seriously.[271] One participant stated that it was only in the following circumstances that the adjournment cycle was broken.

> The probation team give the indication to court that no adjournment is necessary ... and that no further listing in the review court is necessary.[272]

This suggests that this boils down to ineffective communication from the probation services. Although this does not seem inconceivable given the clear problems that probation had experienced following the privatisation, this is a one-sided view from a court staff member, and it would be useful to obtain new data from officers to enrich this discussion point.

Whilst the impact of this issue on economics is unknown, Kerr, et al.[273] reported similar issues at the original drug courts and maintained that adjournment was costly. However, interestingly at Manchester Review Court, the issue had become so prolific that it had been engrained and adapted into customary court practice.

---

269 Participant II, interview data, collected by Anna Kawałek (file held with author).
270 Ethnographic data collected by Anna Kawałek (file held with author); Participant I, interview data, collected by Anna Kawałek (file held with author).
271 Ethnographic data collected by Anna Kawałek (file held with author).
272 Participant I, interview data, collected by Anna Kawałek (file held with author).
273 Kerr et al. (n 38).

We can accommodate adjournments with no issue … there is some spare time – we don't have an issue with listing DRR cases.[274]

Interestingly, the same participant also identified court adjournments as a mechanism for understanding the complexity of addicted lifestyles and relapse tendencies.

The court allows for relapses as it further adjourns.[275]

This illustrates that the adjournment issue could be managed through pre-planned space on the court records with the expectation that a portion of listed individuals would not attend, and then would require adjourning. On Date 5, 19 individuals were listed to attend. I noted:

If everyone attended today, the court would be running into the early hours of tomorrow![276]

Tellingly, 6 of the 19 listed individuals attended their review on Date 5. It thus was clear from my observations that the court could run more smoothly without this problem.[277]

In contrast, sometimes service-users would arrive for review, under ostensible instruction from probation services, to find themselves unlisted.[278] The observed impact was loss of faith in the process, and service-users feeling as though their time had been wasted, especially if they had travelled far to attend court.[279] Magistrates would often review them anyway but with no prepared written instrument to substantiate its content, calling into question the impact of this effort.[280] This is clearly a long-standing problem; even early in the predecessor drug courts' short lifespan, the same problem was recorded, and researchers stated that there were 'difficulties in the communication between partners, which undermined the extent to which they worked effectively together'.[281] They further disclosed that although reviews were an efficient mechanism for facilitating partnership working across agencies, key areas required improvement, particularly communication

---

274 Participant I, interview data, collected by Anna Kawałek (file held with author).
275 Ibid.
276 Ethnographic data collected by Anna Kawałek (file held with author).
277 Ethnographic data collected by Anna Kawałek (file held with author); Participant I, interview data, collected by Anna Kawałek (file held with author); Participant II, interview data, collected by Anna Kawałek (file held with author).
278 Participant V, interview data, collected by Anna Kawałek (file held with author); Participant II, interview data, collected by Anna Kawałek (file held with author); ethnographic data collected by Anna Kawałek (file held with author).
279 Ethnographic data (various dates) collected by Anna Kawałek (file held with author).
280 Participant I, interview data, collected by Anna Kawałek (file held with author).
281 Kerr et al. (n 38) [17].

between the court and probation services to ensure accuracy of the court listings. Since the predecessor report was published years before the probation privatisation reforms were initiated, the split is unlikely to be the cause of this fragmentation, but was rather catalytic to an existing problem.

The problems with fragmentation could be rectified through better coordination between the court and probation services by implementing suggestions already set out; a court manager should be reinstated (if it has not been already) to track expected attendees and liaise with probation officers; individual probation officers should attend court alongside their participant to avoid fragmentation and a Chinese whispers effect; and the Criminal Justice Act[282] should be reformed to legally oblige attendance of shorter DRRs to avoid the non-attendance issue in the first instance. These systemic changes could provide fidelity to Component 10. As such, the discussion points on this final component of the international blueprint, combined with those made for the original drug courts, show another breach of fidelity to a key drug court component. This combines with discussions already made in Chapter 3, which demonstrated that lack of alliance under Component 10 undermined magistrates' knowledge bases.

4.3 Concluding remarks for Chapter 4

The previous chapter (Chapter 3) found that the wine at Manchester Review Court was poured in a style that aligned with therapeutic jurisprudence despite structural (or bottle-level) hurdles creating barriers for good practice. This emphasised the readiness of frontline practitioners. However, success also relies upon support from the wider landscapes; thus, the purpose of this chapter was to dig a little deeper into the emergent systemic factors and beyond by broadening the focus towards the legitimacy of policy and legislation governing the area to ignite discussions that answered Research Questions 1, 2, and 3 ('bottle'), recapped below:

1. Research Question 1 ('bottle'): does the court adhere to the international drug court gold standard?[283]
2. Research Question 2 ('bottle'): is it the remains of the original drug courts?
3. Research Question 3 ('bottle'): what is the therapeutic quality of Manchester Review Court's bottle?

The latest England and Wales drug court analysis is outdated, and since its publication, there have been significant changes to the surrounding landscapes, including but not limited to, austerity measures, cutbacks, and centralisation and

282 (n 8).
283 Ashcroft et al. (n 4).

privatisation reforms to sectors that pillar drug court sustainability.[284] The latest drug court report was published in 2011, but it makes no reference to the current Manchester Review Court; the closest mention is Salford drug court, which closed down alongside Salford Magistrates' Court, but could have been centralised into Manchester Magistrates' Court alongside the mainstream court work. The lack of literature emphasised by my mantra[285] meant that Manchester Review Court was an enigma, and it was uncertain both from my reading of the (limited) existing documentation and from the perspectives of frontline practitioners, whether it was the ghost of Salford drug court or an altogether different method of problem-solving court practice. This lack of clarity on its definition, aims, objectives, and practice protocol made analysis tricky by making uncertain how to frame the evaluation. However, given that this court and the forerunning UK drug courts raised fidelity questions, the international gold standard could be used as an analytical device to unravel the courts' ontological definitions and the extent to which they adhere(d) to the international mould. Moreover, considering the problems that England and Wales have faced in the area (epitomised by the demise of the original drug courts), implementing a well-established framework, whose principles have been documented as providing far-reaching international successes, could effectively position the evaluation by providing some indication surrounding areas of success and failure. This is not to say that wholesale and authentic drug courts are the only way forward for British problem-solving, but the framework could shed some light on the problematic areas given the struggles.

The setting was often challenging to work with empirically, not just because of the lack of literature, but also because of attendance problems undermining data collection effects, organisational problems, and major data storage issues for collating rudimentary information. However, as the study progressed, I realised that each of these frustrations, each of these empirical caveats, said something about the unfriendliness of the bottle, and were important qualitative findings that could be disclosed by the discussions in this chapter.

Research Questions 1 and 2 ('bottle') asked: 'does the court adhere to the international drug court gold standard?' and 'is it the remains of the original drug courts?' To summarise, the following points were made throughout this chapter to suggest that the UK courts (past and present) were/are *not* drug courts.

Component 1

- Manchester Review Court's objectives and those of the predecessor models mimicked the international drug courts: namely, tackling addiction as an

---

284 Kerr et al. (n 38).

285 There is no track record of Manchester Review Court in the available literature repositories evidencing its existence, no empirical research, not in the media or any policy document, and nor is there a court handbook at the site outlining objectives and expected practice.

underlying cause of crime and diverting offenders away from the mainstream criminal justice system to empower rehabilitation. Given the international evidence base, a fidelity model could provide fruitful outcomes for local goals. However, other loose methods of problem-solving courts, with similar goals, could also garner good responses.

- Like the predecessor models, Manchester Review Court had broad eligibility criteria by granting the inclusion of violent and non-acquisitive offenders from low-, medium-, and high-risk sentencing bands. This fairly substantial departure from the international blueprint indicates that the UK models bear more semblance to the probation-led model, HOPE. However, in synchrony with the international drug courts, theft/stealing was the most prominent offence type across both UK models alongside the drug types to which offenders were addicted. This chapter showed that there were stark similarities between the UK models through similar eligibility criteria because the DRR is the centrepiece to both UK courts. However, this fact alone brings to light similarities and raises questions around whether Manchester is the remains of the UK drug courts.

- On this note, participants from both this study and the 2011 study conflated the DRR with the drug court element when answering interview questions for both this component and others; this highlights the conceptual and practical similarities between Manchester and the original drug court models.

- Both UK models provide regular review for participants, all of whom were sentenced to DRRs; most DRRs were less than 12 months. In both models, reviews took place without statutory obligation in a specialist courtroom housing the reviews, on a distinct afternoon with a dedicated (although changing) panel of magistrates. These basic configurations between the old drug courts and Manchester Review Court are startlingly similar.

- Overall, there is some fidelity to this component (court objectives, drug types), though the eligibility criterion of all UK models veers strongly away from a traditional drug court. Therefore, the UK has struggled with long-term fidelity to this area of the international gold standard.

Component 2

- Although review hearings have a refreshed focus on rehabilitation, non-adversarialism could not be achieved because there were no lawyers present to cornerstone this approach. Unlike both the international models and the past UK drug courts, there was no individual from the drugs services present in court and the treatment process was mediated by a point of contact probation officer.

- The absence of lawyers was interpreted positively by participants in both this study and the previous drug courts. The quotations sampled from the data not only show palpable similarities between service-users' interpretation of this, but hint at similarities between the UK models themselves.

- The main lawyering and drugs working occurred outside of the courtroom; this created a chasm between the court itself and the other main DRR work. A similar point was made during research for the original English and Welsh drug courts, and even their forerunners, the DTTOs. The centralisation of Salford into Manchester Magistrates' Court arguably terminated drugs workers attending in court. This was affirmed by an interesting interaction during data collection, whereby a legal advisor from the old Salford drug court mistook me for a drugs worker. This strongly implies that Manchester could be the ghost of Salford drug court because senior practitioners understood it to be a centralised version of the model.

- Moreover, under Transforming Rehabilitation, private probation companies lost their right of audience in court, meaning that individual probation officers did not attend court; service-users were instead represented by a single point-of-contact officer, which is unusual from an international perspective.

- Overall, there is no fidelity to Component 2. And whilst the previous UK drug courts did operate with greater compliance through the presence of drugs workers and individual probation staff in court, the absence of lawyers demonstrates a fundamental infidelity to this key area and an ongoing breach of this component.

Component 3

- The process of enrolment is somewhat difficult to comment on since it occurred off-site of the review court, where the main empirical work took place. However, this finding alone serves to highlight the court's circumscribed role in the full process compared to the international examples where the court is at the forefront of the drug court model. This process has not changed since the Kerr, et al. report, who presented a diagram representing a typical drug court journey in a flow chart.[286] This chart visualises the same process as at Manchester Review Court, making apparent the practical overlaps between the UK models, again hinting that Manchester is the ghost of the precursors.

- The Criminal Justice Act governs the UK court models both past and present. This not only hints that Manchester Review Court could be the survivor of the original drug courts, but scrutiny of the act also brings to light that the essence of Component 3 is enshrined in UK law, including: eligibility, communication of the merits of participating, specialist individuals undertaking screening, and swift linkage to the services. The main (and only) area of disparity is that the predecessor models instated the same sentencing panel for carrying out the reviews; we have already seen why this was not possible at Manchester Review Court due to issues interlaced with Component 7

286 Kerr et al. (n 38) [2] (Figure 1.1).

(cf. Chapter 3). However, the fact that parts of Component 3 were/are legislated for in the act could suggest that all UK models are/were striving to achieve the gold standard and to 'be' a 'drug court'.

- With hesitancy due to the lack of authentic granular data to substantiate the discussion point, it was concluded that there is fidelity to this component across UK models, old and new.

Component 4

- The wraparound drugs services did not sufficiently support the model and both staff and service-users highlighted inadequacies in this sphere.
- Although previous UK researchers also reported shortages in this area, this problem had worsened over time due to funding cuts and diminishing resources, linked to austerity.
- There were also some issues found with accessibility of treatment due to the broad geographical scope of the model, and not all users were supported with a bus pass.
- Accountability had lessened over time as probation companies, shouldering the treatment provision, were subject to a part-denationalised model.
- Drug treatment felt alien to the court and was something that magistrates had little awareness of both at Manchester and in the previous drug courts. This enhances the argument that the court was sidelined from the main work and highlights fundamental differences between the UK and international versions.
- Overall, there has been ongoing infidelity to a critical area of drug courts shown to pillar its sustainability, although this has invariably deteriorated over time as resources have diminished.

Component 5

- Testing kits could be unreliable, the written report was not always produced, and even when it was, it was not always populated assiduously (with full test results) or at all by probation offices. These issues left magistrates powerless to carry out comprehensive and meaningful reviews. This problem is linked to the insufficient statutory support provided under the Criminal Justice Act.
- In the 2011 report, it was documented that reports were an onerous requirement and researchers projected long-term implications for resourcing this area.
- There is non-compliance to Component 5 and the highlighted issues were nascent in the original UK drug courts.

Component 6

- Arguably, the court's most alarming infraction of the gold standard was under Component 6. Manchester was limited in its operation of the carrot-and-stick approach to verbal tokens of praise and/or critique.

- No sentencing took place in the review court; sanctioning for non-compliance would be induced at the discretion of probation officers where three violations then tended (although inconsistently) to lead to the reinstatement of the original court order at a separate breach court. This has always been the case, including at the predecessor drug courts. However, there appeared to be some unused powers under sections 178 and 192, and 211 of the Criminal Justice Act.
- Although the predecessor drug courts appeared to be furnished with more powers in this respect, when the Criminal Justice Act subsumed the DTTOS, this took away from the full breach and sanctioning powers allowed in DRR courts. One of my participants (an erstwhile Salford drug court practitioner) stated these jettisoned powers were the biggest loss when Salford drug court was centralised into Manchester Review Court. This not only shows loss of powers over time, but also implies that some practitioners believed that Manchester Review Court was the remains of the UK drug courts.
- Arguably, ongoing infidelity to this aspect of the international blueprint is the most convincing argument to suggest that Manchester Review Court is not and should not be defined as a 'drug court'. However, by the same token, nor should the original UK versions. This suggests ongoing infidelity.

Component 7 (from Chapter 3)

- Like the former UK drug courts, there was an inconsistent bench of presiding magistrates although problems appeared to have worsened over time; in the older UK models, partial continuity, involving the same magistrate sitting for two consecutive hearings, was achieved 90% of the time. Although it is better than no consistency at all, partial continuity falls short of the ideal, mandating that one presiding judge/magistrate oversee all hearings to help develop rapport with offenders through trust, transparency, and accountability in line with therapeutic jurisprudence principles. This highlights ongoing breach of Component 7.
- In both models, magistrates interacted in similar therapeutic styles, and quotes from the data samples are comparable. The palpable similarities suggest that Manchester is the survivor of the old courts.
- Consistent falling short of the gold standard highlights ongoing infidelity to the area.

Component 8

- Due to the lack of literature even acknowledging its existence, currently there is no useful research to help inform practice at Manchester Review Court.
- There was no manager to oversee key areas exacerbates the issues because it meant no individual could oversee and coordinate key information and data, leading to organisational issues.
- The original drug courts benefitted from a court manager (legal advisor) as well as bespoke process evaluations to inform practice.

- Therefore, Manchester Review Court, unlike the predecessors, lacks fidelity to this area.

Component 9

- In all UK models, training for magistrates has been / is insufficient. At Manchester Review Court, the last session was given in 2010, precluding some magistrates because the pool had naturally changed with time; the situation was catalysed by court centralisation efforts expanding the judicial circle by bringing new practitioners into the pool. Moreover, researchers for the old UK models suggested that, prior to further roll out, national training should be reviewed.
- Some conflation between the UK models was evidenced; erstwhile Salford magistrates identified 'Salford drug court training' as the last training session. This hints at confusion as to the court's origin and could suggest Manchester Review Court is the survivor of the original drug courts, or at least it was understood this way by key frontline practitioners.
- Overall, these findings suggest that there has been ongoing non-compliance to Component 9.

Component 10 (from Chapters 3 and 4)

- Fragmentation between stakeholders caused there to be gaps in magistrates' knowledge bases and highlighted that the court was largely sidelined from the main DRR work.
- Furthermore, goals set outside of the courtroom – at the probation services – did not necessarily collude with those set within court, through loss of authentic communication caused by the exclusion of individual probation officers from court review sessions.
- A further problematic area was court adjournment issues or unlisted participants, caused seemingly by a lack of coalition between probation and the court. This is clearly a long-standing problem; even early in the predecessor drug courts' short lifespan, the same problem was recorded.
- These points illuminate ongoing infidelity to Component 10.

Comparably, the following points were made to suggest that the court was *not* the old Salford drug court and therefore Manchester Review Court was not the ghost of the predecessor drug courts.

- The original drug courts had drugs workers and individual probation officers in attendance, unlike Manchester Review Court.
- The drug courts did not appear to suffer from the same attendance issues as Manchester. This is likely to be because the LASPO Act, shortening the standard length of DRRs came into play in 2012, a year after the forerunning report was published. LASPO contributed to a vacancy where DRRs reviews fall into a legal blackhole.

- The support offered by the wraparound treatment services appeared to be more adequate for the original drug courts.
- The drug courts appeared to be furnished with a wider assortment of breach powers to sanction offenders in court. However, upon closer reading, they simply made use of powers that are still available under the Criminal Justice Act, meaning that no substantive powers have been intercepted since 2011 (although in either case, they are incomprehensive).
- A small amount of training was given to the previous drug court magistrates, unlike to the Manchester magistrates.
- The old models had a legal advisor in place to act as court manager to coordinate key areas and collate basic information as well as bespoke empirical research to inform practice. Although this might be now reinstated, there was no such person when the data collection for this book was taking place.

Therefore, to answer Research Question 1 ('bottle'): is Manchester a drug court? No, it cannot be because it is significantly non-compliant to the drug court fidelity matrix. It should therefore be considered a 'DRR Review Court', a 'problem-solving court' or a 'therapeutic court' (see forthcoming discussion under fidelity matrix: this chapter). To answer Research Question 2 ('bottle'): is the review court the remains of the UK drug courts? This is inconclusive. It is up to readers to decide if they think that Manchester Review Court is the survivor the old drug courts; I have presented the evidence. However, what we can conclude is that Manchester Review Court is similar to the predecessor England and Wales 'drug courts', including in the areas of compliance and non-compliance to the international blueprint, and many of the findings from this book echo those from the 2011 report. This justifies generalisability of the data to all UK problem-solving courts with the DRR at the core. Although the old models operated with more fidelity, they were still in significant breach of the gold standard, and the problematic areas have simply gained traction over time. The fact that the old English and Welsh 'drug courts' have a misplaced ontological foundation means that they should never have operated under this guise, and the name of 'drug court' was a misnomer that bastardised the concept. Perhaps their title does not matter, but what does matter is that objectives, implementation, and protocol are consistently understood by practitioners, implementers, and researchers to ensure coherent, successful, and sustainable delivery, and these factors should be built on a well-thought-out conceptual model. Full fidelity to the drug court framework is perhaps not necessary, but what is necessary is a realistic, coherent, and deliverable model. This ties into Research Question 3 ('bottle'), which sought to answer the question: is the bottle therapeutic-jurisprudence friendly? The following discussion points were made to answer this question:

- Court centralisation reforms were activated under the Courts Act 2003. This broadened the geographical scope of the model. With no rota system in place, this undermined the court's ability to bring about a consistent bench of magistrates. However, since the 2003 court reforms had been on the agenda for some time before the original models were deployed, this suggests that the old courts were incepted based upon a poorly considered framework that failed to account for incompatible legislation that would frustrate fidelity to this area..

- Since the Coalition government ushered in the austerity agenda, judicial training opportunities have been circumspect for the lay magistracy more generally, let alone in the rare field of problem-solving. The raw figures suggest that spending in this area has depreciated by a third, which goes hand in hand with ongoing reductions to the quantity of court staff, including judicial officers. The lack of training meant that some magistrates were operating Manchester Review Court blind. It would be tempting to blame lack of bandwidth of practitioners as the cause of the drug court downfalls, but the findings suggested this was an area that was practised well, and magistrates employed an effective series of interpersonal and behavioural styles similar to those from the original drug courts; problems are instead systemic.

- Due to the way the Criminal Justice Act 2003 is written, the court review aspect of the DRR felt like nothing more than an ancillary component to the probationary-led order. Marginalisation of the court disabled magistrates' full understanding of offender progress. Many of the goings-on occurred outside of court, including the process of enrolment, probationary breaches, and treatment recommendations, which in turn limited the power of the court.

- The splitting up of Probation Trusts through part-nationalisation robbed private officers of a voice in court. This means that service-users were represented by a blanket, single point-of-contact officer from the national service, rather than by their own officer. This structure undermines stakeholder alliance and discredits offender voices by risking a Chinese whispers effect.

- There was no court handbook or website outlining Manchester Review Court's idiosyncratic purpose. I repeated a mantra through this book to illuminate the dearth of literature in this area. Although this meant that objectives and expected practice must be inferred from section 209 of the Criminal Justice Act, this is notoriously vague. Problematically, the paucity of guiding documentation caused confusion amongst practitioners as to the court's definition, some regarding it as a centralised version of the old Salford drug court and others a different method of UK problem-solving practice. Although this is unsurprising given their conceptual and practical similarities, it was problematic that this grassroots knowledge was lacking. This is telling of the lack of political and institutional support governing and prioritising the area, historically.

- Non-legality of the court review process for shorter DRRs under the Criminal Justice Act 2003, alongside the LASPO Act shortening the typical DRR length, created a vacant legal requirement for review hearing for participants with DRRs of under 12 months (i.e. the majority). Combine these factors with penalties for breaching under the payment-by-results model, at private probation companies brought about by Transforming Rehabilitation, alongside difficulties with court accessibility also under the Courts Act expanding the court catchment area to Greater Manchester; these four pieces of legislation/policy are not conducive to good problem-solving and caused poor court attendance.

- Similarly, after the LASPO Act shortened DRRs and removed coverage under the Criminal Justice Act, the DRR report and the drug test results became more arbitrary and worsened in quality, exacerbated by the probation split; arguably because it is no longer a legal requirement as the provision falls into the same legal black hole as the court review itself.

- The court was stuck in a continuous cycle of court adjournment and this highlights obstructed communication channels between the court and the probation services. It indicates that participants should be represented by their own officers in court to help contextualise and explain offender circumstances. The lack of a court manager contributes to the same organisational problems.

- Individuals must attend DRR appointments (including probation, reviews, treatment, and medical) on a broad geographical radius; the Courts Act widens the geographic ambit thus making it difficult for participants to attend all appointments, especially those living on the outskirts of Great Manchester. Only some individuals benefitted from a bus pass.

- UK reforms to Public Health under the Health and Social Care Act 2012 devolved statutory responsibility for health improvement to local authorities. A by-product was cutting public health grants by 5% between 2013 and 2018. Drug and alcohol support for the criminal justice sphere has been especially hard hit, which has been magnified by Transforming Rehabilitation overburdening the existing systems. This in turn has meant that the wraparound services insufficiently support the model. The impacts of the recent withdrawal from the EU and the COVID-19 pandemic will put further pressures on this area.

- The technology used at probation to carry out drug testing generated unreliable results and there was also inadequacy in terms of some of the reports produced by probation companies. These factors undermined the ability to empower an effective court review. The associated problems were most likely linked to heavy probation workloads following the probation split and the non-statutory requirement produced by the Criminal Justice Act.

- The court was furnished with limited power to reward or sanction individual behaviours in court due to insufficient powers under the Criminal Justice Act. Even if magistrates were to spend their unused powers under sections 178, 192, and 211, this would still fall short of the ideal, which is to provide a wide-ranging assortment of sanctions and breaches to respond to behavioural nuances.

- The lack of research in the area undermines the ability to positively change or even understand rudimentary areas of practice. The Ministry of Justice stopped commissioning research once the 2011 process evaluation was published and disseminated (arguably the point at which the drug courts began to peter out).

Reiterating Research Question 3 ('bottle'): is the bottle therapeutic-jurisprudence friendly? No, each of these factors suggest that the bottle is unfriendly, and they put up hurdles for good practice. Although systematic problems have undoubtably worsened over time, this book has provided an explanation for the jettisoned English and Welsh 'drug court' attempts through the same bottle problems. The 'drug courts' were put in place in 2005 under Tony Blair's Labour administration with ostensibe good intentions, save for poor understanding at grassroots level by implementers. Although in theory, UK policymakers advocated drug courts at this point, they did not fully buy in to the practical model, instead making only qualified attempts at delivery. Since the first iteration of drug courts, these issues have worsened and seemingly England and Wales have never been able to support a full-fledged drug court.

Moreover, since 2005, the political landscapes have undergone significant changes, not least in the justice sector, where there have been nine new justice secretaries since 2005, and five since the full unleashing of the Conservatives following the Coalition government. Shortly after the Coalition government was formed, the government ushered in the austerity agenda by announcing £81 billion of spending cuts between 2011 and 2015 through the People Strategy.[287] Alongside austerity, the promised rehabilitation revolution in England and Wales has been stop–start, due to seeming lack of political and public appetite and confidence. Although these factors had negative impacts on the trajectories of the drug courts, and this all looks like rather a bleak story, problem-solving in England and Wales could have a strong place going forward. This could be a watershed moment for the UK, if they follow through with their recent calls in the 2020 White Paper to pilot five new problem-solving courts.[288] If the Ministry of Justice were to rebrand and repackage Manchester Review Court in a way that was conducive to England and Wales' current criminal justice climate, with well-researched principles based upon best practice, with consideration for existing systematic factors, and without eroding other core values and priorities, this would pave the way for a successful future, in turn tackling deep-seated problems with drug-fuelled reoffending, not least in the region of Manchester. Wexler postulates that a jurisdiction authoring problem-solving courts would 'virtually by definition ... be highly therapeutic jurisprudence friendly'.[289] Against the grain, England and Wales offers an example where this statement has failed to apply; despite endorsing problem-solving courts in 2005, England and Wales has provided an unfriendly bottle to support their operation since their inception.

Current issues with drug-fuelled recidivism must be faced and international evidence strongly suggests that can be done well using alternative justice methods that dovetail traditional punitiveness with rehabilitation. However, when shaping future strategy, one cannot ignore the demise of the original England and Wales drug courts, especially if a fresh collection of problem-solving courts is on the

287 Department of Energy & Climate Change, 'People strategy: 2011 to 2014 DECC' (31 January 2012) Corporate report, GOV.uk.
288 Ministry of Justice (n 112).
289 Wexler (n 63) [465].

table. Although it is tempting to suggest that only full adherence to the international drug court framework yields good results, looser nodes of problem-solving court practice can bear fruit if its practical and conceptual features are built upon clear and realistic groundwork. If cultural modalities lean more eagerly towards punitivism, the UK might better tolerate a scheme with overtones of deterrence penology. A full drug court is perhaps not what the UK should be striving for; as with any trend, drug courts are arguably on a downward trajectory as splintering sister models begin to take their place. Although we should look to the drug court component framework for guidance, there is also no harm in borrowing a hybrid set of best-practice principles from various endurable models so long as their principles are well-researched, then consistently understood, communicated, and practised. Inspired by Lattimore, et al., who performed a similar task for HOPE,[290] below I propose a fresh fidelity matrix with ten UK idiosyncratic components. New problem-solving courts implementing these dimensions should not pretend to 'be' drug courts as they veer too strongly away from the drug court mould, and would be more appropriately branded 'therapeutic courts' or 'problem-solving court'.

4.3.1 A renewed UK-specific fidelity matrix for therapeutic courts

Table 4.6 Fidelity Matrix

1	Given its positive feedback, regular judicial monitoring of the DRRs should be retained. A single, highly trained magistrate should take care of all DRR review hearings to provide consistent offender support based on the successes at UK PI/C2 and the international drug courts. There could be a magistrate second-in-command to act as a reserve. If this cannot be ensured, a rota system to provide consistency of magistrates is paramount.
2	Statutory support should mandate court reviews for shorter DRRs under 12 months. This would involve altering the wording in the act to give all DRR reviews coverage under the Criminal Justice Act. It should read 'must' 'if under 12 months' 'if the participant lives within the jurisdiction of a specialist review court'. This change would include all the relevant provisions falling under sections 1a–e to help regulate other aspects of the court review, including testing and reports. With this in place, a standardised report across companies should provide ample information to support the review including: the services that participants are attending, how this is going, and full drug testing history. Moreover, alcohol testing (SCRAM) tags should be considered and legislated for under the same act or the Bail Act to regulate addiction and behaviour. Testing should be administered randomly and more regularly to enhance program compliance.

(Continued)

290 Pamela K. Lattimore, Doris Layton MacKenzie, Gary Zajac, Debbie Dawes, Elaine Arsenault, & Stephen Tueller, 'Outcome findings from the HOPE demonstration field experiment is swift, certain, and fair an effective supervision strategy? (2016) Wiley Online. doi:10.1111/1745-9133.12248.

Table 4.6 Fidelity Matrix (Continued)

3	Regardless of legislative change, courts should sentence service-users to longer DRRs that allow the authorities to better oversee the full reformation process, as well as providing coverage under current statute. Longer DRRs sit in line with the punitivism populism that often characterises UK cultural justice modalities and rhetoric, and thus may be easier to justify to the public.
4	The court should be supported by a dedicated legal advisor who manages cases and coordinates with probation to ascertain information surrounding attendance, adjournment, and other relevant factors. They should also handle key data and should act as the primary contact. For the same reasons as magistrates, this manager should be consistent rather than changing every session. Furthermore, under the renationalisation of probation, service-users should be supported by their own officer in court who can support and oversee proceedings within the component below and provide authentic communication.
5	The courts should be furnished with full powers under the Criminal Justice Act to provide a better assortment of breach and rewards to increase responsivity of the court and to enhance offender compliance through deterrence. Examples of these should be taken from HOPE, and they should be distributed in court along with the advice of probation officers as synchronised by the legal advisor. Magistrates should be trained as to when to use these. Details of when and why breaches take place should be effectively communicated to service-users. Deterrence could be increased through implementing the aforementioned electronic tagging (alcohol monitoring, GPS, and/or curfew) where good behaviour is rewarded symbolically by its removal.
6	All service-users should receive a bus pass to increase accessibility attendance of all appointments, including court reviews, treatment, and probation.
7	The single presiding magistrate (or magistrates if Component 7 continues to be breached) should be highly trained. This could be supported by the Judicial College. Alternatively, there could be opportunities at the Centre for Justice Innovation, who might be able to provide seminars and bespoke education if Manchester asks for this help through the local authority. Linking up with international societies who share similar interests and goals will also be paramount in shaping grassroots levels of knowledge and understanding amongst frontline practitioners. The same style of interpersonal and behavioural styles should be retained by magistrates, although some areas require further improvement in line with findings from this book.
8	Through the legal advisor, the court should seek to develop a bench book configuring key areas of practice to support the area. This could be achieved on a live document, which changes as the court evolves embryonically. This could include the key skills found in Chapter 3 of this book and could be substantiated through a series of Amicus Justitia vignettes to be circulated and shared amongst practitioners in-house and outwards to the international body. This international collaboration can be overseen by the UK Chapter for Therapeutic Jurisprudence.

(*Continued*)

Table 4.6 Fidelity Matrix (Continued)

9	To ensure that the wraparound treatment support can support the model, Andy Burnham (Mayor of Manchester) alongside Baroness Hughes should ask the Centre for Justice Innovation for some advice regarding how to bolster this area by tackling crime at its root cause.
10	Further research should be supported by the Ministry of Justice and could be overseen by the Justice Innovation Charity, other researchers (like myself), and the UK Chapter for Therapeutic Jurisprudence.

Bibliography

Allen R., 'Rehabilitation devolution–how localising justice can reduce crime and imprisonment' (2015) *Transform Justice.* http://www.transformjustice.org.uk/wp-content/uploads/2015/12/TRANSFORM-JUSTICE-REHABILITATION-DEVOLUTION.pdf.

Ashcroft J., Daniels D. and Herriaz D., 'Defining drug courts: the key components.' U.S. Department of Justice (2004). https://www.ncjrs.gov/pdffiles1/bja/205621.pdf.

Baker M., 'Choices and consequences – an account of an experimental sentences programme' (2014) (1) Criminal Law Review. Thomson Reuters (Professionals) UK Limited.

Bartels L., 'Looking at Hawaii's opportunity with probation enforcement (HOPE) program through a therapeutic jurisprudence lens' (2016) 16 QUT Law Review, 30.

Bartels L., *Swift, certain and fair: does project HOPE provide a therapeutic paradigm for managing offenders?* (Cham, Switzerland: Springer, 2017).

Bartels L., 'HOPE-ful bottles: examining the potential for Hawaii's opportunity probation with enforcement (HOPE) to help mainstream therapeutic jurisprudence' (2019) 63 International Journal of Law and Psychiatry, 26–34.

Bean P., *Drugs and crime*, 2nd ed. (Cullompton: Willan Publishing, 2004).

Beckman L.J., 'An attributional analysis of alcoholics anonymous' (1980) 41 Journal of Studies on Alcohol, 714–772.

Bowen P. and Donoghue J., 'Digging up the grassroots? The impact of marketisation and managerialism on local justice, 1997 to 2013' (2013) British Journal of Community Justice, 9–2.

Bowen P. and Whitehead S., 'Problem-solving courts: a delivery plan' (2016) Justice Innovation Charity.

British Medical Association, 'Feeling the squeeze – the local impact of cuts to public health budgets in England' (14 March 2018). https://archive.bma.org.uk/-/media/files/pdfs/collective%20voice/policy%20research/public%20and%20population%20health/public-health-budgets-feeling-the-squeeze-briefing-march-2018.pdf?la=en, Accessed 6 July 2018.

Bryan M., Bono E. and Pudney S., 'Drug-related crime' (2013) No. 2013-08 Institute for Social and Economic Research.

Burke A.M., 'Would violent offenders benefit from participation in drug court?' (2013) (Master's Thesis). https://cornerstone.lib.mnsu.edu/cgi/viewcontent.cgi?article=1233&context=etds.

Carey S., Finigan M.W. and Pukstas K., 'Exploring the key component s of drug courts: a comparative study of 18 adult drug courts on practices, outcomes and costs' (2008) NPC Research.

Center for Substance Abuse Treatment, *Enhancing motivation for change in substance abuse treatment*' (Rockville, MD: Substance Abuse and Mental Health Services Administration (US) (Treatment Improvement Protocol (TIP) Series, No. 35, 1999). Chapter 1--Conceptualizing motivation and change. https://www.ncb i.nlm.nih.gov/books/NBK64972/.

Cillario M., 'Former city solicitor Gauke becomes fourth justice secretary in two years amid latest cabinet reshuffle' (9 January 2018). https://www.legalbusiness.co. uk/blogs/former-city-solicitor-gauke-becomes-fourth-justice-secretary-in-two -years-amid-latest-cabinet-reshuffle/, Accessed 6 July 2020.

Cloud C. and Granfield R., 'Social context and 'natural recovery': the role of social capital in the resolution of drug-associated problems' (2001) 36(11) Substance use and Misuse, 1543–1570.

Cloud W. and Granfield R., 'Conceptualizing recovery capital: expansion of a theoretical construct' (2008) 43(12–13) Substance use and Misuse, 1971–1986. doi:10.1080/10826080802289762.

Cooper C. and Trotter J., 'Recent developments in drug case management: re-engineering the judicial process' (1994) 17(1), Justice System Journal, 83–96, doi:10.1080/23277556.1994.10871194.

Coviello D.M., Zanis D.A., Wesnoski S.A., Palman N., Gur A., Lynch K.G. and McKay J.M., 'Does mandating offenders to treatment improve completion rates?' (2013) 44(4) Journal of Substance Abuse Treatment, 417–425. doi:10.1016/j.jsat.2012.10.

Department of Energy & Climate Change, 'People strategy: 2011 to 2014 DECC' (31 January 2012) Corporate report, GOV.uk.

Donoghue J., *Transforming criminal justice?: Problem-solving and court specialization* (New York: Routledge, 2014).

European Commission, 'EU health programme 2014–2020'. https://ec.europa.eu/ health/funding/programme/2014-2020_en, Accessed 6 July 2020.

Facilitate the Therapeutic Design and Application of the Law TJ (2014). Paper 6. https:// papers.ssrn.com/sol3/papers.cfm?abstract_id=2564613, accessed 16 August 2018.

Gibbs P., 'Return magistrates' courts to local control' *The Law Society Gazette* (3 June 2013). https://www.lawgazette.co.uk/analysis/return-magistrates-courts-to-loc al-control/71223.article, Accessed 1 July 2020.

Gleuk S. and Gleuk E., *Juvenile delinquents grown up* (New York: Commonwealth Fund, 1940).

Goldkamp J., 'Challenges for research and innovation: when is a drug court not a drug court?' in C.T. Terry (ed.) (Thousand Oaks, CA: Sage, 1999).

Goldkamp J., White W. and Robinson J., 'Do drug courts work? Getting inside the drug court black box' (2000) 31(1) Journal of Drug Issues, 27–72.

Greater Manchester, 'Greater Manchester drug and alcohol strategy 2019–2021' (2019).   https://www.greatermanchester-ca.gov.uk/media/2507/greater-m anchester-drug-and-alcohol-strategy.pdf.

The Greater Manchester Combined Authority, 'The Mayor'. https://www.greaterm anchester-ca.gov.uk/the-mayor/, Accessed 6 July 2020.

Hansten M.L., Downey L., Rosengren D.B. and Donovan D.M., 'Relationship between follow-up rates and treatment outcomes in substance abuse research: more is better but when is 'enough' enough?' (2000) 95(9) Addiction, 1403–1416.

Health Scrutiny Committee. https://democracy.manchester.gov.uk/Data/Heal th%20Scrutiny%20Committee/20151029/Agenda/5._Reform_of_Public_Hea lth.pdf, Accessed 2 July 2020.

Hiller M., Belenko S., Taxman S., Young D., Perdoni M. and Saum C., 'Measuring drug court structure and operations: key component s and beyond' (2010) Criminal Justice and Behavior.

Home Office National Statistics, 'Drug misuse: findings from the 2013/14 crime survey for England and Wales' (2014). https://www.gov.uk/government/publi cations/drug-misuse-findings-from-the-2013-to-2014-csew/drug-misuse-finding s-from-the-201314-crime-survey-for-england-and-wales, Accessed 2 July 2020.

Hora P., 'A Dozen years of drug treatment courts: uncovering our theoretical foundation and the construction of a mainstream paradigm' (2002) 37 Substance Use and Misuse, 12 & 13; 1469–1488.

House of Commons Justice Committee, 'Government should undertake a review of transforming rehabilitation reforms' (22 June 2018). https://publications.parliamen t.uk/pa/cm201719/cmselect/cmjust/482/48202.htm, Accessed 6 July 2020.

House of Commons Justice Committee, 'The role of the magistracy: follow-up Eighteenth Report of Session 2017–19' (2019).

House of Commons. https://publications.parliament.uk/pa/cm201719/cmselect/ cmjust/1654/1654.pdf.

Hser V.I., Joshi V., Maglione M., Chih-Ping C. and Anglin D., 'Effects of program and patient characteristics on retention of drug treatment patients' (2001) 24(4) Evaluation and Program Planning, 331–341.

https://digitalcommons.georgiasouthern.edu/crimjust-criminology-facpubs/120.

https://www.ncjrs.gov/pdffiles1/nij/grants/223853.pdf.

Kawałek A., 'A tool for measuring therapeutic jurisprudence values during empirical research' (2020) 71C International Journal of Law and Psychiatry, 101581.

Kedia S., Sell M. and Relyea G., 'Mono- versus polydrug abuse patterns among publicly funded clients' (2007) Subst Abuse Treat Prev Policy. doi:10.1186/1747-597X-2-33.

Kerr J., Tompkins C., Tomaszewski W., Dickens S., Grimshaw R., Nat W. and Matt B. 'The dedicated drug courts pilot evaluation process study' (2011) Ministry of Justice Research Series, 1. Ministry of Justice, London.

KPMG Consulting, 'Evaluation of the drug court of Victoria. Government advisory services. Final report.' (2014) Magistrates' Court of Victoria, 18.

Lattimore P.K., MacKenzie D.L., Zajac G., Dawes D., Arsenault E. and Tueller S., 'Outcome findings from the HOPE demonstration field experiment is swift, certain, and fair an effective supervision strategy?' (2016) Wiley. https://doi. org/10.1111/1745-9133.12248.

Maldonado-Molina M.M. and Khey D.N. (ed.), Hoboken, NJ: John Wiley & Sons, Inc, 1–8. doi:10.1002/9781118519639.wbecpx275, isbn: 9781118519639.

Manchester City Council, 'Tackling alcohol and drug related crime. Manchester city council' (2015). https://secure.manchester.gov.uk/download/meetings/id/2 0099/6_alcohol_and_drug_related_crime, Accessed 15 August 2017.

Maruna S., *Making good: how ex-convicts reform and rebuild their lives* (Washington, DC: American Psychological Association, 2011).

Matharu M., 'private companies running failing probation services must be made publicly accountable' (Byline, 2013), https://www.byline.com/column/71/ar ticle/1827, Accessed 2 July 2020.

Matrix Knowledge Group, 'Dedicated drug court pilots a process report' (2008) Ministry of Justice Research Series 7/08. Ministry of Justice; Perlin (n 44) Franco, London, 2010.

McSweeney T., Stevens A., Hunt N. and Turnbell P., 'Drug testing and court review hearings: uses and limitations' (2008) 55(1) Probation Journal, 39–53.

Mendoza N.S., Linley J.V., Nochajski T.N. and Farrell M.G., 'Attrition in drug court research: examining participant characteristics and recommendations for follow-up' (2013) 3(1) Journal of Forensic Social Work, 56–68. doi:10.1080/19 36928X.2013.837418.

Michael P., 'Mental health courts, dignity, and human rights' on page 193 in B. McSherry and I. Freckelton (eds.) *Coercive care: law and policy* (Abingdon: Routledge, 2013).

MIDAS. https://www.investinmanchester.com/about-us/midas, Accessed 1 July 2020.

Ministry of Justice, 'Swift and sure justice: the government's plans for reform of the criminal justice system' (2012). https://assets.publishing.service.gov.uk/gove rnment/uploads/system/uploads/attachment_data/file/217328/swift-and-su re-justice.pdf, Accessed 6 July 2020, cited in Jane C., 'Court modernisation project 'risks missing 2023 deadline'' (9 May 2018). https://www.ft.com/content/1e1 542c2-4f93-11e8-9471-a083af05aea7, Accessed 6 July 2020.

Ministry of Justice, 'Transforming rehabilitation A strategy for reform' (2013). https ://consult.justice.gov.uk/digital-communications/transforming-rehabilitation/ results/transforming-rehabilitation-response.pdf.

Ministry of Justice, 'A smarter approach to sentencing' (2020) White Paper.

Ministry of Justice, 'Justice secretary announces new model for probation' (16 May 2019). https://www.gov.uk/government/news/justice-secretary-announces-ne w-model-for-probation, Accessed 6 July 2020.

Mitchell O., Wilson D.B., Eggers A. and MacKenzie D.L., 'Drug courts' effects on criminal offending for juveniles and adults' (2012) 8(1) Systematic Review, i-87.

National Association of Probation Officers [NATO], 'Napo's online submission to the MoJ consultation – strengthening probation'. https://www.napo.org.uk/ sites/default/files/Napo%20Response%20to%20MOJ%20Consultation_0.pdf, Accessed 1 July 2020.

National Offender Management Service, 'Supporting community order treatment requirements' (2014) Commissioning Group.

National Treatment Agency, 'Breaking the link' (2009). http://www.fead.org.uk/wp -content/uploads/2015/09/nta_criminaljustice_0809.pdf, Accessed 1 July 2020.

NHS Support Federation, Cuts to Frontline Practitioners (2020). https://nhsfund ing.info/symptoms/10-effects-of-underfunding/cuts-to-frontline-services/, Accessed 6 July 2020.

Office for National Statistics, 'Coronavirus and the impact on output in the UK economy: April 2020' (12 June 2020). https://tinyurl.com/ycxrdxzq, Accessed 6 July 2020.

Perron B. and Bright C., 'The influence of legal coercion on dropout from substance abuse treatment: results from a national survey' (2008) 92(1–3) Drug and Alcohol Dependence, 123–131. doi:10.1016/j.drugalcdep.2007.07.011

Peters R.H. and Murrin M.R., 'Effectiveness of treatment-based drug courts in reducing criminal recidivism' (2000) 27 Criminal Justice and Behavior, 72.

Phillips J., Kawalek A. and Greenslade A.-M., 'An evaluation of the choice and consequences and PI programmes in Bedfordshire and Hertfordshire' (2020) Ministry of Justice.

Regan D., 'Manchester city council report for information' (2015) Manchester City Council Item, 5.

Rocque M., Chad P. and Justin H., 'Age and crime' in W.G. Jennings, G.E. Higgins, M.M. Maldonado-Molina, and D.N. Khey (eds.) *Encyclopedia of crime and punishment* (1-8) (Hoboken, NJ: John Wiley & Sons, Inc., 2015). doi:10.1002/9781118519639.wbecpx275. isbn: 9781118519639. https://digital commons.georgiasouthern.edu/crimjust-criminology-facpubs/120.

Saum C.A. and Hiller M. 'Should violent offenders be excluded from drug court participation? An examination of the recidivism of violent and nonviolent drug court participants' (2008) 33(3) Criminal Justice Review, 291–307. http://www .antoniocasella.eu/archila/saum_2008.pdf.

Saum C.A., Scarpitti F.R. and Robbins C.A., 'Violent offenders in drug court' (2001) 31(1) Journal of Drug Issues, 107–128.

Shaffer D.F., 'Looking inside the black box of drug courts: a meta-analytic review' (2011) 28(3) Justice Quarterly, 493–521. doi:10.1080/07418825.2010.525222.

Shannon L., Jackson A., Newell J., Perkins E. and Neal C., 'Examining factors associated with treatment completion in a community-based program for individuals with criminal justice involvement' (2015) 10(Suppl 1) Addiction Science Clinical Practice, A60. doi:10.1186/1940-0640-10-S1-A60.

Smith B. and Chamberlain J.M., 'Completion rates: an analysis of factors related to drug court program completion' (2017) 3 Cogent Social Sciences, 1. doi:10.108 0/23311886.2017.1304500.

Stevens-Martin K., 'The SWIFT court: tackling the issue of high-risk offenders and chronic probation violators' (2014) Corrections Today. http://www.aca.org/a ca_prod_imis/Docs/Corrections%20Today/2014%20Articles/Sept%20Articles/ Martin.pdfn, Accessed 2 July 2020.

U.S. General Accounting Office, 'Adult drug court evidence indicates recidivism reductions and mixed results for other outcomes' (2005) Report to Congressional Committees. https://www.gao.gov/new.items/d05219.pdf.

Velázquez T., 'The verdict on drug courts' (9 December 2010). https://www.the nation.com/article/archive/verdict-drug-courts/, Accessed 2 July 2020. Volume 2013, Article ID 493679. doi:10.1155/2013/493679.

Wexler D.B., 'Moving forward on mainstreaming therapeutic jurisprudence: an ongoing process to facilitate the therapeutic design and application of the law' (2015) Therapeutic Jurisprudence: New Zealand Perspectives v (Warren Brookbanks ed., 2015), Arizona Legal Studies Discussion Paper No. 15–10. Available at SSRN: https://ssrn.com/abstract=2564613.

Wexler D.B., 'New wine in new bottles: the need to sketch a therapeutic jurisprudence 'code' of proposed criminal processes and practices' (2014)7 Arizona Summit Law Review, 463–480.

Wexler D.B. and Winick B.J., *Judging in a therapeutic key: therapeutic jurisprudence and the courts* (Durham, NC: Carolina Academic Press, 2003).

Whitehead S., 'Community sentences case study: embedded CRC presence at Teeside Magistrates Court' *Justice Innovation* (2019). https://justiceinnovation.org/artic les/community-sentences-case-study-embedded-crc-presence-teeside-magistrate s-court, Accessed 1 July 2020.

Witkin S. and Hays S., 'Drug court through the eyes of participants' (2017) 30(7) Criminal Justice Policy Review, 971–989. doi:10.1177/0887403417731802.

Wittouck C., Dekkers D., Ruyver B.D., Vanderplasschen W. and Laenen F.V., 'The impact of drug treatment courts on recovery: a systematic review' (2012) Hindawi Publishing Corporation, Scientific World Journal.

Zehr H., *The little book of restorative justice* (Intercourse, PA: Good Books, 2002).

Conclusion

England and Wales currently face problems with recidivism.[1] A plethora of research, of both national and international origin, point to the demonstrable link between drug addiction and recidivist crimes (for instance: shoplifting, burglary, vehicle crime, robbery).[2] If the aetiology of reoffending is often drug addiction, this opens up broader questions: could the criminal justice system be a window of opportunity to rehabilitate offenders; could the criminal justice system itself be a vehicle for recovery; and, can we marry together health and justice? These questions are encapsulated by broad paradigm shifts in criminal justice and beyond, transforming deficit-based models into strengths-based theory, which has in turn reconceptualised the 'criminal man' into a restorable human being.

This changing of lenses has overseen the emergence of a multitude of new therapeutic, reintegrative, and restorative practical interventions, which have altered the tone, structure, and delivery of many punishment disposals, and have forced us to think of new ways of dealing with recidivist cycles within the above-posited questions. The leading example is the drug court, which was first implemented in Miami-Dade County in the late 1980s to tackle problems with recidivism in the US, similar to the problems that England and Wales currently face. Research indicates that the drug court model has been successful for dealing with drug-fuelled

---

1 Ministry of Justice, 'Criminal justice statistics quarterly, England and Wales' (2017) National Statistics; Ministry of Justice, 'Transforming rehabilitation: a strategy for reform' (2013). Retrieved from https://consult.justice.gov.uk/digital-communications/transforming-reh abilitation/results/transforming-rehabilitation-response.pdf; Ministry of Justice, 'Prison safety and reform' (2016) Ministry of Justice; Ministry of Justice, 'New partnership to boost offender rehabilitation' (2019). Retrieved from: https://www.gov.uk/government/news/new-partnership-to-boost-offender-rehabilitation; David Gauke, 'Smarter sentences, safer streets' Ministry of Justice; Georgina Eaton & Aiden Mews, 'The impact of short custodial sentences, community orders and suspended sentence orders on reoffending' (2019) Ministry of Justice.
2 Michael Gossop, 'The National Treatment Outcomes Research Study (NTORS) and its influence on addiction treatment policy in the United Kingdom' (2015) National Addiction Centre, Institute of Psychiatry.

offending[3] as these courts have proliferated across jurisdictions worldwide in new and various guises.[4] From the evidence base, we can see the facets that a drug court 'should' possess to match the international mould with a 'typical' drug best captured by the Ten Key Drug Court Components, which provides a yardstick for good practice.[5] International empirical results demonstrate that fidelity to the framework optimises drug court outcomes.[6]

Despite the far-reaching and widely documented successes of the burgeoning international drug courts, the English and Welsh examples have lagged far behind. Unlike many international nations, in England and Wale drug courts are a misunderstood area, where perhaps as a result, perhaps as a cause, there has been limited empirical research. Although the literature reports discreetly on England and Wales drug courts, from the little evidence, we do know six pilots were established in the early noughties were still very much alive in 2011 when the last piece of empirical research was published,[7] where it was claimed that the courts operated in line with international understandings. However, since 2011, a series of newspaper articles have detailed the closedowns of some but not all models, and there has been no formal announcement from the Ministry of Justice

---

3 Douglas Marlowe, 'Research update on adult drug courts' (2010) National Association of Drug Court Professionals.

4 Erin Collins, 'Status courts' (2017) Geo. Law Journal, 105, 1481–1528; Arie Freiberg, 'Problem-oriented courts: innovative solutions to intractable problems?' (2001) Journal of Judicial Administration, 11(8); Michael Perlin, '"The judge, he cast his robe aside": mental health courts, dignity and due process' (2013) Mental Health Law and Policy Journal, 3(1), 1–29; Lorana Bartels, 'Looking at Hawaii's opportunity with probation enforcement (HOPE) program through a therapeutic jurisprudence lens' (2016) QUT Law Review, 16, 30; Lorana Bartels, 'Swift, certain and fair: does project HOPE provide a therapeutic paradigm for managing offenders? (Springer, 2017); Lorana Bartels, 'HOPE-ful bottles: examining the potential for Hawaii's opportunity probation with enforcement (HOPE) to help mainstream therapeutic jurisprudence' (2019) International Journal of Law and Psychiatry, 63, 26–34.

5 John Ashcroft, Deborah Daniels, & Domingo Herriaz, 'Defining drug courts: the key components. U.S. Department of Justice' (2004). Retrieved from: https://www.ncjrs.gov/pdf files1/bja/205621.pdf.

6 John Goldkamp, Michael White, & Jennifer Robinson, 'Do drug courts work? Getting inside the drug court black box' (2000) Journal of Drug Issues, 31(1), 27–72; John Goldkamp, 'Challenges for research and innovation: when is a drug court not a drug court?' in W. Clinton Terry (ed.) *The early drug courts: case studies in judicial innovation* (Sage, 1999); Shannon M. Carey, Michael W. Finigan, & Kimberly Pukstas, 'Exploring the key components of drug courts: a comparative study of 18 adult drug courts on practices, outcomes and costs' (2008) NPC Research; Peggy Hora, 'A dozen years of drug treatment courts: uncovering our theoretical foundation and the construction of a mainstream paradigm' (2002) Substance Use and Misuse 37, 12 & 13, 1469–1488; Matthew Hiller, Steven Belenko, Faye Taxman, Douglas Young, Matthew Perdoni, & Christine Saum, 'Measuring drug court structure and operations: key components and beyond' (2010) Criminal Justice and Behaviour; Freiberg; Susan Witkin & Scott Hays, 'Drug court through the eyes of participants' (2017) Criminal Justice Policy Review, 30(7), 971–989. doi:10.1177/0887403417731802

7 Jane Kerr, Charlotte Tompkins, Wojtek Tomaszewski, Sarah Dickens, Roger Grimshaw, Nat Wright, & Matt Barnard, 'The dedicated drug courts pilot evaluation process study' (2011) Ministry of Justice Research Series, 1. London: Ministry of Justice.

or any empirical evaluation explaining their downfalls.[8] To highlight this confusing gap, I reiterated the following mantra throughout this book for emphasis: there is no track record of Manchester Review Court in the available literature repositories evidencing its existence, no empirical research, not in the media or any policy document, and nor is there a court handbook at the site outlining objectives and expected practice. Of the six original drug courts, arguably only the ghost of Salford drug court remains in the form of Manchester Review Court, which became the object of empirical study. Through a case study design, the book addressed many of the questions left open by the literature – why did the drug courts fall by the wayside? What exactly is Manchester Review Court? Is it linked to the drug courts, or is it something different? Is it the ghost of Salford drug court or an independent practice? What remains for British problem-solving courts?

Through original data leveraged by three methods and in line with the seminal therapeutic-jurisprudence analogy, research questions were split into two tiers; the first referred to the wine and the other to the bottle; they are reiterated below.

Wine

1. What impact does an inconsistent bench have on the therapeutic application of magistrates' interpersonal skills and behavioural styles?
   a.   Does proficiency at these approaches change according to magistrates' gender?
2. What is the therapeutic quality of the wine?

Bottle

1. Does the court adhere to the international drug court gold standard?[9]
2. Is the review court the remains of the original drug courts?
3. What is the therapeutic quality of the bottle?

The dual focus of research questions enabled a comprehensive discussion of the possibilities and pitfalls of the British problem-solving courts in the past, present, and future by focusing on both the practices existing within the courts (wine)

---

8 Jon Robins, 'Where next for community justice? Pioneering court closes' *The Justice Gap* (24 October 2013); Jon Robins, 'Whatever happened to community justice?' *The Justice Gap* (3 October 2012); Owen Bowcott, 'US-style problem solving courts plan losing momentum.' (*The Guardian*, 12 October 2016) <https://tinyurl.com/y3e68qc4> Accessed 2 June 2019; Penelope Gibbs 'Has the West London drugs court closed and does it matter?' (*Transforming Justice*, 10 June 2014) <http://www.transformjustice.org.uk/has-the-west-london-drugs-court-closed-and-does-it-matter/> Accessed 4 September 2019; Owen Bowcott, 'Why are special courts that can help drug users at risk of being scrapped?' (*The Guardian*, 10 June 2014) <https://tinyurl.com/y3n6o9bp> Accessed 3 September 2019.
9 Ashcroft et al. (n 5).

and the wide systemic structures supporting the court (bottle). The discussions were enabled by knitting together results from three datasets through a triangulation analysis. The data showed that magistrates' interpersonal and behavioural styles aligned with the therapeutic jurisprudence philosophy. However, the bottle for Manchester Review Court bottle was significantly therapeutic-jurisprudence unfriendly. It was concluded that where the current UK criminal justice system is emphasising managerialism, centralisation and austerity measures, the bottle remains inconducive for pouring good therapeutic-jurisprudence wine, and the system puts up significant hurdles for good practice despite the talent, enthusiasm and bandwidth amongst the frontline practitioners, particularly magistrates.

Given the lack of literature in the area and since Manchester Review Court was an enigma, the data also enabled a drug court fidelity analysis to be carried out using the international Ten Key Components as an evaluative framework to discover areas of compliance and non-compliance to its principles. It was concluded that Manchester Review Court cannot be a drug court because it is significantly non-compliant to the drug court matrix, hence it being named a 'review court' throughout this book. However, this raised questions around the definition and practices in the predecessor drug courts. Although the data is inconclusive as to whether it is the ghost of Salford drug court, by comparing results from this book to the predecessor drug court research, the similarities between the models are palpable. As such, we can conclude that Manchester Review Court is like the predecessor England and Wales 'drug courts', including areas of compliance and non-compliance to the international blueprint. Although the data showed that the old UK 'drug courts' operated with more fidelity in keeping with the international mould compared to Manchester Review Court, this was marginal. As such, both models breached the gold standard. Therefore, the evidence shows that a stable bottle, enabling fidelity, always been lacking for the UK, with the same problems either already existent or nascent in 2011, but worsening with time. As such, the old English and Welsh 'drug courts' had a misplaced ontological foundation, meaning that they should never have operated under this guise, and they were misnomers. Although in theory policymakers appeared to advocate the implementation of drug courts in 2005, they did not fully buy into the model fully, making only a qualified attempt at successful operation. As such, there have been long-standing jurisdictional problems at the grassroots level with the English and Welsh drug courts, where the surrounding policy, social structures, and legal dimensions have consistently failed to support their authentic operation.

Although this looks like rather a bleak story, this book has argued that problem-solving courts in England and Wales have a strong place going forward, which is made apt by the 2020 White Paper seeking fresh delivery.[10] Whilst it is tempting to suggest that only full adherence to the international drug framework yields good responses, therapeutic jurisprudence can also be found within

---

10 Ministry of Justice, 'A smarter approach to sentencing' (2020) White Paper.

looser nodes of problem-solving court practice so long as the courts are delivered on a well-researched best practice principles and a conceptual model that accounts for bottle factors. Perhaps their title does not matter, but what does matter is that objectives, implementation, and protocol are consistently understood by practitioners, implementers, and researchers to ensure coherent, successful, and sustainable delivery. With this in mind, based on the empirical evidence, I posited a UK-specific fidelity matrix for problem-solving courts going forward, which accounts, and seeks to overcome, the problematic factors found within this research. The hope is that the matrix offers a realistic framework for future English and Welsh problem-solving courts, and a pathway for improving Manchester Review Court.

Current issues with drug-fuelled recidivism must be faced and international evidence suggests that can be done well using alternative justice methods, such as problem solving courts. However, when shaping future UK strategy and policy, one cannot ignore the demise of the original England and Wales drug courts, especially when a fresh collection of problem-solving courts is on the table. If the Ministry of Justice were to rebrand and repackage Manchester Review Court (and problem-solving courts) in a way that is conducive to the criminal justice milieu by using the posited fidelity matrix to guide implementation and operation, I argue strongly that this would pave the way for a fruitful future, which would in turn tackle current problems with recidivism, addiction and austerity.

Bibliography

Ashcroft A., Daniels D. and Herriaz D., 'Defining drug courts: the key components. U.S. Department of Justice' (2004). https://www.ncjrs.gov/pdffiles1/bja/2056 21.pdf.

Bartels L., 'HOPE-ful bottles: examining the potential for Hawaii's opportunity probation with enforcement (HOPE) to help mainstream therapeutic jurisprudence' (2009) 63 International Journal of Law and Psychiatry, 26–34.

Bartels L., 'Looking at Hawaii's opportunity with probation enforcement (HOPE) program through a therapeutic jurisprudence lens' (2016) 16 QUT Law Review, 30.

Bartels L., *Swift, certain and fair: does project HOPE provide a therapeutic paradigm for managing offenders?* (Cham, Switzerland: Springer, 2017).

Bowcott O., 'Why are special courts that can help drug users at risk of being scrapped?' *Guardian* (10 June 2014). https://tinyurl.com/y3n6o9bp, Accessed 3 September 2019.

Bowcott O., 'US-style problem solving courts plan losing momentum' *Guardian* (12 October 2016). https://tinyurl.com/y3e68qc4, Accessed 2 June 2019.

Carey S.M., Finigan M.W. and Pukstas K., 'Exploring the key component s of drug courts: a comparative study of 18 adult drug courts on practices, outcomes and costs' (2008) NPC Research.

Collins E., 'Status courts' (2017) 105 Geo Law Journal, 1481–1528; Arie F., 'Problem-oriented courts: innovative solutions to intractable problems?' (2001) 11(8) Journal of Judicial Administration.

Eaton G. and Mews A., 'The impact of short custodial sentences, community orders and suspended sentence orders on reoffending' (2019) Ministry of Justice.

Gibbs P., 'Has the West London drugs court closed and does it matter?' *Transforming Justice* (10 June 2014). http://www.transformjustice.org.uk/has-the-west-lo ndon-drugs-court-closed-and-does-it-matter/, Accessed 4 September 2019.

Goldkamp J., 'Challenges for research and innovation: when is a drug court not a drug court?' in W.C. Terry (eds.) *The early drug courts: case studies in judicial innovation* (Thousand Oaks, CA: Sage, 1999).

Goldkamp J., Michael W. and Jennifer R., 'Do drug courts work? getting inside the drug court black box' (2000) 31(1) Journal of Drug Issues, 27–72.

Gossop M., 'The national treatment outcomes research study (NTORS) and its influence on addiction treatment policy in the United Kingdom' (2015) National Addiction Centre, Institute of Psychiatry.

Gauke D., 'Smarter sentences, safer streets' (Speech: 18 July 2019) Ministry of Justice.

Hiller M., Belenko S., Taxman D., Young D., Perdoni M. and Saum C., 'Measuring drug court structure and operations: key component s and beyond' (2010) Criminal Justice and Behaviour; Freiberg (n 25); Susan W. and Scott H., 'Drug court through the eyes of participants' (2017) 30(7) Criminal Justice Policy Review, 971–989. doi:10.1177/0887403417731802.

Hora P., 'A Dozen years of drug treatment courts: uncovering our theoretical foundation and the construction of a mainstream paradigm' (2002) 37 Substance Use and Misuse, 12 & 13; 1469–1488.

Kerr J., Tompkins C., Tomaszewski W., Dickens S., Grimshaw R., Wright N. and Barnard M., 'The dedicated drug courts pilot evaluation process study' (2011) Ministry of Justice Research Series, 1. Ministry of Justice, London.

Marlowe D., 'Research update on adult drug courts' (2010) National Association of Drug Court Professionals.

Ministry of Justice, 'Transforming rehabilitation: a strategy for reform' (2013). https://consult.justice.gov.uk/digital-communications/transforming-rehabili tation/results/transforming-rehabilitation-response.pdf.

Ministry of Justice, 'Prison safety and reform' (2016) Ministry of Justice.

Ministry of Justice, 'Criminal justice statistics quarterly, England and Wales' (2017) National Statistics.

Ministry of Justice, 'New partnership to boost offender rehabilitation' (2019). https ://www.gov.uk/government/news/new-partnership-to-boost-offender-rehabi litation.

Ministry of Justice, 'A smarter approach to sentencing' (2020) White Paper.

Perlin M., '"The judge, he cast his robe aside": mental health courts, dignity and due process' (2013) 3(1) Mental Health Law and Policy Journal, 1–29.

Robins J., 'Where next for community justice? Pioneering court closes' *The Justice Gap* (24 October 2013); Jon R., 'Whatever happened to community justice?' *The Justice Gap* (3 October 2012).

Appendices

Appendix 1: Levene's statistic for gender question

Test of homogeneity of variances				
	Levene's statistic	*df1*	*df2*	*Sig.*
Support means	2.046	2	48	.140

Appendix 2: One-way ANOVA: gender

		df	Mean Square	F	Sig.
Support means	Between groups	2	1.778	4.673	.014
	Within groups	48	.381		
	Total	50			
Dialogue means	Between group	2	.132	.802	.454
	Within groups	48	.164		
	Total	50			
Change means	Between groups	2	.477	1.083	.347
	Within groups	48	.441		
	Total	50			

Appendix 3: Tukey corrections

Dependent variable	(I) Magistrates' gender	(J) Magistrates' gender	Mean difference (I–J)	Sig.
Support means	All male	All female	.18971	.671
		Mixed	–.41180	.163
	All female	All male	–.18971	.671
		Mixed	–.60150*	.012
	Mixed	All male	.41180	.163
		All female	.60150*	.012
Dialogue means	All male	All female	.17274	.468
		Mixed	.04993	.938
	All female	All male	–.17274	.468
		Mixed	–.12281	.622
	Mixed	All male	–.04993	.938
		All female	.12281	.622
Change means	All male	All female	.13158	.847
		Mixed	–.18421	.722
	All female	All male	–.13158	.847
		Mixed	–.31579	.316
	Mixed	All male	.18421	.722
		All female	.31579	.316

Index